THE BUSINESS OF NEWSPAPERS ON THE WESTERN FRONTIER

WILBUR S. SHEPPERSON SERIES IN HISTORY AND HUMANITIES

The Business of Newspapers on the Western Frontier

BARBARA CLOUD

University of Nevada Press

Reno, Las Vegas, London

Winner of the Wilbur S. Shepperson Humanities Book Award for 1992

Wilbur S. Shepperson Series in History and Humanities No. 33
(formerly Nevada Studies in History and Political Science)
Series Editor: Jerome E. Edwards

The jacket and part title illustrations are from Benjamin Butterworth, *The Growth of Industrial Art* (Washington, D.C.: Government Printing Office, 1892).

The paper used in this book meets the requirements of
American National Standard for Information Sciences—
Permanence of Paper for Printed Library Materials, ANSI Z39.48-1984.
Binding materials were chosen for strength and durability.

University of Nevada Press, Reno, Nevada 89557 USA

Designed by Kaelin Chappell

Printed in the United States of America

9 8 7 6 5 4 3 2 1

Library of Congress Cataloging-in-Publication Data
Cloud, Barbara Lee.
The business of newspapers on the western frontier / Barbara Cloud.
p.   cm. — (Wilbur S. Shepperson series in history and humanities : no. 33)
Includes bibliographical references and index.
ISBN 0-87417-184-9 (alk. paper)
1. Newspaper publishing—Economic aspects—West (U.S.)—History—19th century.
2. American newspapers—West (U.S.)—History—19th century.
3. West (U.S.)—Economic conditions—19th century.
4. Frontier and pioneer life—West (U.S.)
I. Title.   II. Series.
z478.3.w47c56   1992
338.4'70718—dc20   91-47583
CIP

This book is the recipient of the
Wilbur S. Shepperson Humanities Book Award,
which is given annually in his memory by the
Nevada Humanities Committee and the University of Nevada
Press. One of Nevada's most distinguished historians,
Wilbur S. Shepperson was a founding board member and
long-time supporter of both organizations.

CONTENTS

LIST OF TABLES

PREFACE

The growing number of mergers and takeovers of media companies in recent years reminded Americans that newspapers and broadcast stations providing news, information, and entertainment are as subject to business trends as automakers, soap manufacturers, and home builders. At the same time, because of journalism's First Amendment pedestal, business changes affecting the media often seemed to generate a sense of surprise, dismay, even shock, as though people were discovering for the first time that news as a commodity bears a considerable resemblance to soy beans.

But, of course, there is no reason for surprise. Since the time Benjamin Harris first offered *Publick Occurrences* to his coffeehouse audience in 1690, U.S. news media, whatever else the motivations of those involved in them, have been businesses. Eighteenth-century newspaperman Isaiah Thomas knew that a medium had to be financially successful in order to provide news and information, ideas and entertainment; the nineteenth century's James Gordon Bennett and Joseph Pulitzer knew it; in the twentieth century Ted Turner and Al Neuharth know it. To their credit, many media owners have recognized and accepted the special role media play in a democracy, yet this has not diverted their efforts to assemble staff and facilities, and develop processes and procedures for the economic survival of their newspapers and stations so that they can play that role.

"To understand the media, to see them more nearly whole in historical terms, means that the economic dimension must no longer be neglected,"[1] Ames and Teeter wrote in 1971. Journalism historians have been slow to respond to this call to expand their studies, however much they recognize that looking only at journalistic content fails to tell the full story of U.S. media. However, recent attention paid to media business has provoked more serious interest in the balance sheets of the past. After all:

- Advertising occupies a significant portion of media content.
- More media people are employed outside the newsroom than in it.
- Production of news is one of the biggest industries in the United States.
- A medium's loss of economic viability can damage the political system, as well as the men and women put out of work and the advertisers and customers who must find other ways to communicate economic information.

We also must acknowledge, like it or not, that business influences journalistic content. In a newspaper, advertising sales determine the space allocated to news; production and distribution requirements determine deadlines; and boosterism, advertisers, and other sources of economic pressure have been known to influence editorial decisions.

To be sure, the study of media business is not virgin territory. Isaiah Thomas acknowledged the importance of business in his history, and in the 1930s, Alfred McClung Lee's *The Daily Newspaper in America* paid close attention to economic considerations.[2] Rare is the newspaper history that neglects business matters entirely. We learn of ownership changes, shifts in frequency of publication, and sometimes circulation, but these matters are usually treated as peripheral to other questions.

The Business of Newspapers on the Western Frontier tackles the subject head-on by focusing on a particular group of newspapers in a particular time and place: those that lived and died on the far western frontier. Included are newspapers started by publishers whose "excited hopes" (to use their phrase) were triggered by the tremendous opportunity for wealth and power that came with the start of something big—in this case, the development of the western third of the continental United States.

This focus indulges a personal interest because I have long wondered about—indeed, considered with some awe—the people who uprooted themselves and undertook a difficult and often dangerous journey to an undeveloped land. But it also helps balance a general bias in journalism history toward big-city eastern newspapers. Most Americans did not read the city papers that figure so prominently in our histories; they read the small-town press, the kinds of papers

that take center stage in *The Business of Newspapers*. The importance of this kind of newspaper in American life is evident when it is
realized that, even today, weekly newspaper circulation growth out-
strips that of daily newspapers. From 1960 to 1990, daily newspaper
circulation increased nearly 30 percent; weekly circulation rose 160
percent.[3]

Clones of the Eastern Press?

It has been suggested that studying western institutions such as the
press offers little of value because of the derivative nature of western
development. "[W]esterners were, on the whole, imitators, not origi-
nators, and conformists rather than nonconformists," comments one
observer,[4] while another, discussing city building, remarks that the
"result was the establishment of a society that mirrored and made
the same mistakes as those made earlier in the rest of the country."[5]

To be sure, western publishers used eastern newspapers as their
models, and their experiences differ mainly in degree from those of
their contemporaries in the East. To the extent that they are similar, of course, *The Business of Newspapers on the Western Frontier*
helps illuminate small-newspaper business practices everywhere.
But there are differences; for example, what Australian historian
Geoffrey Blainey described as the "tyranny of distance."[6] Western
publishers operated, as a rule, in greater isolation and farther from
material, labor, and major news sources than most publishers in
other parts of the continent. San Francisco quickly developed as a
supply center, but hundreds of miles separated the city from the mining camps of Idaho or Montana and from the agricultural settlements
of eastern Washington or Southern California. In addition, the boomtown development so common on the mining frontier created a western industry particularly susceptible to audiences that disappeared
as ore veins played out or as better prospects were discovered elsewhere. Dependence on extractive influences, a factor Michael Malone
has identified as fundamental to regional identity, clearly extended
to newspapers.[7] And, finally, even accepting the largely derivative
nature of western development, there remains a sense of a unique
experience that argues for special attention for western institutions.[8]

I have used "western" here as a regional resident does, ignoring that to a Connecticut resident that could mean the western half of his state. "West" for these purposes begins essentially at the Rocky Mountains—the eastern slopes because Denver, after all, is a western city—and covers eleven western states: Montana, Wyoming, Colorado, New Mexico, Utah, Arizona, Idaho, Nevada, Washington, Oregon, and California. It is an arbitrary grouping whose members show enormous diversity. The coastal states claim little affinity with those farther inland. California, Nevada, and Oregon became states well before any of the others. Terrain, climate, and resources differ. The Mormon settlements in Utah or the farms of Oregon bear little resemblance to the mining camps of their neighbors. The rain forests of the Olympic Peninsula are a far cry from the Mojave and Sonora deserts. Yet somehow we all consider ourselves westerners.

The term "frontier," which many use almost interchangeably with "western" and "pioneer," also needs some comment. If we accept the notion of the frontiersman as a self-sufficient individual, able to fend for himself and survive in isolation, then "frontier press" is a misnomer. Dependent as he was on materials that only close connections to civilization could provide—type, presses and paper, and news itself—the newspaper publisher was anything but self-sufficient, no matter how ingenious he might be in making do with what he had. But even the legendary frontiersman, the mountain man, carried with him the trappings of civilization—guns, supplies, perhaps a book to read by firelight—and expected to sell the result of his labors to a national or international market. William Cronin, in an examination of frontier theories, provides justification for our clinging to the term "frontier" and applying it to the press when he reminds us, "In reality, even the most remote frontier was always connected to the economic activities and demographic changes in the rest of the world."[9]

In considering the frontier press, one must deal with the legends and mythology that have developed, both about the region and about the press itself. Western literature, both fiction and nonfiction, has created people and places larger than even the wide-open spaces of the West can accommodate with honesty, and journalism history has added its own mystique. Although scholarship has clarified the record in many cases, debunking the cowboy and Indian and the heroes of dime novels and films, the aura remains. In a sense, *The Business of Newspapers on the Western Frontier* seeks to peel back the glamour and excitement sometimes associated with the frontier press and to show real people doing real things. Contrary to films and television, crusading editors concentrated more on getting their political cronies into office than on driving gun-toting bullies out of town; the suspense in our story comes from the tension created when the shipment of paper was late rather than whether the hero would beat the bad guy to the draw; the record shows that more wounds resulted from tongue lashings than from bullet holes. Even so, the challenges that ordinary people faced in coming to grips with frontier conditions generate excitement for those of us who seek a greater understanding of the past.

An examination of frontier newspapers raises another question: just what is a newspaper anyway? In fact, not everyone agrees. Perhaps "newspaper" escapes explicit definition; perhaps, like obscenity, it is one of those things we know when we see it. But let me clarify what kind of newspaper is included in this study.

All the newspapers discussed in *The Business of Newspapers on the Western Frontier* were mechanically produced and, so far as I know, all were on paper of some kind, although not always newsprint. I leave to others the interesting story of the holographic papers and papers printed on odd materials such as shingles. My newspapers had, or at least intended, regular frequency, and they sought to reach as wide an audience as possible. They carried news and advertising, they sold subscriptions, and they looked much like the *New York Times* of their day. None of these criteria can be applied absolutely. A few publications looked more like pamphlets or magazines than newspapers, schedules were interrupted, and content sometimes stretched the meaning of "news" (but that's another definitional problem).

As a general rule, the religious press is excluded from the study because of its limited audience; but the *Deseret News*, an organ of the Church of Jesus Christ of Latter-day Saints (the Mormons), was included because it was also a mainstream paper for Salt Lake City.[10] Literary newspapers—San Francisco's *Golden Era* for example—as well as the foreign language press, and other clearly special-interest newspapers are also largely ignored, but any periodical may surface in these pages if it contributes to the understanding of the economic life of the frontier press.

The Business of Newspapers on the Western Frontier spans more than four decades, 1846–1890. Although the first attempts at news-papering in the region date to the 1830s, the year 1846 also marks the real beginnings of the frontier press, with the establishment of the *Californian* in Monterey.[11] Bernard De Voto called 1846 the "Year of Decision" because it was a watershed year in western development—the United States seriously challenged Mexico for California, the Mormons started for Utah, and the nation generally turned its eyes toward the Pacific. In the closing year, 1890, the U.S. Census Bureau declared that the frontier was no more, a statement that induced Frederick Jackson Turner to develop his famous frontier thesis and spawned a new field of study.[12] The period covered is therefore as arbitrary as the geographical boundaries but, I hope, will seem as rational to readers as it does to me.

The discerning reader may notice that the pronouns herein are almost always masculine. In her research for *Equal to the Occasion: Women Editors of the Nineteenth-Century West*, Sherilyn Cox Bennion uncovered more than two hundred western women editors, many of whom ran newspapers falling within the scope of this study.[13] However, most of these women practiced their craft in the 1890s, and few of the 40 or so earlier editors left the kind of information central to this study. Hence, women's role in these pages is regrettably light.

Sex Is More Fun

Collecting historical material is rarely easy; gathering information about business practices of newspapers is particularly difficult because publishers then, as now, saw little excitement in an account book. They were generally content to let their product speak not only for itself but also for themselves as individuals. "It is no doubt significant that more is known about the love life of many a prominent publisher than is known about the financial lives of their newspapers," commented Ames and Teeter. "But then, perhaps sex is more fun."[14] Research on the frontier press is also handicapped by frequent changes of ownership and by the fires and floods that damaged the often haphazardly built towns, destroying newspaper files and records in the process. Indeed, we know secondhand of newspapers that apparently existed but of which no copies have been located. Yet, one should not protest too much because obviously enough information has been collected to produce this volume.

In the course of this study I read hundreds of copies of western newspapers, at least a few in each state or territory covered in the study and a great many in some locales. I was heartened to find publishers remarkably vocal about their economic problems and practices. I am also greatly indebted to the scholars who read hundreds of other newspapers and recorded their findings; I would still be reading, and reading, and reading, had their work not been so helpful. I also discovered that many specific situations still await a closer look. For example, the involvement of companies like Anaconda Copper in Montana or the Central Pacific in California with their local press is yet to be fully told, and I hope *The Business of Newspapers* will interest others in this field.

The following pages are organized under four main headings: 1) the overall development of western newspapers—markets, owners, and their funding; 2) sources of income—advertising, circulation, and job printing; 3) expenditures—materials and equipment, labor, newsgathering costs, auxiliary industries and services; and 4) the balance sheet—outside pressures that affected operations, growth, and a final assessment of the frontier newspaper business.

Unlike the frontier publisher, I cannot blame the ultimate success or failure of this volume on discounted currency or an exhausted gold mine. If it is a success, I must share the credit with all those fine librarians and archivists who helped locate materials—the interlibrary loan librarians at a number of institutions, but most particularly my own, the University of Nevada, Las Vegas; archivists in the Western History Department at the Denver Public Library, the California Historical Society, the University of Washington's Northwest Collection and Manuscript Division, and other librarians who were so helpful even when their collections were not. I am also grateful for the aid and encouragement offered by William Huntzicker at the University of Minnesota and Cynthia Wood and Thomas Radko at the University of Nevada Press. A grant from the Nevada Humanities Committee, a sabbatical leave from UNLV, and my tolerant husband, Stan, gave me the time to collect and review the materials, to make sense of them, and to write these pages.

PART I

Getting Started

1

THE NEWSPAPER FRONTIER

The mountain men of the nineteenth century sought to escape civilization by disappearing into the wilds of the West. Those who came later, to mine, farm, ranch, or otherwise take advantage of the region's rich natural resources, sought instead to establish civilization where none had been before. Indeed, could they have tucked a bottle of instant-civilization elixir amongst their underwear when they packed for the westward journey, they no doubt would have done so. Lacking a magical potion, however, they looked to one of the most useful conduits through which such influences could flow: the newspaper.

In 1863 a Nevada woman expressed the feelings of many settlers when she wrote to her newly established local paper, "I am so glad that you've brought here your civilizer—your printing press . . . however civilized a place may be, the addition of an enlightened public journal to its institutions will serve as the best of all civilizing processes in use."[1]

Initially, western immigrants had to rely on the civilizing influences of the occasional copy of an eastern newspaper slipped into a traveler's baggage for the journey west. These rarities were much in demand; express company employees paid naive passengers a dollar or so for copies which they resold for two or three times as much.[2] Papers passed from hand to hand until they were "so thoroughly read as to be completely deprived of all signs of printing-ink. They would be worn to a dirty white paper."[3]

The potential for profit to be made from western readers was not lost on publishers, either in the East or West. Eastern newspapers prepared special editions which they loaded onto steamers and shipped to the West Coast to help meet the demand for the printed word. Before long, farmers, ranchers, and miners throughout the region also had freshly printed local journals to read, as newspapers with names like Calico *Print*, *Hydraulic Press*, and Tombstone *Epitaph* made their appearance.

Westerners warmly welcomed their local newspapers. A San Francisco writer remembered that when the stage carrying the Sacramento *Union* arrived in the Nevada mining camp where she lived as a child, "it was the great event of the day that every man lived for, and every line was scanned as if it were precious as Biblical lore."[4]

Another California writer described similar enthusiasm:

> [S]oon we beheld a burly personage of about forty years, with a grizzly head, and a face full of energy, striding onward, looking neither to the right nor the left, and bearing on his arm an enormous basket containing papers. As he went, he exclaimed at the top of his voice, "Here's the California *True Delta*, the greatest paper ever published in the United States of America, or in any part of the civilized world. Any body that has money can throw a dollar into that basket and take a copy, and any poor man may take a copy for nothing." Paper after paper disappeared, and dollar after dollar jingled in the basket.[5]

Arrival of a newspaper press created considerable excitement in frontier towns. In Denver in 1859, as two papers raced to be first to publish, miners placed bets and cheered the efforts of their favorites. Thirty years later townsfolk still treated a new newspaper like a long-lost relative. When the first copy of the *Wasatch Wave* was pulled from the press in Heber, Utah, "Three cheers were given with such vigor that they were heard a block away and a cloud of hats went flying in the air."[6] Publishers considered such enthusiasm their due. After all, wasn't the newspaper "just as necessary to fitting a man for his true position in life as food or raiment"?[7]

The Newspaper Rush

As it contributed in so many other ways to western development, the California gold rush that began in 1849 generated much of the western newspaper market, not only by attracting great numbers of people to the region, but also by changing the character of the economy. Industry and commerce challenged the preeminence of pastoral and agricultural interests, and the people attracted to the West created a market in which, as Earl Pomeroy has said, "[f]or a while almost anything would sell, at almost any distance, from Oregon City to Los Angeles, and everyone who had come West seemed justified."[8]

Boomtown San Francisco became the heart of economic vitality and the West's cradle of newspaper development. Several factors enhanced the city's early growth: an influx of young veterans of the recent Mexican War, looking for work and adventure; expanded steamship service; and the arrival of promoters like Sam Brannan, who came West with a Mormon group but soon branched out on his own.[9] The promoters brought one of their major tools—a printing press. Eager for the advantages a newspaper conferred, frontier residents proclaimed the press "that mighty engine which controls Powers and Principalities, converts howling wilderness into smiling fields and busy marts of commerce,"[10] and "first in the order of civilizing and enlightening pioneer communities."[11]

Westerners had diverse reasons for welcoming newspapers, boosterism only one of them. Public officials and politicians wanted to deliver information and partisan propaganda to the public, the literati desired regular reading material, and advertisers needed to reach customers. Newspapers also had a symbolic value. They gave a town an aura of stability and an identity. A town with a newspaper was a real town, just like the ones residents had left behind.

Urban historian Richard C. Wade has called the newspaper the "most important unifying element in urban culture." Wade says: "Read by nearly everyone, it was a plumb line which touched all levels of society. . . . Along with makeshift schools and churches, a newspaper was the first outward sign of civilization in frontier settlements."[12] Another historian suggests that newspapers served an essential function by helping pioneers maintain contact with their former societies.[13]

Whatever the newspaper's value to the community, publishers saw a market, and a willing cadre of printers and journalists moved to supply the product. "[W]e think we can see opportunity," said one publisher, expressing the motto of the day.[14] Thousands of newspapers were started between 1846 and 1890, exactly how many we may never know because some exist only as a mention in another newspaper's columns, copies having been destroyed over time.[15] (See

TABLE 1.1

Population, Daily and Weekly Newspapers, and Percent of Increase
in Eleven Western States and Territories, 1850–1890[a]

YEAR	POPULATION	NEWSPAPERS	% INCREASE POPULATION	% INCREASE NEWSPAPERS
1850	166,237	11		
1860	577,842	138	248	1,155
1870	991,310	285	72	107
1880	1,787,697	684	80	140
1890	3,027,613	1,281	69	87

Source: U.S. Census.

  a. 1850 includes one semi-monthly; other years cover newspapers with at least weekly frequency.

table 1.1.) Most of these newspapers were short-lived; the publishers who tried but gave up within a year or two are legion. In Nevada, for example, roughly two hundred newspapers were started between 1858 and 1890, but only eleven were publishing in the latter year. In Virginia City alone, thirty-seven newspapers were started in the same period. Twenty-one of these survived less than a year; only three lasted more than five years, and only three still published in 1890.[16]

A similar pattern developed in other parts of the West. In Washington Territory, more than 330 newspapers were started—about 260 in the 1880s as Washingtonians anticipated statehood—but fewer than half still published in 1890.[17] Washington fared better than Nevada; by 1890 Nevada's mining boom had ended and the state's population actually declined, taking newspapers down with it, whereas Washington, with a more broadly based economy, continued to grow. (See table 1.2.)

One western observer commented that "just as every community in the land must, only a few years from now, have a railroad of its very own, so did every hamlet and crossroads in the West pant . . . for its own newspaper."[18] The enormous desire for newspapers and the large number that were started no doubt provides the basis for the commonly held assumption that *every* little frontier town had at least one newspaper, a notion the statistics contradict. In the 11 territories and states in 1880 about three-fourths—73 percent—of the counties had at least one newspaper (160 of 218), which means one-fourth of the counties had none.[19] This percentage changes dra-

TABLE 1.2

Number of Newspapers [a] *Eleven Western States and Territories, 1850–1890*

STATE	1850	1860	1870	1880	1890
Arizona		1	17	35	35
California	7	116	181	361	490
Colorado			13	87	239
Idaho		6	10	48	48
Montana		10	18	55	55
Nevada		12	37	25	25
New Mexico	2	2	5	18	40
Oregon	2	14	30	74	126
Utah		2	9	22	28
Washington		4	12	29	164
Wyoming		6	11	31	31
WEST	11	138	285	684	1,281

Source: U.S. Census.

a. 1850 includes one semi-monthly; other years include newspapers with at least weekly frequency.

matically if only the territories are considered. By 1880, 91 percent of the counties in the western states (Oregon, California, Nevada, and Colorado) had newspapers. In the territories, however, only about half of the counties (50 of 96, or 52 percent) could claim a newspaper. Table 1.3 shows the percentage of counties with newspapers in each state or territory in 1880.

Clearly, publishers found some locations more attractive than others, and identification of a suitable market was the first step in establishing a newspaper. Sometimes publishers seized an opportunity that presented itself; the establishment of the *Californian* in Monterey was occasioned not so much by a careful examination of the market as by the discovery of a printing press coincident with the desire of military authorities to have an outlet for their decrees. But more often publishers were judicious in their site selection, and the subsequent transfer of the Monterey press to San Francisco came as a result of its owners' estimate of better prospects.[20]

A publisher's assessment of his market potential did not necessarily require an on-site examination. The right enticement, such as a sufficient guarantee of booster support, could convince him of the outstanding prospects of a locale. Portland boosters found Thomas Jefferson Dryer in San Francisco and with promises of fiscal sus-

TABLE 1.3

Percent of Counties With Newspapers, 1880

STATE	% OF COUNTIES
Arizona	71
California	100
Colorado	84
Idaho	46
Montana	82
Nevada	80
New Mexico	50
Oregon	87
Utah	30
Washington	48
Wyoming	71
WEST	78

Source: U.S. Census.

tenance, persuaded him to take a press to Oregon.[21] The developer of Steilacoom, Washington, employing similar assurances, induced another San Francisco printer to move north a few years later.[22]

Gold provided an almost irresistible lure, bringing more than one publisher to pack up a press and head for a gold-strike town on the strength of rumored riches. Towns from Whatcom on Bellingham Bay in northwestern Washington to Silver City, New Mexico, gained papers in response to mineral discoveries—and lost them just as quickly. Newspaperman William Bausman traveled north from San Francisco with a shipload of prospectors headed for the Fraser River diggings. Bausman's presence on board added confidence to the mining contingent: "When they heard there was a printing press aboard going to Whatcom, they supposed the owner had inside information and changed their destination [from Victoria, Canada, actually closer to the goldfields, to Whatcom]."[23] Ironically, the British soon required all prospectors to register in Victoria; the miners deserted Whatcom, and Bausman's three-month-old newspaper, the *Northern Light*, was extinguished.[24]

More commonly, however, publishers scouted an area or issued a prospectus to gauge the level of interest before setting up their presses. They rarely committed to publishing solely on the basis of local boosters' words or reports of gold. Portland's Dryer saw for himself the prospects of Puget Sound before he agreed to back a news-

TABLE 1.4

Average Population of Counties With, Without,
or With New Newspapers,[a] 1880

STATE	WITH NP		W/O NP		NEW NP	
	N	AVG.	N	AVG.	N	AVG.
Arizona	5	6,793	2	3,237	1	5,689
California	52	15,475	0	0	0	0
Colorado	26	7,118	5	1,854	8	7,009
Idaho	6	3,746	7	1,448	2	4,597
Montana	9	4,057	2	1,272	3	3,046
Nevada	12	4,993	3	782	0	0
New Mexico	6	10,713	6	9,214	0	0
Oregon	20	8,464	3	1,832	3	2,772
Utah	7	12,561	16	3,502	3	7,239
Washington	12	4,817	13	1,332	3	3,709
Wyoming	5	3,893	2	438	2	3,000
WEST (Avg.)	160	9,636	59	2,810	25	5,090

Source: U.S. Census.
a. New newspapers are those established after 1877.

paper for Olympia;[25] William Byers covered a good deal of western territory before hauling a press to the Colorado goldfields in 1859;[26] J. R. Watson sought public response with a sample copy of the *Washington Gazette* before he moved his press to Seattle.[27]

Market Conditions

The frontier publisher lacked the extensive statistics that influence modern business decisions, but he must have looked informally at factors that today's publisher evaluates. The frontiersman's analysis of demographic information may have been seat-of-the-pants instead of computerized, but he would have had a sense of the numbers necessary to conduct a viable enterprise.

Each time and place had its own demographics, many of which elude us after more than a century. Nevertheless, using census data, it is possible to trace the decision-making process of a publisher examining the potential market for a newspaper and to make comparisons and generalizations about press development.

Consideration of population is the most obvious starting point in

TABLE 1.5

Counties With (Without) Newspapers
by Population, 1880

ELEVEN WESTERN STATES AND TERRITORIES

Under 1,000	1 (19)
1,001–2,000	10 (14)
2,001–5,000	50 (15)
5,001–7,000	39 (4)
7,001–10,000	21 (1)
Over 10,000	39 (4)

Source: U.S. Census.

recreating the process a publisher might have followed as he contemplated establishment of a newspaper. He probably would have inquired of local government officials and boosters, and perhaps consulted census data, if available, to be assured that the potential audience was large enough to sustain his operation.

An examination of census data verifies the relationship between population and newspapers. Table 1.4 compares the average 1880 populations of counties in the region that had newspapers with those that did not. The figures show a substantial difference, 9,636 to 2,810, counties with newspapers having more than three times the population of those without. To control for the possibility that some of the differences may be attributed to the newspaper's booster efforts, the table also lists counties with newspapers no more than two years old (new newspaper counties), a period in which the newspaper may not yet have had time to make an impact. Although the differences narrow, counties with new newspapers still show a larger average population than those that have none, 5,090 to 2,810.

The populations of newspaper counties clustered below 5,000 and again between 5,000 and 8,000 (table 1.5). Overall, 76 percent of the newspapers were in counties with populations of less than 10,000, and most of the remaining newspapers were in San Francisco County, the largest county in the West.

Reliance on county populations could mislead if a county had more than one newspaper, so a prospective publisher wanted to know the average county population per newspaper (table 1.6). This typically fell between 2,500 and 3,500 people per newspaper, suggesting a countywide population base of at least 2,500 for a viable weekly news-

TABLE 1.6

Average Population Per Newspaper, 1880

STATE	DAILY[a]	WEEKLY[b]
Arizona	4,618	3,580
California	12,974	2,761
Colorado	5,329	2,540
Idaho	0	2,809
Montana	3,849	2,640
Nevada	3,364	1,165
New Mexico	10,502	4,682
Oregon	6,714	4,892
Utah	8,864	7,268
Washington	4,736	2,818
Wyoming	3,678	1,778
WEST (Avg.)	7,545	1,330

Source: U.S. Census.

a. Based on population of counties with at least one daily newspaper.

b. Based on population of counties with weeklies (1x, 2x, 3x) only.

paper. Table 1.6 also shows comparable figures for daily newspapers, which had larger population requirements.

Both weekly and daily publishers on the frontier were willing to undertake a newspaper for populations considerably less than the optimum numbers recommended by their counterparts elsewhere. The 1880 special census report on newspapers claimed an agricultural county needed 10,000 for a weekly and 15,000 for a daily, figures little changed from those suggested by Horace Greeley nearly thirty years earlier. At the same time, the census report acknowledged western newspapers as exceptions to these guidelines.[28]

A population of 2,500 people in a county provided a minimum foundation for a newspaper, but variations in the relationship between size and newspaper development reinforce the notion that population alone is not enough on which to stake one's journalistic fortune. In 1880 Washington, New Mexico, and Utah all had populations larger than Nevada's, but smaller percentages of their counties had newspapers. Eighty percent of Nevada's counties had newspapers, in contrast to only 30 percent in Utah and about 50 percent in Washington and New Mexico. The lack of consistent correlation between population and newspapers was evident in Whitman County, Washington, which had only one weekly for a population of 7,014, and in Utah County, Utah, where one twice-weekly served a population of 17,973. Conversely, the 17,000 residents of Pima County, Arizona, had access to three dailies, two of them in Tombstone, population 973.

Clearly, however important population was to a publisher, other elements also contributed to his choice of location for his newspaper. Of the several population characteristics modern research defines as important to newspaper success, few prove to be distinguishing factors for the frontier press. For example, a publisher would want a literate public that could read his paper, but in most communities literacy was not an issue. With the exception of New Mexico and Arizona, with high proportions of Spanish-speaking people, the western states and territories had an English literacy level higher than the nation's as a whole. In 1880, when 9.4 percent of the U.S. population was listed as illiterate, the percentage in most of the West fell well below 9.0, in Montana as low as 2.2. At the same time, although the rates did not correspond in all cases to the level of newspaper activity in each state or territory, those with the highest literacy levels also had the largest number of newspapers per population.

Historians of the mining camps have frequently noted the high cultural level of the forty-niners and those who followed. Allan Nevins has commented that "never in the history of the world has there been such an articulate body of pioneers" as the gold-seekers who headed for California "with an Ames shovel in one hand and a pen in the other."[29] Encouraged by the eastern press which advised westward travelers to take reading material with them, many people packed books with their other belongings. That the books were sometimes destroyed by water in the holds of ships or forgotten in the eagerness of their owners to get to the diggings only heightened the need for books and newspapers to be supplied locally.

To meet literary and informational needs, stationers in mining supply centers as remote as Helena, Montana, and Silver City, Idaho, advertised the latest in literature. For example, in 1867 the *Owyhee Avalanche* in Silver City carried advertisements for three booksellers and in 1879 two local suppliers advertised in the *Daily Leader* in Eureka, Nevada. Mining-camp dwellers so valued newspapers that the *Placer Times* in 1849 offered to pay correspondents with copies of eastern papers, "probably the only reward we can name that will be listened to."[30]

Although most frontier newspapers were in English, literacy among Spanish-speaking westerners was high enough to sustain several Spanish-language newspapers. In addition, as major centers grew, a foreign-language press developed. German was the most pervasive, but San Francisco also had newspapers in French, Italian, Danish, Swedish, and Chinese by 1880.

Stability of readership was another factor for a prospective publisher to consider. Newspapermen hoped to stay and help build a community. The publishers of the Cheyenne *Leader* emphasized that theirs was not a speculative venture; the Reno *Daily Record* publishers looked forward to permanence, and others around the region, like the publishers of the Chehalis, Washington, *Bee*, planned to "make money and prosper" wherever they happened to be located.[31]

However, one of the best indicators of stability, the proportion of women in a community, proved contrary to expectations. Women were perceived as an inherently steadying factor in the creation of a community, a single man finding it easier to move on to another location than a married couple or family. When the Gold Hill, Nevada, *News* started in 1863, a woman reader chided other local papers for failing to point out that the increasing number of women and families moving into the area made it a more desirable place to live.[32] In fact, however, in 1880 the states or territories with the largest proportion of women also tended to have the fewest newspapers per population.

Territories like New Mexico, Utah, and Oregon, with high proportions of women and relatively stable agricultural and pastoral economies, supported fewer newspapers than the more transient and volatile mining towns. The apparent contradiction is not difficult to resolve. Mining camps offered a more compact market with fewer distribution worries, their residents were more likely to have the cash a newspaper needed to pay for supplies, and prospectors had a keen interest in the kinds of information a newspaper might provide— new mineral discoveries, mining market trends, news of other opportunities to make one's fortune. It is also conceivable that miners had more discretionary time and that their distance from loved ones increased their desire for the contact with "home" that a newspaper could provide. In family-based communities, such as the agricultural towns, individuals could get at least some emotional support from other members of the family, perhaps reducing the need for the newspaper bridge with the former life. However, the lack of cash in agricultural areas probably played a more important role in publishers' preferences for mining camps.

Population meant readers, a vital component for any newspaper, but by the latter part of the nineteenth century, newspapers looked to advertising to provide a substantial proportion of their income. Western newspapers received about half of their revenue from advertising, and prospective publishers would have examined a business community, looking for retailers and service companies who might advertise. A lively business community also meant customers for the job-printing business that accompanied virtually every newspaper. Smart publishers took into account the potential for legal advertising—land, mining, and timber claim notices, in particular—which could make a considerable impact on their revenue picture.

Population and businesses provided incentives; the longer term promised profit. Daniel Boorstin has suggested that the "first task of the printer in the upstart city was to bring into existence a community where the newspaper could survive."[33] In fact, publishers wanted more than survival. They expected a community to provide them with immediate sustenance, but they also looked for promise of growth and prosperity. Those publishers who "came to stay" sought assurance that circulation, advertising, and job printing would increase, and their profits with them. "A newspaper has to look to things eventual as well as matters immediate," the publisher of the Butte, Montana, *Miner* explained upon starting in a town that had been somewhat depressed but was reviving.[34]

Frank Leach decided to forego starting a newspaper in Woodland, California, in favor of Vallejo, because he saw few prospects for growth in Woodland. Vallejo might be harder at the beginning, he thought, but it offered long-term benefits.[35] At the insistence of a local attorney, several printers investigated Snohomish, Washington, as a possible site for a newspaper, but when they arrived, they found a town in decline and too lethargic to provide good prospects for newspaper success.[36]

Yet in Spokane, Francis Cook started a newspaper when the town had only about 100 people. The difference? A signal that the publisher could expect growth, in this case the anticipated arrival of the Northern Pacific Railroad. That indicator was missing in Snohomish, and lack of a growth signal helps explain why simple measures of stability failed to attract publishers. They wanted a stable population base, but it was more important that it not be a stagnating one. A study of Washington Territory newspapers started before 1883 showed that 80 percent were linked to some event that promised substantial growth, and as time went on, publishers demanded ever stronger signals before setting up their presses.[37]

Throughout the West, three kinds of activity sent particularly strong growth signals: political development, mineral finds, and railroad construction. Anticipation of the formation of a state, territory, or local government generally accounted for the establishment of one or more newspapers in a given community. In Washington Territory, for example, as confidence grew that statehood was imminent, newspapers multiplied rapidly. In 1887 the territory had about seventy newspapers; in the next two years leading to statehood the number more than doubled.[38]

Official status, at whatever level, conferred political legitimacy on a locale and almost certainly induced a boost in population by assuring hesitant immigrants that the United States government gave its full blessing and protection. For the publisher this not only meant readers and advertisers, but also heightened prospects for power and profit, the power via the influence a publisher could exercise through his paper, the profit via the public printing which would come as a reward for his lending that influence to the winning side.

Publishers supported efforts to form separate territories, win statehood, and create new counties, recognizing that new political entities could be economically beneficial to them because of the forms and laws to be printed. The *Columbian* argued for separation from Oregon Territory, the Mesilla *Times* in New Mexico agitated for formation of Arizona Territory, the *Golden Age* in Lewiston campaigned for Idaho Territory, and the first papers in Los Angeles and San Diego called for the splitting of California into two states.[39] Countless papers pushed their towns' advantages as county seats.

Although much riskier even than political activity, a mineral find —gold, silver, copper, lead, even coal—provided another powerful incentive. Indeed, few growth signals were more obvious than the mining camps that mushroomed in the mountains and canyons of the West. Led by the California gold rush, every state experienced some kind of boom linked to minerals, and as already noted, publishers were there to help exploit the earth's riches. The *Owyhee Avalanche* in Silver City, Idaho, the *Miner* in Butte, Montana, and the *Territorial Enterprise* in Virginia City, Nevada, are just three of the hundreds of newspapers started in the mining camps, and great numbers of publishers also rushed to establish themselves in towns and cities like San Francisco, Denver, Salt Lake City, Sacramento, and Portland in anticipation of the growth of these centers to serve the burgeoning hinterlands.

Railroad expansion provided a further signal that a publisher could expect prosperity. A railroad line meant easier access for potential migrants, as well as better service in and out of town for mail and freight, including the news and printing supplies on which a newspaper depended. The Spokane *Times* and the Cheyenne *Leader* were among the many papers started in response to railroad construction. Boosters knew the value of a good transportation system and often worked closely with the newspaper to promote construction of trails, roads, and tracks, sometimes building short lines themselves if they found the major railroads reluctant to provide connections.

Anticipation of economic growth was the primary element that marked the establishment of a newspaper; nevertheless, circumstances peculiar to a location occasionally governed a publisher's decision. For example, the Mormon church's domination of Utah and control over resources undoubtedly influenced the fact that in 1880 Utah had relatively few newspapers in relation to its population. Most—but not all—Utah papers had the blessing of church president Brigham Young who recognized the value of channels for communication with his people but balanced that benefit with the need to devote all-too-limited resources to even more basic needs of survival.[40] The large Spanish-speaking population and Catholic influence in New Mexico that for many years prevented the establishment of a public-school system helps account for the territory's low literacy rate which in turn accounts for only half its counties having newspapers.[41]

Partisan politics also contributed to the spread of newspapers, but one not necessarily conducive to building a foundation for survival because those papers that lasted the longest were rarely the most rabid partisans. In general, the first newspaper in a community was started with economic objectives, but subsequent papers, as well as short-term campaign papers, often came as a response to the first editor's increasing partisanship. On the frontier, as elsewhere, the symbiotic relationship between press and politics was not to be denied, and an editor's initial neutrality waned as he gained opportunities to exercise political influence.[42] Nevertheless, the small populations in most towns meant that a publisher had to appeal to as many people as possible to ensure adequate support, and the more successful publishers tended to be those with a moderate voice.

Occasionally publishers started newspapers for highly personal reasons, ignoring statistics and rational business considerations. When no experienced publisher would start a newspaper in Snohomish, Washington, a local attorney who wanted an outlet for his own writing raised the funds to hire a printer to produce the *Northern Star*.[43] The publisher of the *Rebel Battery* in Seabeck, Washington, went into the business to pursue a personal vendetta against the local sawmill owners.[44] Both newspapers soon failed.

Few publishers exercised the self-indulgence of the owners of the *Northern Star* or *Rebel Battery*, however. While the journalists among them may have daydreamed about working oblivious to business concerns, most publishers adhered to the view expressed by a Nevadan who proposed to run his journal "in the interest of ourself and those dependent upon us, as far as any pecuniary advantage to be derived therefrom is concerned."[45] Or, as an Idaho publisher insisted, "In these degenerate days newspapers are run, not for glory, but for money. It is purely and strictly a matter of business."[46]

2

INK-STAINED ENTREPRENEURS

An Arizona publisher was killed resisting arrest after a stage robbery, and a Utah journalist moonlighted as an actor.[1] An Oregon publisher joined the first group to climb Mount St. Helens, while a San Francisco man personified the counting room: "Not a hair out of place, not a button-hole unmated to its button, his Prince Albert coat severely neat and irreproachable. . . Conservatism . . . enthroned."[2] A diverse group of characters, indeed, but all western newspapermen.

People who elected to publish frontier newspapers brought varied talents and interests to the task. Some were printers, with the know-how to set type and run a press; some were journalists, experienced in using pen and scissors to write news and editorials or decide what should be clipped from other newspapers; still others were newspaper neophytes whose primary occupation was the law, medicine, education, politics, or some other livelihood that gave them an affinity for the written word. Like the clientele they served, they encompassed a panorama of traits, from adventurism to caution, selflessness to egotism, intelligence to stupidity, philanthropy to baseness.

They went by several titles: publisher, proprietor, manager, or editor, or a combination thereof, such as editor and publisher, but titles rarely defined the individual's status vis-à-vis ownership of his newspaper. A publisher—the term we shall use most commonly because of its suggestion of fiscal responsibility—might be sole owner or a partner with one or two others, own a share in a larger syndicate, or be an employee of an unnamed owner or owners, arrangements that could change from time to time, even by the week, in the volatile business climate of the frontier. Documentation as to exactly which kind of ownership held at any given time or place is generally lacking but examples will show the diversity of financial arrangements that lay behind the development of western journalism.

Of the publishers who could be said to have sole title to their enterprises, few actually started their newspapers without financial assistance. Their offices were often fully mortgaged, but so long as they made the payments due on their debts, they alone controlled their operations. So far as can be determined, John Miller Murphy had no partners in the *Washington Standard* in Olympia, and Frank A. Leach became sole owner of the Vallejo, California, *Chronicle*. In 1875 Nevada newspaperman Alf Doten greeted the New Year by writing in his diary that he had paid off his debts and owned the Gold Hill *News* free and clear of encumbrances: "Have cleared my property & insured it, have a wife and baby, and am worth $20,000 or more— Am much better fixed than I ever was before in my life."[3]

Partnerships among more or less equals were a common form of newspaper ownership. A study of thirty-one pioneer Washington publishers found eight partnerships involving eighteen individuals, including the four printers who started the *Washington Statesman* in Walla Walla.[4] The two printers at the *Territorial Enterprise* in Nevada and the founders of the *Rocky Mountain News* in Denver also formed apparently straightforward partnerships.[5] Out-of-work or disgruntled printers such as those who started the Sacramento *Union*, the San Francisco *Call*, and the Los Angeles *Express* similarly pooled resources in partnerships.[6]

Partnerships were sometimes formed after an individual took over a newspaper and found he needed additional capital. When Edward Kemble assumed control of the *Star* and *Californian* in San Francisco in 1848, both papers were saddled with debts he could not handle alone. Kemble persuaded Edward C. Gilbert, a printer from New York, to take one-half interest and senior editorship in exchange for underwriting half the debts; George C. Hubbard, another New York printer, bought one-fourth interest. In 1849 the re-formed partnership then introduced the *Alta California*.[7] Decades later when Frank Leach bought the Oakland *Enquirer*, he needed funding and took two partners in return for their investments.[8]

Sometimes an individual's labor was his principal contribution to the partnership. And sometimes a partner supplying the financing stayed in the background. "Silent" partners were often candidates for office and undoubtedly influenced editorial policy on politics, but they paid little attention to the day-to-day operations of the paper. A local doctor-turned-political-candidate backed western Washington publisher Travers Daniel, and in eastern Washington Andrew Jackson Cain's partner was a fellow land promoter who sought political office.[9]

Another form of newspaper ownership, syndicates or stock companies, often supported booster and political papers. Local businessmen or partisan activists took shares in return for providing the money to purchase the type and presses needed for the enterprise. Occasionally they also pledged support to see the publisher through the early months, usually at minimum a promise of advertising and/or subscriptions, but also cash payments that could be called in if needed.[10] In these arrangements the publisher might receive a share in return for his labor, he might contribute capital, he might lease the equipment, or he might be only an employee, at least at first.

In Waitsburg, Washington, residents formed a community joint-stock company that raised $1,250 for the purchase of equipment which was leased to a printer who started the Waitsburg *Weekly Times*.[11] Residents of Genoa, Nevada, in 1865 bought the equipment of a defunct newspaper and leased it to a printer who started a short-lived paper.[12] California's *Placer Weekly Argus* started with capital provided by an association of wealthy businessmen.[13] Where the papers succeeded, ownership gradually consolidated into fewer hands. After a newspaper was under way, boosters and politicians often seemed content to sell or even give away their interests. This made it possible for employee-publishers to gain control of the enterprise.

Regardless of initial arrangements, ownership conditions could change rapidly, an individual maintaining his share sometimes only for months or weeks, others buying when he was ready to sell. John L. Dailey was short of cash when William Byers was putting together his team that would start the *Rocky Mountain News* in Denver, so Byers and his partner Thomas Gibson hired Dailey as printing foreman. Dailey bought a share of the paper as soon as he was able.[14] Similarly, Jonas Winchester bought into the *Pacific News* for which he worked, only to sell out less than a year later as the *News* declined.[15] James Anthony arrived in San Francisco in 1849, unsuccessfully tried mining for two years, then took a job as bookkeeper for the Sacramento *Union* and became a major shareholder in 1853.[16] In Las Vegas, New Mexico, a local school principal hired to translate for the Spanish section of the *Weekly Mail* owned three-fourths of the paper by his eighth issue.[17]

Some publishers had interests in two or more newspapers. For example, publishers of the *Alta California* started Sacramento's *Placer Times*, the *Oregonian's* Dryer also owned the *Columbian* in Washington Territory, John Booth owned both the Belmont *Courier* and the *Reese River Reveille* in Nevada, the owner of the Colfax, Washington, *Gazette* started the Moscow, Idaho, *Mirror*, and the founder of the Cheyenne *Leader* concurrently published the Laramie *Sentinel* and the South Pass City *News*.[18]

Movable Typesetters

In the press history of every western state and territory, names of publishers swirl like leaves in the wind, now landing here, now drifting somewhere else, leaving few signs that they had passed by. A study of thirty-eight early Washington publishers showed that nearly two-thirds of them were associated with a particular newspaper two years or less, and half of them stayed no more than a year.[19] Sometimes publishers simply walked away from debt or their press was repossessed, and some sold in order to go somewhere they considered more promising, and, of course, economic exigencies such as mine closures or too much competition forced publishers to seek a change of scene. But failure to stay should not necessarily be taken as a sign of failure of the newspaper.

A willingness to move, to try a new location, characterized western newspapermen. They even called themselves "co-temporaries" instead of "contemporaries" in acknowledgment of the ephemeral nature of their existence. Generally unencumbered by family—at least in the early days because even if married, their wives tended to remain in the East—printers and journalists enjoyed a flexibility and mobility that they exploited as desire or circumstances demanded. Thus personal inclinations or the need to return to their families might result in publishers leaving their newspapers. Prosperity attracted buyers whose offers publishers could not refuse.

James Allen exemplifies the mobile publisher. An Ohio newspaperman and former state campaign manager for William Henry Harrison, the 49-year-old Allen first tried mining after he arrived in California in 1850. Like most journalists lured by gold, he soon returned to his earlier vocation and by 1852 was editor of the Marysville

Record. In 1855 he was elected mayor of Marysville. Subsequently elected state printer, he moved to Sacramento where he edited the *California American.* He sold his interest in that newspaper and in 1858 returned to Marysville to buy a share in the Marysville *Daily News.* Frustrated by the economic uncertainties of mining-camp publishing, he quit newspapering in favor of farming, but the farmer's plow turned out to have no more appeal than the miner's pick, and in 1860 he was back in the business, editing the *Hydraulic Press* in North San Juan for a few weeks, then moving on to the *Morning Transcript* in Nevada City, California. The following year he operated the *Washoe Times* in Nevada, at least his sixth newspaper in a decade. Who knows how many more newspapers he would have been able to list on a resume had he not died of blood poisoning in 1863.[20]

Another mobile westerner, J. Wing Oliver, who was associated with six newspapers in eight years, founded the Grass Valley *Telegraph* in 1853 and the next year edited the Georgetown *News*; in 1855 he was a member of the California State Assembly, but in 1856 operated the *Columbian* in Tuolumne County for a brief period; two years later he had left still another newspaper, the *Columbia Gazette,* in favor of the *Siskiyou Chronicle,* and in 1860 he started the *Scott Valley Mirror* at Fort Hall.[21] Frank A. Kenyon, called "the man of many newspapers," had ties with the *Lyon County Times,* Bodie *Standard,* Esmeralda *Herald,* and Pioche *Review* in Nevada; the *Golden Age* and the *Mining News* in Idaho; the *Weekly Independent* in Montana; *Daily Journal* and *Review* in Utah; *Daily News* in Oregon, and additional papers in California. He was heading for Guatemala to start another newspaper when he died of jaundice.[22] In Oregon, Milton H. Abbott was associated with papers in The Dalles, Albany, LaGrande, Baker, Oregon City, and Portland in a twenty-year period.[23]

The frontier publisher most famous for his mobility was Legh Freeman, whose "press on wheels" anticipated the Union Pacific as it moved toward its juncture at Promontory Point, Utah, in 1869. Freeman published at sixteen or more locations during his controversial career. With the completion of the railroad, Freeman eventually settled in Washington, publishing at least two newspapers there.[24]

At the other end of the mobility spectrum were the publishers who became veritable pillars of their communities: Byers at the *Rocky Mountain News* for more than 20 years; George Crosette, publisher of the Butte, California, *Record* for 30 years; Robert E. Fisk at the

Helena, Montana, *Herald* for 36 years; and John Miller Murphy at the *Washington Standard* in Olympia for more than 50 years.[25]

Glitter and Destiny

Many men who started newspapers, particularly before 1870, were drawn westward by gold and other metals, as a succession of strikes attracted prospectors, adventurers, and entrepreneurs. Quickly disillusioned by the struggle to make money in the diggings, newspapermen were nevertheless encouraged by general prospects in the West, and, desiring to stay, they returned to their craft for a means of livelihood.

John A. Lewis and William H. Rand were a Boston reporter and printer, respectively, who tried mining before joining the *Alta California* staff and eventually starting the Los Angeles *Star*.[26] Pennsylvanian William Bausman sought gold in the northern California mines but soon became an editor on a mining-camp newspaper, and then bought an interest in the *Daily Sun* in San Francisco. Having learned firsthand both the difficulties of mining and the potential profit in supplying a service to miners, Bausman responded quickly when word of gold on Canada's Fraser River reached San Francisco in 1858. He headed for northwestern Washington with a printing press, not a gold pan, in his baggage.[27] Thornton McElroy intended to prospect for gold but news of sickness in the mining camps led him to detour to Portland, where he set type for several papers including Dryer's newly established *Oregonian*. Before going to Olympia as Dryer's agent, McElroy returned to California to spend a few months at Placerville where, once he learned where and how to pan for gold, he could earn as much as $16.00 a day, rather better than the $6.50 a day he was paid for setting type in Oregon.[28]

Probably most printers and journalists in the West in the 1850s tried their luck in mines at least briefly. But few newspapermen persevered as prospectors, preferring the perhaps smaller but relatively surer income a newspaper could provide. Increasingly, men realized they would not find gold lying on the ground waiting to be collected, and that successful working of a mining claim required a kind of labor to which they were unaccustomed. Operating a press was hard work, but it was work they understood. Printing also offered more freedom.

As mining became less individualized and more industrialized, men preferred the relative independence of the printing office.

While exceedingly important, gold and other metals were, of course, not the only lures to the West. The westward trend was well established before the discovery of gold at Sutter's Mill. By the mid-1840s, the Pacific Northwest and California had significant numbers of American settlers, most of whom urged the United States to take control of the region. Nor was gold a factor in the settlement of Utah where the Mormons founded their Zion. The nation's manifest destiny, many believed, was to fill the continent, and who were printers to disagree.

Printer Sam Brannan did not need the incentive of gold. He came west with fellow Mormons to establish a colony in California.[29] John Miller Murphy, future pioneer Washington publisher, arrived with his sister's family who staked their future on commerce in the Pacific Northwest. Murphy was just a lad when they settled in Olympia where his merchant brother-in-law opened a shop, and the youngster watched McElroy and Wiley unload their equipment for the *Columbian*.[30] N. C. Meeker came west to organize the Union Colony, a co-operative movement that settled Greeley, Colorado. Meeker became interested in co-operative movements under the influence of Horace Greeley at the New York *Tribune*, for whom he had worked both as a Civil War correspondent and later as agricultural editor. When Meeker decided to lead a colony to northern Colorado, a newspaper was recognized as an essential communication tool for the colony. Meeker started the Greeley *Tribune*, named, like the town, to honor his mentor.[31] Other publishers, such as John P. Clum of the Tombstone, Arizona, *Epitaph* and Richard C. McCormick of the *Arizona Miner*, moved west to take up appointments as territorial officers.[32]

The first essential for publishing a newspaper was to have someone to do the printing, and in the early days of frontier journalism, the typical publisher filled that role. A journeyman printer, even when he might have no personal interest in writing, could copy stories out of other newspapers to fill his pages, whereas a writer, even an experienced one, probably lacked the specialized knowledge required to do a printer's work. In the later years, as the number of journeyman printers available for hire in the West increased, more nonprinters became interested in operating newspapers. In Washington Territory, only one of thirteen publishers who started newspapers before

1870 had a background other than printing; during the next decade, six of eighteen were not printers.[33]

Curiously, people who started a newspaper without a printing or journalistic background did not, as a rule, seek out experienced newspapermen as partners. They preferred to employ printers, although they sometimes offered conditions similar to partnerships. Dr. Michael Beshoar, who started the Pueblo, Colorado, *Chieftain*, found a printer in Golden presumed to be dying of consumption. Beshoar examined the printer and concluded that he suffered only from bronchitis, laryngitis, and tracheitis, and that a good climate and healthy living would ensure his survival for quite a few years to come. Beshoar therefore made him a healthy offer: he could be foreman, job printer, and co-proprietor of Beshoar's proposed newspaper. Beshoar would pay his expenses and a salary equal to half the net profits for three years, while retaining control and absorbing any losses.[34] The Legh Freemans advertised that they would sell an interest in the Ogden *Freeman* to a printer qualified to be foreman, but they did not offer to share control.[35]

Observers of the American frontier, from the first wilds of Massachusetts to the Pacific shore, have noted that settlers undertook multiple responsibilities because there was so much to do and so few people to do it. The British visitor, James Bryce, wrote of western business, "No one has any fixed occupation; he is a storekeeper to-day, a ranchman to-morrow, a miner next week," and "to prosper in the West you must be able to turn your hand to anything, and seize the chance to-day which every one else will have seen tomorrow."[36] For many newspapermen, publishing was part of a dual, or indeed multiple, career.

The Seattle publisher Isaac M. (Ike) Hall is a case in point. Hall moved to Seattle in 1864 from Iowa where he had been a schoolteacher. In Seattle he took advantage of the easy-going territory rules to become a lawyer and eventually made a name for himself as a witty, capable attorney and judge. During his first few years he also tried a number of other enterprises including real-estate speculation, and for some reason he apparently learned to "stick type" (the term for hand typesetting, so named because the typesetter places the type in a holder called a composing stick). In 1866 he acquired the remains of Seattle's first newspaper, the *Gazette*, and turned it into the *Puget Sound Weekly*. He tried publishing semi-weekly and daily editions in spring and summer of 1866, giving the territory its first daily newspaper, but had shut them down by the time he sold the weekly in September.[37]

Hall then concentrated on his law practice but controlled the print-shop again the next spring—apparently the buyers couldn't pay for it—and resumed publication with the *Puget Sound Weekly Gazette*. Like most lawyers and newspapermen, Hall gravitated to politics, and he used the *Gazette* effectively in the 1867 election. A staunch Union party supporter, he received the party's backing in his bid for King County auditor. When he won the position, he sold the *Gazette* to a publisher who turned it into the *Weekly Intelligencer*, the antecedent of today's *Post-Intelligencer*.[38]

But Hall was not finished with newspapers. In the early 1870s, when another local attorney came into possession of a newspaper office for payment of client debts, Hall and a partner undertook management of it. They changed the name of the *Alaska Times and Seattle Dispatch* to the *Territorial Dispatch and Alaska Times*. Hall announced plans to make the *Dispatch* Puget Sound's premier newspaper, but turned the paper back to its previous owner before he had a chance to make good on his statements. In 1877 Hall again was involved in repossession of the *Dispatch*, but he may have been acting as attorney for other owners.[39] Hall also founded something of a newspaper dynasty. His son and nephews established the Seattle *Daily Call*, a pro-labor, anti-Chinese newspaper in the late 1880s, and his ex-wife, Laura, edited a communitarian newspaper in Port Angeles about the same time.[40]

Attorney was perhaps the most common alter ego for publishers, but certainly not the only one. Teachers gravitated to newspapering. The owners of the *Columbia Chronicle*, in Dayton, Washington, taught school; seven teachers published newspapers in New Mexico before 1880.[41] James S. Reynolds, founder of the *Idaho Tri-Weekly Statesman* in Boise, had been a printer, attorney, and schoolteacher; he was city recorder at The Dalles when he and two other Oregonians decided to start a paper at Boise.[42]

Ministers, too, went into the business. Missionaries in the Pacific Northwest, California, and New Mexico introduced printing to the West, although religious tracts, not newspapers, came from their presses. Later, however, minister-publisher ranks included Padre José Antonio Martinez, who started the first school in Taos, New

Mexico, as well as its first newspaper, and the Reverend Ferdinand Washington Dallas Mays, who published the *Washington Independent* in Pomeroy, Washington, for more than twenty years.[43]

Few newspapermen stopped with one alternative career choice. A Wyoming publisher worked as a teacher, lawyer, accountant, agriculturalist, miner, and land salesman at various times; the owner of one California paper also entertained as an actor, lecturer, and impersonator; and another California publisher was an undertaker, as well as the local photographer.[44]

Publishers throughout the West also held political office, many serving in their state or territorial legislatures, or holding local political sinecures as rewards for party service. Among New Mexico publishers before 1880, at least fourteen became territorial officials.[45] A study of seven influential Wyoming publishers showed they held a variety of government positions: mayor, alderman, justice of the peace, judge, city and county attorney, territorial auditor, penitentiary commissioner, legislator, postmaster, and federal land commissioner.[46] Several Washington Territory publishers served in the territorial legislature, as well as in other government posts.[47] A few men, such as McCormick in Arizona and Tom Fitch in Nevada, started newspapers specifically to foster their own political careers.

The level of energy required to maintain one's multiple occupations was served by the youth of western settlers in general and of early publishers in particular. Of twenty-one early Washington publishers whose ages have been determined, ages ranged from 21 to 46 with an average of 30; 52 percent were under 30 years and all but one were younger than 40.[48] While he probably overstates the case, Robert L. Housman says pioneer publishers "needed youth, of mind and body, to face the hardships of pioneer newspaper making; the long hours, the irregular routines, the work with inadequate equipment."[49] The stamina of youth unquestionably helped an individual cope with newspaper production plus the rigor of pioneer life. At the same time, the experience that usually comes with maturity often enabled publishers to find better ways of coping, and newspapermen were not so young that they lacked experience. Of the Washington publishers studied in depth, 71 percent had prior newspaper experience.[50]

Education levels ranged widely, but evidence suggests that publishers generally had better educations than the average person. The newspaper itself was a good school, exposing printers to a variety of information and writing as they set type. Some, like the *Oregonian's* Dryer who had only about three months of formal education, were largely self-taught, but at the other extreme, a Wyoming publisher had been the first president of the University of Washington.[51]

The origins and mobility of the Washington publishers reflect the territorial and western populations as a whole. Only two were born in the West, one in San Francisco, the other in Seattle. The most frequently represented birthplaces were Pennsylvania, Indiana, Ohio, and New York. Only two were foreign born. Most of the publishers had lived in the Mississippi Valley before moving west. Once in the West, 82 percent had moved more than once, commonly starting in California, then moving to a center such as Portland or Denver where they worked in an existing print shop. There they gathered the experience and resources with which to move to a smaller community to start a newspaper.[52]

Born in Pennsylvania, the *Columbian's* publisher, McElroy, spent his childhood in Ohio and young manhood in Illinois before the gold rush beckoned.[53] Seattle's first publisher, John R. Watson, lived in Ohio, Illinois, California, and British Columbia.[54] Another Ohioan, Francis H. Cook, publisher of newspapers in Olympia, Tacoma, and finally Spokane, served his apprenticeship in Iowa before moving to the Pacific Northwest.[55] Similarly, of seven Wyoming newspapermen studied in detail, three were New Yorkers and the others were from Virginia, Maine, Illinois, and Pennsylvania. All had stopped in at least one other state in middle America before arriving in Wyoming.[56] The majority of the Washingtonians, and probably most western publishers, had lived in the region at least five years before starting their own businesses.

Women in publishing positions were usually wives or widows. The only woman publisher in the Washington study, Mrs. M. L. Money, co-proprietor with her husband of the Kalama *Beacon*, took primary credit as the editor.[57] The co-publisher of the *Arizona Star*, E. Josephine Brawley Hughes, served as business manager, bookkeeper, and circulation director until 1883 when she took over the paper, her husband having become governor.[58] A few women published more or less independently of their husbands' activities. The San Diego *Sun* was started by the wife of a prominent attorney.[59] Sarah Moore Clarke published the *Contra Costa* in Oakland, using the San Francisco *Evening Journal* facilities, owned by her husband, for printing.[60] Ada Chase Merritt and a male partner bought the *Idaho Recorder* in Salmon, and Caroline Romney founded the Durango, Colorado, *Record*, but relatively few general circulation newspapers had women publishers until after 1890.[61]

The typical publisher was politically active, even if his paper was not the avowed spokesman for a party. Of the nineteen Washington Territory publishers whose political preferences were clear, the majority (58 percent) declared themselves Republicans; the remainder split evenly between Democrats and Independents.[62] Thirty percent of California publishers in 1869 claimed independence or no party affinity; 34 percent aligned themselves with Democrats, and 36 percent with Republicans.[63] California Republicans gained adherents as the decades passed, but greatest growth came in the Independent category. By 1879, this group accounted for 63 percent of California's general circulation press, Democrats and Republicans combined totalling only 38 percent.[64] Meanwhile, in the West as a whole, by the late 1870s, 36 percent of the major daily newspapers supported the Republican party, 21 percent the Democratic party, and the remaining 43 percent were Independent, a higher proportion of independents than any other region except the middle Atlantic states.[65]

When western publishers declared their papers to be "independent," often they were simply denying any formal party affiliation or support; they were hardly neutral. As the Grass Valley, California, *Tidings* declared in 1874, "*TIDINGS* will not be NEUTRAL in, or independent OF politics. It will be independent IN politics and independent OF party."[66] Few newspapermen could resist the symbiotic relationship between politics and the press. Indeed, as Tocqueville had observed for earlier frontiers, the newspaper provided a channel for ideological dialogue, and most newspapermen involved themselves with political parties willingly, even enthusiastically.[67] The result was not so much a press funded by and thereby beholden to a partisan organization, but, as Gerald Baldasty has pointed out for the time period generally, an adherence on the part of publishers to party *principle*.[68]

Nevertheless, as the region developed politically, some publishers were out-and-out partisans. Clarence Bagley in Washington Territory provides a prime example of the publisher thrilled by involvement in political skirmishing. Bagley allied himself to a rising political star, Selucius Garfielde, who, with his supporters, started a newspaper. Bagley, only 25 years old, became Garfielde's publisher and signed a formal agreement, pledging to support the politician's nomination for territorial delegate to Congress.[69] But the agreement was hardly necessary. Bagley's excitement about his political role pervades his correspondence with his father, Daniel, a pioneer Seattle minister and active Republican. "We did some of the tallest and prettiest working that ever was done," Bagley wrote in connection with a county nominating convention. "Four of us met in our office and planned everything and then went into convention and carried everything."[70]

Garfielde, who won the election, helped subsidize the newspaper but after he lost his bid for re-election, worried that he was carrying more than his share of the financial burden.[71] Although Garfielde faded from the Washington political scene, the Olympia clique that he developed dominated territorial politics for a decade, thanks in part to Bagley's continued support which was duly rewarded with public-printing contracts.

Even Nevada's Alf Doten, a loyal but generally low-key Republican, could be moved by political adrenaline. Describing a behind-the-scenes meeting much like Bagley's, Doten wrote that deciding who should be nominated at the Republican State Convention was the "liveliest dabbling in politics I ever had to do with."[72]

A party could be good to a supportive publisher, rewarding him with a cash subsidy, public-printing contract, or political office. Appointments such as postmasterships were a common payback, but some publishers sought elective office with the party's approval and support. Seattle publisher Ike Hall, after promising "to avoid the filthy pool of political chicanery and trickery and to discuss the important political questions of the times in a calm, dispassionate, and conservative manner," proceeded to dirty the campaign by accusing the Democratic candidate for territorial delegate of lying, vote tampering, and other skullduggery, a show of loyalty that fellow party members repaid by voting for him for auditor.[73]

Successful candidates like Hall gave up their newspapers if they had no time to operate them properly, but otherwise they seemed to see no conflict of interest in holding office while also running their newspapers. The publisher of the *Sage Brush* in Susanville was also county judge, and an Arizona publisher served concurrently as territorial attorney general.[74]

As might be anticipated in such a large and diverse group, not everyone boasted a sterling character. The confidence local business people showed by giving a printer $1,500 or more to buy equipment usually paid off, but occasionally they made a poor choice in their selection of publisher. In Martinez, California, the "Co." in local newspaper publisher W. B. Soule and Co. referred to a number of public-spirited citizens who gave Soule money to buy a press and other essentials. Described later as an "unmitigated confidence sharp," Soule ordered the equipment but failed to pay for it, instead disappearing with the funds. The investors, philosophically making the best of their loss, arranged to pay for the press and hired two printers to publish the newspaper.[75]

Another publisher, W. L. Jernegan, who started the *Yolo Democrat* in 1857, persuaded a local businessman to buy equipment, and staff to work on credit and even lend him money. ("Think of that," recalled his editor later, "an editor loaning cash.") Jernegan then left the area in debt to everyone who had "trusted him under the very mistaken supposition that he hadn't got sense enough to cheat anybody!"[76] Jernegan soon became one of the original partners in Nevada's *Territorial Enterprise*, but he had to be forcibly evicted by the local sheriff when he lost his share in the newspaper because of poor business judgment. He tried to get even by spreading malicious stories about his former partner, but his efforts to destroy the man failed. On his deathbed Jernegan cursed the *Enterprise* and anyone associated with it.[77] All frontier newspapers should have been so cursed; the *Enterprise* achieved considerable success.

Soule and Jernegan represented the minority, however. Most publishers had too high an opinion of themselves and their calling to betray their backers deliberately, although financial exigencies may have led some to leave town in the middle of the night. They understood the value and potential power of their medium in the community, and they tried to use it responsibly. The press was, as one publisher wrote, an "exalting influence" and "indispensable appendage to society," that should be treated with care.[78]

Early publishers felt keenly the educational function of the press, and its role in supplying "a hungry people in their yearnings for brain food."[79] Said a Washington publisher, "Next to the schools the newspaper is the most potent of public educators, and next to the churches is the most efficient of all moral conservitors [sic]."[80] His view was later echoed in a Seattle paper which, after commenting that in settlements east of the Mississippi the itinerant Methodist preacher was often first on the scene, suggested that west of the great river the press filled that role: "It may be said that these courageous educators have frequently taken the place of both the pedagogue and preacher and they have become both the schoolmaster and the church."[81]

At the same time, they expressed their disappointment that the reading public failed to assure that publishers' rewards were commensurate with their efforts and their newspapers' value to society. Few could declare with the publisher of the San Diego *Herald* that "we have been successful beyond our most ardent hopes . . . and retire from the post we have occupied for the past four years with pleasure and profit."[82] More often they shared the view of the disillusioned publisher who wrote, "Newspapers have been all-important in their support of the mining industry, but the newspaper men remained poor, the crumbs falling to them from the rich man's table being merely a profitless aggravation in the way of excited hopes."[83]

PART II

Income

3

BUILDING CIRCULATION

Wherever they settled, however carefully they assessed a community, publishers still had to deal with the problem of turning population into readership, for both the income it could provide and the advertisers it could attract. As we have seen, attracting readers was not difficult; an audience was ready and waiting. Nevertheless, readers needed to be encouraged, even cajoled, into actually parting with some of their income in exchange for the newspaper, and the publisher who took his readers for granted invited their disdain. Publishers recognized that they had to treat their publications as products and, like salesmen, cultivate their markets. To this end they used various strategies and tools in building a list of subscribers, both at home and abroad.

In opening salutatories, in subsequent editorial comment, and in advertising, frontier publishers stressed that people had an obligation to support the newspaper which, they promised, provided the means to bring prosperity to everyone in town. According to a California paper:

> Particularly in reading matter does the local press represent its community abroad. The home industries, the new enterprises, the resources and successes of the locality all find a herald in the press. . . . Thus the wealth of the locality is increased and its progress insured.[1]

Publishers contrasted their community efforts with the failure of out-of-town papers to provide a similar service. In the 1870s, an item made the rounds of the region as papers borrowed one another's ideas for boosting business:

> Do the city papers say anything in regard to your own county? Nothing. Do they contain notices of your schools, churches, . . . and hundreds of other local matters of interest, which your

home paper publishes? Not an item. Do they ever say a word calculated to draw attention to your county and its numerous thriving towns, and aid in their progress and enterprise? Not a line.[2]

The writer concluded by scolding people who subscribed to city papers just because they were bigger. A Washington newspaper followed the same theme, pointing out that it only had time and space to cover county news but that citizens should be interested enough to take the local paper as well as big-city publications.[3]

An Idaho publisher facing lagging subscription income reminded local residents of the risks he took in starting the paper in the "dullest season of the year."[4] The *Rocky Mountain Herald* in Denver told readers that support for the newspaper "would help themselves and their neighbors to more advantage than twenty times the amount invested in grand streetcars, or chambers of commerce, stylish saloons, or even churches";[5] the Cheyenne *Leader* called on readers to supply their "cordial support" for the paper's efforts to promote the town.[6]

By stressing boosterism, publishers hoped to persuade local readers to buy the paper for friends and relatives as well as themselves. The purpose of a booster newspaper was to print stories about the town and to distribute copies around the country, both to other newspapers that might reprint the stories and to friends and relatives who might be interested in moving west. The Calico, California, *Print* promised to provide a paper that readers would "take pleasure in sending to distant friends,"[7] and the Belmont, Nevada, *Courier* suggested a subscription would make a

> NICE PRESENT. If you have a father, mother, sister, brother, cousin, aunt, uncle, or a dear friend, living at a distance, either on this coast, in the Atlantic States, or in Europe, you should subscribe for the *Courier*, to be sent regularly from the publication office, which would not only save frequent correspondence, but it would carry a weekly reflex of all local matters, as well as invaluable information regarding the resources of the country in which you are living.[8]

The appeals brought results. A Washington publisher remembered a number of residents who purchased several subscriptions to help boost the town; one couldn't read but nevertheless bought the paper to send to friends as a substitute for writing to them.[9] The *Deseret News* noted in its first issue that ten emigrants had paid for copies for friends they had left in the East.[10] In Oregon the *Statesman* commented on the popularity of subscriptions in other states, which had been purchased by Oregonians wanting to maintain ties.[11]

Publishers forthrightly expressed displeasure when they felt townsfolk had failed them. Residents who subscribed to out-of-town newspapers drew particular wrath. A list of journalists' "likes and dislikes" circulated among western newspapers, drawing readers' attention to publishers' "dislike" of men who subscribed to two or three eastern papers while neglecting the hometown sheet.[12] Another publisher complained when he found that he was sending only eight copies of his paper to a nearby town but that some fifty copies of the other town's paper were sold in his camp.[13]

Pleas for subscribers stressed boosterism and convenience, but they also pointed out that the newspaper filled an informational need by supplying news. The Sacramento *Daily Union* promised it would provide good coverage of San Francisco and have a correspondent in all the important mining areas.[14] The arrival of emigrants to the Salt Lake Valley elicited intense interest so the *Deseret News* offered to publish the names of newcomers for 25 cents each and at times filled a half page or more with the names of those who responded.[15] The editor of a Vallejo, California, newspaper in the 1870s said one of his "best business strokes" was to send a writer to interview farmers in the surrounding countryside. Subscriptions generated from the tour more than covered its cost.[16]

A Montana publisher tied readership to improvements in the paper when he put out a call for more subscribers: "If the people expect a more readable sheet they must 'put up,'" he said, because the more "newsy" the paper, the more labor was required. "Help us increase our list, thereby securing a better paper."[17]

Occasionally, publishers appealed to readers' better nature, their intelligence, and their morality, citing a newspaper's contribution to society; concurrently they complained about the morals of those who read the paper but did not subscribe. When they found that allowing residents to lounge around the newspaper office not only disrupted work but also cost subscriptions because the hangers-on read copy over the shoulders of the typesetters, they tried to ban them from the office. One mining camp publisher sought to turn expulsion from his office to his advantage: "BUY PAPERS.—Let those who wish to know what is to appear in the Echo, buy it every Saturday, and they will save us the very unpleasant task of telling them that our rules are, not to read the copy on the stand or file before it appears in the paper."[18]

Newspapers' exhortations to subscribe were by no means the only device used to build readership. Most frontier circulation activities would be familiar today, even if their execution was less sophisticated than modern approaches. For example, a publisher did not wait for subscribers to come to him; he went to them through door-to-door canvassing, a challenging task in the spread-out environs of many communities.

When the first publisher went into Spokane in 1880, he recognized that the village of 100 residents would be unable to support a newspaper until the railroad arrived and brought additional population. He hired a man to canvass nearby Colfax for subscriptions and arranged for special courier delivery.[19] The *Washington Statesman* in Walla Walla sent agents into the Idaho mining country to turn prospectors into subscribers.[20]

A California newspaperman canvassed Napa for subscriptions to the San Francisco *Argus* in the 1860s but refused to take advance payment because he thought the paper's future uncertain. The paper later told him to go back to collect and keep whatever he could get in lieu of pay.[21] One canvassing trip yielded an Idaho publisher 200 subscriptions.[22] When starting his newspaper career in Como, Nevada, and then later in Virginia City, Alf Doten, future publisher of the Gold Hill *News*, had no compunction in canvassing for California newspapers even though they might be competition for his Nevada employers.[23]

Amateur agents like Doten were common, and publishers prevailed upon local residents—particularly those who frequently traveled to surrounding areas, such as doctors and the sheriff—to help them gather subscriptions. A Washington publisher's agent in a nearby Puget Sound town quit, writing that he had agreed in good faith to represent the paper, "But on enquiry, I found a much larger sum could be raised on the other paper owing probably to its being more explanatory and consequently better calculated to attract attention."[24]

Publishers hired professional agents in larger centers. The *Territorial Enterprise* in Nevada employed the Thomas Boyce agency in San Francisco, which accepted subscriptions and advertising for twenty-four other newspapers from Portland to Los Angeles. The *Enterprise* also had a Sacramento agent who served a number of California newspapers as well. A San Francisco agent represented the *Oregon Statesman*, and the *Central Nevadan* used agents in New York and Chicago as well as on the West Coast. The *Deseret News* in Salt Lake City developed an extensive system of agents in thirty-eight Utah settlements as well as in California, Nevada, Idaho, New York, St. Louis, and Liverpool.[25]

Knowing that potential subscribers wanted to see the product before they purchased it, publishers distributed free copies when they first established their newspapers. New owners sometimes also offered samples to give a boost to circulation.

Premiums also attracted subscribers.[26] In 1868 anyone paying the $3.00 annual subscription in advance for the *Echo* in Olympia, Washington, received a steel engraving or lithograph.[27] The San Francisco *Chronicle* in the 1870s offered a $75.00 sewing machine and a subscription to the weekly for $22.00 or to the daily for $26.00, plus freight from Chicago. Later, a sporting outfit—shotgun, coat, belt, hat, and twenty-five shells—could be had together with the weekly for $13.50, with the daily for $18.50.[28]

Premium proposals became quite elaborate, with newspapers promoting "clubs," or multiple subscription arrangements. Premiums increased in value commensurate with the number of subscriptions collected. For example, a person getting ten subscriptions for a Pacific Northwest weekly earned a $10.00 gold ring; fifteen subscriptions brought a $15.00 moss agate ring, and twenty-five gained a $25.00 watch. Larger premiums were especially aimed at organizations such as women's clubs who might work to collect subscriptions to earn a triple-silver-plated, six-piece tea service.[29] In San Francisco in 1878, the *Chronicle* offered a choice of gold coin or premiums and claimed that an enterprising individual could make up to $5,000 a year getting subscribers for its weekly edition. Awards ranged from "An elegant SQUARE PIANO, seven and a quarter octaves," or $375 in coin for 300 subscriptions, to a variety of items such as a lady's riding whip, games or sports equipment, valued at about $2.00, for three subscriptions. Items for the home or the farm, books, and guns were used to entice people to serve as subscription agents for the newspaper.[30]

Newspapers less generous—or perhaps with more confidence in

their worth—sometimes promised free subscriptions to people collecting a number of readers for them or free binding to subscribers who saved a full year's set of issues.[31]

Although views on the appropriateness of the practice differed sharply, some publishers arranged for subscriptions to New York or San Francisco papers together with the local product. In Washington the Kalama *Semi-Weekly Beacon* took the position that circulation of good eastern publications would whet the reading appetite of local residents, thereby benefiting the hometown newspaper,[32] but Clarence Bagley at the *Puget Sound Courier* argued that encouraging people to read outside publications only ensured that revenue was lost to the town.[33]

Publishers seized other kinds of promotional opportunities to attract subscribers. One evidenced considerable sensitivity to community spirit when he let representatives from the local sewing society help print the first copy of the newspaper; the society auctioned the historic document as a fund-raiser. The same publisher also offered a free subscription to the oldest man in the county to publicize the paper.[34] William Byers let Cherry Creek prospector O. P. "Old Scout" Wiggins ink the first form of the *Rocky Mountain News*, winning substantial goodwill not only in the town generally but also from Wiggins who later named a town for Byers.[35]

The San Francisco *Chronicle* promoted subscriptions in the 1880s by printing miniature newspapers—about 5 by 7 inches, sometimes smaller—that carried subscription information on the inside pages. The paper also issued miniatures to commemorate special occasions such as the anniversary of publisher Charles deYoung's assassination by a political foe.[36]

Newspapers also used puzzles to interest readers. As early as 1850, the *Deseret News* published an "enigma," a word-number puzzle which drew several replies. Together with the second puzzle, the *News* published a poem, attributed to a subscriber:

> Ned Piper, my boy, the answer to use
> Of your last Enigma, is "Deseret News,"
> So give us another, 'twill rouse up our muse,
> And thus may we patronize Deseret News.[37]

By the late 1880s, following the example of the New York City papers, promotion had become more sophisticated. In 1888 the San

Francisco *Examiner* printed a mathematical puzzle involving the newspaper's circulation and offered a pencil box to every schoolchild who brought the answer to the office on a specific afternoon. The paper ordered 10,000 boxes and was indeed besieged by youngsters claiming their prizes.[38] On other occasions, the *Examiner* sponsored a competition to send a student to the Paris Exposition, and, seeking to establish itself as champion of the underdog, opened an employment bureau to help San Francisco's "army of unemployed."[39]

Delivery

Once they had a list of subscribers, newspapers had to be prepared to deliver the product. Early subscribers commonly stopped by the newspaper or post office to pick up copies, and the *Deseret News* even arranged for the post office to be open Sunday from noon to 1:00 P.M. so people could collect their papers.[40] For local subscribers, however, most publishers quickly established home-delivery services.

With rough streets, no sidewalks, and toting 100 to 150 copies of the paper, carriers earned their pennies. A carrier for the *Territorial Enterprise* estimated that he walked 35 miles a day for two and a half years delivering the paper.[41] Both youths and adults carried the paper, one Nevada man delivering copies for twenty years.[42] Sometimes the apprentice or "printer's devil" inherited the delivery job. The Mesilla, New Mexico, *Times* told its readers, "The 'Devil' is authorized to accommodate the public with extra copies of the paper at oue [sic] bit each; and his Satanship positively declares he won't do a credit business."[43]

To encourage their carriers to provide good service, western publishers adopted the eastern practice of issuing a carrier's address on New Year's Day. These ranged from a poem to a special supplement that carriers delivered to their customers in hopes of getting a bonus. The bonus doubtless was given in spite of the poetry:

> Monday morning I gets on my mettle
> And calls on my customers to come and settle.
> Put up or shut up my motto shall be;
> If you don't ante up, no paper you'll see.
> And to paying subscribers, from far and near
> I here wish a jolly and happy New Year.[44]

An early *Oregonian* carrier remembered getting $5 from one sub-
scriber but only a grudgingly given 25 cents from another who was
upset about the delivery time.[45]

In some cases, carriers apparently worked as employees of the
newspaper, but more often they seem to have operated on a contract
basis—the Philadelphia plan of circulation—buying the paper and
reselling it.[46] Carrier rates for city subscriptions were usually listed
in the papers in weekly terms, small sums that would have been convenient for the carrier to collect but a bookkeeping headache for the
newspaper itself; subscription announcements sometimes specified
that payment for local papers was to be made to the carrier; mail
subscriptions went directly to the newspaper.

Scant evidence exists on how publishers divided subscription income with carriers, although the few available examples indicate
the paper sought to retain at least half of the price. In 1871 the
San Francisco *Evening Post*, started by economic philosopher Henry
George, set a wholesale price of a half cent per copy and a retail
price of a penny. Although the *Post* advertised that its newsboys
would give change, oftentimes the boys made an extra profit because
San Franciscans did not want to be bothered with pennies. The next
year George boosted the retail price of a single copy to 5 cents—
even though a subscription to the *Post* was still 10 cents a week—
apparently in response to the public's distaste for pennies; how he
split this increase with the newsboys is not documented.[47] In Colorado, the Gunnison *Daily News-Democrat* fought with its newsboys
in the 1880s when they demanded half of the 5-cent sales price, the
publisher claiming the division left him no profit.[48]

Because many of the carriers worked through agents, the amount
that reached those who actually made the deliveries was probably
small unless customers were generous with tips. In San Francisco
at one point dealers paid 30 cents a week for a six-day-a-week paper
that sold by subscription for 50 cents a week. They paid the carriers
an estimated 10 cents, leaving them with 10 cents to cover agents'
expenses and profit.[49]

For some newspapers, sales on trains or steamers became important. The Los Angeles *Daily Times* announced its availability on all
trains of the Southern Pacific, Central Pacific, Texas and Pacific, and
the Atcheson, Topeka and Santa Fe.[50] The denial of the right to sell
papers on the trains and boats owned by the Central Pacific helped

force the anti-railroad Sacramento *Union* into bankruptcy.[51] In out-lying areas, subscribers received their copies through the mail or via agents. If demand warranted, publishers arranged special delivery. The publisher of Silver City, Idaho, *Daily Avalanche* promised nearby Boise readers that if they would provide enough subscriptions and advertising, he would send the *Avalanche* by pony express in time to reach them every morning before the Boise *Tri-Weekly Statesman* arrived.[52]

Subscription rates were affected by a predictable variety of fac-tors, such as general and local economic conditions and distance from major markets, which in turn determined the cost of labor and paper. Nevertheless, amounts were surprisingly consistent across the re-gion, outside of San Francisco. In the 1840s, subscribers typically paid $5 a year for one of the handful of weeklies available; the gold rush, with its strain on resources, pushed prices up a dollar or two for weeklies. The rush also brought about the introduction of two- and three-times-a-week publication, as well as a number of dailies in major centers, all of which charged from $12 to $16 a year. The Sacramento *Union*, established in 1851, opened at a relatively low $12 a year, but four months later boosted its price to $16 a year, ex-plaining that for self-preservation in a cutthroat printing market it had come to terms on rates with the town's other paper, the *Times and Transcript*.[53]

In the 1860s weekly rates held fairly steady at $5, and dailies stabilized at $16 a year. By 1870, the gold-rush conditions that had boosted prices subsided and the depression of the 1870s brought them down. In 1880 a typical daily subscription cost $10 a year and a weekly from $3 to $5, depending on location. Readers in Arizona, Idaho, Montana, and Nevada paid the higher figure; others rarely paid more than $3 for a weekly, and the Oregon and Washington weekly press, consistently among the poorest, typically charged from $2 to $2.50.[54]

Arizona, Idaho, and Montana likely charged more because they had no major centers of their own to provide big-city competition. However, that does not explain the high rate for Nevada which, while it had no major population center of its own, had ready access to San Francisco and Salt Lake City. The small populations in Nevada and the other high-priced regions may have discouraged city papers from actively wooing subscribers. They thus presented little threat to the local papers, which could charge what market or conscience would bear.

Daily newspapers outside San Francisco, delivered in town, typically carried a price of 25 cents a week; occasionally publishers charged 50 cents or, rarely, even 75 cents. Single copies generally sold for one or two bits—12 1/2 or 25 cents. Annual rates for dailies generally matched those in eastern states, but western weeklies charged substantially more than the $1.50 or $2 common in other parts of the country, thanks largely to freight and labor costs.

Newspapers usually published subscription rates on the front page, commonly at the top of the left-hand column. They graduated rates to encourage longer subscriptions. The annual charge of $5 for a weekly might increase to $3 for those only taking six months, and the $10 daily cost $6 if taken for half a year. For example, in 1869 the Hamilton, Nevada, *Daily Inland Empire* charged $16 a year, $10 for six months, $6 for three months, all by mail and paid in advance; a subscriber could have the paper delivered by carrier in town for 75 cents a week.[55] The weekly Pomeroy, Washington, *Republican* in 1882 charged $2.50 a year, $1.50 for six months, or $1 for three months.[56]

Publishers insisted that payment was "invariably in advance." "No paper furnished until paid for," declared the *Carson Valley News* in 1875 in its inaugural issue; the following year it reiterated its pay-in-advance position, explaining, "Our profits are not large enough to justify us in waiting six or twelve months for our pay, and our capital is too limited to enable us to conduct our business on that basis; besides we wish to avoid the necessity of continually annoying our readers with duns."[57] The *Placer Times*, noting that its parent newspaper, the *Alta California*, had gone to a cash system, called collecting unpaid subscriptions more trouble than the subscription was worth and expressed the hope that the "wretched vocation of bill collecting" was dead.[58] A few who did accept credit posted a higher rate for subscriptions not paid within six months.

Few newspapers successfully enforced advance payment. Periodically publishers took to their columns to plead with, cajole, or berate subscribers delinquent in paying their bills. One publisher complained about honest men paying for cheaters' papers,[59] another regretted "requiring cash customers to pay the expenses of publishing papers to supply a certain class of deadbeats,"[60] while still another urged charitable donations from those whose consciences hurt them for "having deceived the printer, and diddled him out of one or more dollars."[61]

Publishers emphasized their need for money and scolded readers for doing so little to support the newspaper they claimed they wanted. In an item headed "How to Sustain your Local Paper," one newspaperman advised readers to "Lay aside your fears that the editor will get rich faster than his neighbor."[62] Asking for payment, the *Oregon Statesman* noted, "These dues are mostly small amounts, and may seem of but little importance to individual debtors, but at the aggregate they form a sum which a printing office cannot well do without."[63]

Desperate for funds, the publisher of an early Seattle weekly tried sarcasm to loosen the purse strings: "By the term support we don't mean such support as a man gives to a paper by subscribing for it, or advertising in it, and never paying the bill. We mean an entirely different kind of support. If anybody that owes this office should take a hint at this, we should, of course, ironically speaking, feel very bad about it."[64] Another took an angry turn. Noting that a good harvest should enable subscribers to pay, he said he would not continue the paper unless they did so. "It is disgraceful to a community of this size to allow an enterprise of this character to fail for want of necessary aid."[65]

The mining-camp papers had a particularly difficult time collecting for subscriptions. The transient nature of mining undoubtedly contributed to both publishers' frustration and their aggressiveness in seeking payment. The Ione *Advertiser* in Nevada, noting that a prior hint to delinquents "failed to accomplish the desired object," threatened to publish their names and to sell the claims at auction.[66] The paper died before it could carry out its threat, but the *Idaho Avalanche* did list a few people who had left Silver City owing amounts from $4 to $250.[67]

William Byers at the *Rocky Mountain News* also published a list of overdue subscribers and offered to sell the accounts to anyone willing to collect them. In a March 1, 1873, article, Byers explained that those owing the *News* money had been asked to pay or to explain why they could not. "We don't propose to work for 'dead beats'," Byers said and proceeded to publish nearly two columns of names of people who had failed to respond.[68] The list divided the names by occupation, such as "Showmen and Professionals" and "Military Accounts," and included the city in which the person was last known to reside. A New York advertising agent owed the largest single sum, $425. "Showmen" owed a total of $596, and the military nearly $700. A few individuals on the list owed only a dollar, but the amounts totaled nearly $8,000. In January 1874, Byers reported that many accounts had been collected, but he published another list, this one much shorter and with different names.[69] Such drastic measures gained Byers not only some revenue but also a challenge to a duel—which was settled peacefully.

Publishers tried various means of getting subscribers' attention at billing time—one Salt Lake City paper warned readers of expiring subscriptions by putting the paper in a colored wrapper—and praised those who made their payments.[70] "Mr. W. A. Townsend, of Centralia, called at The Bee office this week and paid three years back subscription and one in advance. May others do likewise," wrote a Washington publisher.[71] The *Idaho Avalanche* had off-handed approval for a new subscriber who had read the paper for years for nothing but "didn't think it would be manly to sponge his reading any longer."[72] And at the close of its subscription lists for the first six months, the *Deseret News* offered the "opportunity for the friends of the press, to manifest their good feelings for the continuance of a newspaper in Deseret."[73]

Payment came in various forms. Cash was favored, but publishers were also happy to accept gold dust as payment under proper circumstances:

> Our patrons, in sending us gold dust on subscriptions, or otherwise, containing one half to two thirds sand, will confer an especial favor by making a proper allowance for the weight of the sand. We can't make those who buy the dust of us believe that the sand is as valuable as the gold; nor do we believe it, either.[74]

In Denver, the amount of gold dust a seller could pinch from a buyer's buckskin using thumb and forefinger equaled 25 cents, the single copy price of the *Rocky Mountain News*. To accommodate miners, the *News* had a pair of scales for weighing gold, plus a piece of carpet to catch any gold flakes that fell during weighing.[75]

Publishers recognized that cash was often scarce on the frontier and most small-town newspapers accepted goods and services in exchange for subscription payments. In the 1850s the *Deseret News* outlined its willingness to take in-kind payments but, weighing the cost of disposing of bartered goods, expressed a preference for bushels of wheat, an easily traded commodity.[76] At the same time, the *News* recognized that employees could benefit from barter and welcomed immediately usable items. "Our printers are in want of eatables; they cannot work without bread," the publishers said.[77] Another Utah publisher, offering to accept produce for subscription payments, said, "The potatoes, squash and cabbage are wanted for brain food for the editor of the Utonian who must live high, no matter what the cost."[78] Peaches, hams, butter, eggs, berries, garden produce, and wood helped two Washington newspaper families get by when little cash circulated in town.[79]

Still, cash was essential to pay suppliers. "We are in immediate need of cash to pay for paper and other fixin's," the *Deseret News* told readers in July 1851. "Will some of our friends please to notice the pencil bills accompanying this paper; and our agents remit as speedily as possible."[80]

If accepting chickens in lieu of cash might seem foreign to today's circulation manager, so would another practice of frontier newspapers: continuing to deliver newspapers until the subscriber paid. Declared the publishers of Washington Territory's first newspaper, the *Columbian*, "No paper will be discontinued, unless at the option of the publishers, until all arrearages are paid."[81] And the *Deseret News* warned readers that their subscriptions would be renewed if they failed to return the next issue of the paper.[82] The practice lasted at least until the late 1870s.

Publishers printed "The Law of Newspapers" to alert subscribers to their obligations:

1. Subscribers who do not give express notice to the contrary, are considered as wishing to continue their subscriptions.
2. If subscribers order their papers discontinued, publishers may continue to send them until all charges are paid.
3. If subscribers neglect or refuse to take their papers from the office or place to which they are sent, they are held responsible until they settle their bill and give notice to discontinue them.
4. If subscribers move to other places without informing the publisher, and the paper is sent to the former direction, they are held responsible. Notice should always be given of removal.

5. The Courts have decided that refusing to take a paper or
   periodical from the office, or removing and leaving it un-
   called for, is PRIMA FACIE evidence of intentional fraud.[83]

This must have been a costly practice at times, particularly in
mining camps where subscribers packed up suddenly and left no for-
warding address. It is not clear how long publishers continued to
send papers to people known to have left town; as in the case of the
Centralia man, they apparently rarely stopped the subscriptions of
residents who wanted the paper and made some effort to pay.

Circulation Success

The level of success the individual frontier publisher achieved with
his circulation practices is difficult to assess because of exaggerated
readership claims common to the mid-to-late nineteenth century.
Publishers seldom bragged about circulation, except in the most general terms, not wanting rivals to know how they fared. When a California merchant suggested that one of his town's newspapers had the
highest readership, the other newspaper took him to task, saying he
didn't know what he was talking about. Neither newspaper provided
evidence for its assertions.[84]

As a matter of course, newspapers proclaimed themselves the
largest in town or county, few as modest in doing so as the Nevada
newspaper that said, "We claim the largest circulation of any paper
published in Churchill County, yet we are assured that our contracts
with the paper mills will not overtax their capacity."[85]

In 1850, 11 newspapers in the West—7 in California, 2 each in New
Mexico and Oregon—reported a combined circulation of 6,903—an
average of 628 subscribers per paper. The range of average circulations varied little around the region, from 547 in Oregon to 668 in
California. Ten years later, 138 newspapers of weekly or greater frequency served the West and average circulation had risen to 1,599,
with a much wider range, from 575 in New Mexico to more than
3,000 readers per newspaper in Utah. By 1870 the region's 285 daily
and weekly newspapers averaged 1,790 readers each, but the 1880
census showed a decrease to 1,296 per paper. The decline per newspaper, which was reversed in the 1880s, resulted in part from ad-

TABLE 3.1

Average Circulation, United States and West, 1850–1890

	1850	1860	1870	1880	1890
WEST					
Daily	505	2,469	2,157	1,870	2,884
Weekly	698	1,416	1,700	1,156	1,118
All	628	1,599	1,790	1,296	1,411
UNITED STATES					
Daily	2,986	3,820	4,532	3,673	4,845
Weekly	1,501	2,360	2,433	1,878	2,279
All	1,665	2,512	2,670	2,056	2,581
Population per Newspaper					
WEST	15,112	3,985	3,069	2,614	2,363
UNITED STATES	10,075	8,455	7,817	5,113	4,258
Circulation as Percent of Population (%)					
WEST	4	46	61	45	60
UNITED STATES	16	30	34	40	61

Source: U.S. Census.

vertisers' demand for honesty in reporting circulation, but the newspaper growth rate in the decade also exceeded that of the general population. Daily newspapers experienced particular development in the 1870s, thanks to the rise of urban centers and improved communication systems. (see table 3.1).

Circulation as a percentage of population provides another perspective. In 1850 western publishers claimed to print enough copies of newspapers to reach 4 percent of the population; by 1860 they could reach 43 percent, 61 percent by 1870 and back to 53 percent in 1880. The latter figure compared favorably to the national percentage.[86]

Circulation figures for individual frontier newspapers are elusive. Published figures were subject to fabrication and variation. The press run of the first issue of the *Rocky Mountain News* has been reported as 500 or 800 copies.[87] The *Southern Californian* in Los Angeles claimed it printed nearly 800 copies by its third issue, a number challenged by a local attorney who put the figure at 400.[88] Some contend that the *Territorial Enterprise* was larger in its prime than the San Francisco newspapers, but others estimate the *Enterprise*'s maxi-

TABLE 3.2

Circulation and Population Growth
Western States and Territories 1850–1890

YEAR	POPULATION	% CHANGE	CIRCULATION	% CHANGE
1850	166,237		6,963	
1860	577,842	+248	267,313	+3,739
1870	991,310	+ 72	608,883	+ 128
1880	1,787,697	+ 80	808,850	+ 33
1890	3,027,613	+ 69	1,807,992	+ 124

Source: U.S. Census.

mum circulation at 1,500 at a time San Francisco papers claimed more than 5,000.[89] The San Francisco *Chronicle* said it had 8,000 subscribers when it became a general circulation daily in 1868 and double that number a year later.[90]

Records show the *Deseret News* started in 1850 with about 225 subscribers. The following year it reported about 700, and 4,000 in 1856. In 1870 the *News* weekly edition had increased to 5,000, and daily and semi-weekly editions added another 3,000. By 1880 the total figure had risen only slightly, to 8,200, but a nearly 50 percent increase in the following decade brought circulation to 12,000 by 1890.[91]

The Civil War boosted circulation at most newspapers, but the San Francisco *Bulletin* and the Sacramento *Union* were particularly successful because they effectively monopolized the telegraphed war news. In 1860 the *Bulletin* claimed it sold 5,100 papers, in March 1861, 6,000, in August 1861, 7,300, and October 1863, 8,700; the *Union* claimed 6,000 daily and 7,000 weekly at the end of 1860; 9,500 daily and 11,200 weekly by August 1863.[92]

Overall, western newspaper circulation more than kept pace with population growth (see table 3.2). During the 1860s, while regional population increased 72 percent, newspaper circulation rose 128 percent. In the next decade, western fever cooled somewhat, slowing circulation growth to 33 percent, compared to 80 percent for the population. The rapid growth of western cities in this decade was reflected, however, in the 90 percent increase in circulation for daily newspapers.

Growth took another spurt in the 1880s, fueled particularly by immigration to the Pacific Northwest. Western population increased

TABLE 3.3

Circulation Revenue 1880–1890

STATE	CIRCULATION $ 1880	CIRCULATION $ 1890	% CHANGE
Arizona	37,700	54,950	+ 46
California	1,785,321	2,496,152	+ 40
Colorado	447,668	678,746	+ 52
Idaho	18,810	49,980	+166
Montana	93,620	74,250	+114
Nevada	123,661	41,374	− 67
New Mexico	35,089	74,250	+112
Oregon	190,094	407,499	+114
Utah	95,788	211,785	+121
Washington	38,560	389,501	+910
Wyoming	14,350	61,214	+327
WEST	2,880,661	4,665,348	+ 62
UNITED STATES	49,872,768	72,343,087	+ 45

Source: U.S. Census.

69 percent, but the completion of two railroad lines, the Northern Pacific and the Great Northern, and anticipated creation of new states pushed population in Washington, Oregon, and Idaho up 165 percent, led by a spectacular 365 percent boom in Washington. Newspaper circulation scored even more impressive increases: 123 percent in the West, 336 in the Pacific Northwest, and 1,023 percent in Washington alone. Only one area countered the trend: Nevada where population declined 26 percent, the number of newspapers slid 32 percent, and circulation 47 percent.

In the final frontier decade, lower paper and labor costs allowed publishers to hold down prices to retain subscribers, but increased competition meant that revenue grew somewhat more slowly than overall circulation. Subscription income increased only 62 percent in the region from 1880 to 1890, half of the circulation increase. In the anomaly, Nevada, circulation revenue plummeted 67 percent (see table 3.3). Clearly, by 1890 a publisher needed to hone his management skills to maintain his share of the market.

4

ADVERTISING

Mark Twain may be best known for his literary abilities, but he also understood where to find a dollar. He showed an early appreciation for newspaper business practices, in particular, advertising. While still Samuel Clemens in Missouri, he supposedly once assured a newspaper subscriber that the spider hiding in the fold of the newspaper was just checking advertisements for a place to spin a web. According to Twain, even spiders knew that no one entered the shop of a merchant who did not advertise, so the spider could be sure his doorway would be a comfortable home.[1]

Frontier merchants wanted no spider webs in their doorways. They flooded their local newspapers with advertising, at times more than the papers could handle. Publishers apologized in print for omitting news or advertising because there was so much of the latter. A Nevada publisher wrote in his inaugural issue:

> UNEXAMPLED PRESSURE.—We have been 'out-generaled' in all our plans for the first issue of the News by the singular kindness of our advertising patrons. The pressure upon us in this respect is unexampled in our knowledge of newspaper starting, and it has driven us to the exclusion of several arrangements with which we had intended to occupy our columns.[2]

Similarly apologetic but grateful, a Seattle publisher recognized that although all the advertising in his paper indicated a prosperous community, it was also a "privation to our country subscribers who want more news and reading matter."[3]

Although common wisdom says that retail advertising developed with urbanization and concentration of markets, Scottish traveler James Stirling observed that advertising was perhaps most needed in areas where people were dispersed geographically.[4] Certainly Stirling's notion would help explain why frontier advertisers greeted newspapers so eagerly. Publishers, however, did not take this enthusiasm for granted. Always seeking more support, they laced their newspaper columns with calls to local businessmen to advertise.

Like the circulation appeals, these calls often tried to create a sense of guilt and obligation to support the press. According to a Denver newspaper, "When you see a man who is too close and stingy to advertise, you can safely put him down as being too selfish to deal generously or very fairly or honestly."[5] A Wyoming neighbor agreed: "Right here in our town, there are men trying to do business whose existence is scarcely known because they do not keep themselves before the public through the press, and such men ought to be ignored."[6]

Some exploited the same booster spirit they used to promote subscriptions. "There is something inspiring and cheerful, encouraging and hopeful, in the very look of well-filled advertising columns," wrote one mining-camp publisher in his attempt to play on boosterism.[7] But publishers also recognized the need to appeal to the advertiser's immediate self-interest and emphasized the newspaper's value as a channel to customers. A retailer, declared the deYoungs in the first issue of the San Francisco *Daily Dramatic Chronicle*, must keep "himself, his store and his New Goods constantly BEFORE ALL THE PEOPLE" and he must "not fail to LET THE PEOPLE KNOW IT" when he has something to sell.[8] At the end of its first week the *Chronicle* commented that advertising was selling well and "our patrons, we feel assured, have suffered no loss from this extensive diffusion of information concerning their business."[9] A few years later, across San Francisco Bay, the appeal was similar as the new Oakland *Daily Tribune* promised advertisers that readers would see their messages because the paper was so small it offered few distractions.[10]

Playing on the practice of established newspapers to note the introduction of a newcomer which in turn reprinted its press notices, the *Chronicle* created bogus welcomes as part of its promotional efforts. One was credited to the "Daily Halter" which "criticized" the new paper for printing interesting items that might draw attention from its advertisements, something the "Daily Halter" would never do.[11] Publishers also printed articles on advertising, many of them taken from popular books on the subject or from other newspapers.

Publishers recognized the link between circulation and advertising, and stressed their distribution, locally and regionally. They touted low subscription rates as certain to build readership, and pointed to the quality of their circulation. Explaining that he would distribute his paper among the mine and mill men, the publisher of the Butte, Montana, *Miner* said, "Advertisers having goods or machinery to sell to them will find it an excellent medium for reaching those who will be interested and buy."[12] A Nevada publisher offered a paper specifically for people who did not subscribe to a daily newspaper, either because the timing of the mail service made the news old before it was received or because they couldn't afford it, and he invited advertising patronage aimed at this particular market.[13]

They pledged good service and tried to live up to their promise; on one occasion a Nevada publisher bought a special font of type and delayed the paper an hour to meet an advertiser's needs.[14] They appealed to advertisers' egos, calling them enterprising and clear-sighted when they had the intelligence to advertise. And at least one newspaperman hoped to tap advertisers' sense of public service when he defined an advertiser as one who "confers a favor upon the buyer as he is thereby saved the trouble of going from store to store to inquire for such goods as he wants."[15]

Publishers had three basic ways of getting advertising: it was brought to the newspaper office; they went out looking for it; or agents, either regional or national, collected it for them. The first option provided the bread-and-butter advertising that gave life to the newspaper. Local merchants, keen to have an advertising vehicle, would bring copy directly to the newspaper, their message often scribbled on a piece of paper, leaving it up to the typesetter to develop an eye-catching layout—after he determined what the hand-written message said.

With all the other things they had to attend to, frontier publishers had little time in which to solicit advertising, but they had no choice in the matter, at least when the newspaper was new. They regularly made the rounds of the business district to tell merchants of their services, but not all publishers took kindly to the salesman's role. One California man recalled that after he and his partner got their print shop in order, they had to canvass for subscriptions and advertising. "This kind of work was repugnant to both my partner and myself, but, knowing that it had to be done, we started out."[16] His partner was soon discouraged and returned home, leaving him alone to find enough support to get the newspaper under way.

Local businesses formed the core of advertising support but rare was the country paper that lacked advertising from nearby towns and regional centers. Western Washington and Oregon newspapers carried San Francisco ads; newspapers on the eastern end of the Columbia River had Portland advertising. In Nevada and inland California, newspapers had advertisements from San Francisco. Idaho papers sold space to Ogden and Salt Lake City merchants. San Francisco advertising filled half of the first issue of the San Diego *Herald* and played a major role in the paper's early survival. It also gave the publisher an excuse for frequent visits to San Francisco where he reportedly enjoyed a "convivial time."[17] As communication and transportation developed, New York and Chicago advertising was increasingly common in the remote papers as well as in western cities.

Although publishers might personally visit other towns and cities with a view to acquiring advertising contracts, they also employed agents to accept advertising, usually the same ones who took subscriptions. Agents in major centers such as San Francisco or Sacramento represented tens of western newspapers. San Francisco agents included L. P. Fisher's Newspaper Advertising Agency, Thomas Boyce, C. W. Crane, Myron Angel, and J. J. Knowledge & Company. K. K. Phipps and George M. Mott operated out of Sacramento. New York City agent George P. Rowell & Company and Chicago's Charles K. Miller & Company were among the eastern firms listed as representatives. Agents actively sought the newspapers' business. In 1868, Hudson & Monet, New York advertising agents with an office in San Francisco, offered to represent a Denver publisher.[18]

The arrangements individual newspapers made with their agents are obscure but appear to be basically either on the newspaper agency or space-jobbing plan. In the former, publishers paid agents a commission, usually letting them negotiate rates with advertisers, sometimes insisting they follow established rates. A space jobber was an independent middleman who sold space to advertisers, then turned around and bought it from newspapers at a discount because he could buy in large quantities. Space wholesaling, whereby the agent first bought discounted space from the newspapers and then sold it to advertisers at whatever the market would bear, was not unknown.[19] In 1874, S. M. Pettengill of New York wrote the Antioch, California, *Ledger* with two offers for ad space, noting that he had advertising in hand only for one.[20]

Publishers also actively pursued out-of-town advertising by sending copies of the paper to potential advertisers or to agents, and by calling on advertisers when they had the opportunity to visit the cities. The *Deseret News* was particularly enterprising; anticipating completion of the transcontinental railroad in 1868, the *News* sent a representative to eastern states to solicit advertising. In one issue that summer, Chicago advertising filled four of the twenty-four columns of the paper.[21]

Most out-of-town advertising probably came through agents, but some advertisers dealt directly with individual newspapers, either in person or by mail. Nevada's Alf Doten noted that W. A. Dooley of Dooley Brothers (New York yeast-powder manufacturers) had been in town and had contracted for about $100 in advertising space.[22] The *Antioch Ledger* dealt directly with a San Francisco firm that wanted to exchange goods for advertising.[23]

Patent-medicine companies may well qualify as the first truly "national" advertisers. Patent-medicine advertisements appeared early in western newspapers and increased severalfold as the use of stereotyping expanded in the 1870s and 1880s. The stereotype process allowed advertisers to send out prepared metal plates that the publisher could place in his type form without having to set any type. By having the work done in city print shops, national advertisers could take advantage of superior facilities to include engraved artwork and exotic typography. Not all such advertising came from the East Coast. Sacramento and San Francisco pharmacies produced their own ctrealls which they advertised around the region.

The success with which publishers and agents solicited advertisements varied from place to place and time to time, but in general frontier papers were well patronized. Six of the eleven western states or territories were among the top ten in per capita expenditure on advertising.

Although they might open with modest amounts of advertising, publishers were usually gratified by rapid expansion of business. In 1876 the Butte *Miner* devoted only about 35 percent of its space to advertising in its first issues; within three months the amount had increased to 54 percent. The content of the *Owyhee Avalanche* also was about one-third advertising at its start in 1865; two years later advertising amounted to just over half of the space, and in 1874 to about three-fourths.

Newspapers that started in small format enlarged repeatedly to meet the demand for advertising space. The Oakland *Tribune* started on February 21, 1874, about 5 x 7 inches in size, with three columns, carrying 43 ads. By May the paper enlarged to accommodate 82 ads; in July it carried 110 ads then expanded again. By November, 141 businesses placed advertisements, taking up 60 percent of the space. Most ads were from Oakland businesses, with just a few patent medicine or San Francisco messages.

To be sure, at times publishers struggled with sparse patronage. A mining boomtown gone bust clearly was in no position to provide advertisers to a newspaper. When fire hit a frontier town, the newspaper itself might or might not be damaged, but real problems resulted from loss of advertisers whose enterprises burned. At the same time, advertisers who survived a fire or other disaster valued the newspaper as a means of letting customers know they continued in business; when fire destroyed a third of Eureka, Nevada, in 1879, the local paper enlarged to meet survivors' demand for advertising space.[24]

Financial depressions also affected advertising patronage. In 1878, a publisher noted that times were "fearfully dull, and every branch of business completely paralyzed," but nevertheless "people have advertised as much as they could."[25] At other times towns like Virginia City, Nevada, could produce enough advertising to support several daily newspapers, and only a newspaper in the direst of straits devoted less than one-third of its columns to advertising. Calculations of up to 65 percent are not uncommon, and occasionally the share of advertising space reached as high as 80 percent.

A four-page paper more than half filled with advertisements had little room for news, so to accommodate what sometimes became an excessive amount of advertising, it became a common practice for a newspaper to issue supplements. The extra page or pages might be entirely devoted to advertising or they might carry an installment of a serialized story or other minimal reading matter. Twain claimed that every day from five to eleven columns of advertising were omitted and crowded into spasmodic supplements of the *Territorial Enterprise*.[26]

In addition to producing supplements, publishers tried other means of keeping news and advertising space in balance. In 1855, the *Deseret News* sought to get more news into the paper by reducing the type size for advertising matter.[27] Later the *News* began regular publication of an advertising supplement, and in 1865, it started a semi-weekly along with the weekly. The weekly was to have more news than ads, the semi-weekly more ads than news.[28] The *Owyhee Avalanche* made a similar distinction between its weekly and daily editions.

Although frontier publishers rarely invoked the edict of James Gordon Bennett, publisher of the New York *Herald*, that advertising be as timely as the news, they recognized that to their readers the content of the ads was indeed newsworthy. One Nevada publisher declared that his new newspaper would be free from "dead" or old advertisements.[29] At the time the publisher feared no contradiction of his claim because he had no ads at all and ran several blank columns in his first issue, but within a few weeks, his pages were filled with commercial messages, and their mortality was in question.

The *Deseret News* refused in 1853 to give price advantages to advertisers who signed long-term contracts because the publishers wanted the advertising to be as fresh as possible. They offered a special three-week rate, but unlike most newspapers, which gave ever-better rates to advertisers who let their messages run without change for a long period, provided no further discounts for renewals.[30] Other publishers, however much they might prefer "live" ads, rarely had the personnel required to set new copy every issue. Starting each issue with a page or more of advertising already in type allowed fewer printers to produce the newspaper in less time. A reading of frontier newspapers shows the same advertisements continuing for months. The *Idaho Register* even stated that it would not allow ads longer than three inches to be changed more often than quarterly.[31]

Advertising rates reflected the preference for long-running messages. Of those newspapers that published rates, a few listed only multiple insertion rates, and almost all used a graduated scale dependent on the number of insertions and the amount of space purchased. A newspaper charging $2 a square for the first insertion generally charged $1.50 or less for subsequent insertions. Advertising in the form of business cards for lawyers or other professional services could run every issue for $5 a month in a paper that charged $3 for a single insertion. One paper that charged $2.50 a square offered to print a full column every week for a year for only $100.

Newspapers generally based advertising rates on the "square," a measure similar to the "column inch" used today—one column wide by one inch deep—but there were variations. Sometimes publishers specified the number of lines in their "square"; in Oregon in 1846 a square was given as sixteen lines, in 1850 in San Francisco it was ten lines. A ten- or twelve-line square was most common. Newspapers rarely stated the size of type used, but because twelve lines of nonpareil type (six point) filled one inch, most newspapers probably used this standard.

The real difficulty in assessing advertising rates is the fact that not all newspapers published rates and even when they did, they seldom held to them. Twain claimed the *Territorial Enterprise*, which did not publish its rates after it moved to Virginia City and became a daily, had "exorbitant" advertising charges; rates for the Los Angeles *Star* have been described as "eccentric."[32] Advertising costs almost everywhere were subject to negotiation and newspapers promised substantial but unspecified discounts for quantity purchases of space.

Publishers extended credit to most of their advertisers but tried to get obviously transient clients to pay in advance, and, at least in the early years, some followed the practice used for delinquent subscribers: continuing the service and letting the bill build up until the customer paid. Gradually publishers adopted the practice of printing insertion dates on an advertisement, usually removing the ad at the end of the contract.

Publishers found it almost as difficult to collect from advertisers as they had from subscribers. The frontier was largely a cashless society, dependent on credit and barter. Small local businesses who extended credit to their customers had little ready cash to pay the newspaper, and offered goods and services in exchange for space. At times even city advertisers proposed in-kind payment for advertising. In the 1870s a San Francisco music store offered the Antioch *Ledger* 55 percent off the price of an organ in exchange for advertising. The *Ledger* ignored the proposition, so the company modified it by proposing to credit the cost of six months of advertising against the purchase of the publisher's choice of musical instruments.[33] Another advertiser offered a sewing machine at half price in exchange for ten months of advertising.[34] A New York agent wanted to trade a $104 *New American Encyclopedia* for twenty-four inches of space, two advertisements to run alternately for a year; this offer the *Ledger* apparently accepted.[35]

One early California publisher contracted for one of the more unusual trades when he became a Royal Arch Mason in exchange for advertising in his newspaper.[36] Whether the bottle of pure Grizzly Bear Oil the same publisher received from an advertiser was a free sample or payment for advertising, he did not say.[37] Washington publishers claimed that at times almost all of their merchant advertising was paid for by goods or services.[38] Although one Washington Territory publisher said patent-medicine advertisers accounted for most of the cash he received, national advertisers were not necessarily quicker than local advertisers to pay their accounts.[39] A Nevada publisher wrote to a New York advertising agent threatening to throw out his ads, send the account to a legal agent in New York to collect, and then expose him if he neglected to pay.[40] The list of delinquent advertisers and subscribers published by the *Rocky Mountain News* in an attempt to shame debtors into paying their bills included a prominent New York agency.[41]

Publishers showed little consensus about the advisability of printing names of those who failed to pay their bills, whether for advertising or for subscription. Few actually did so and when the *Oregonian* named a man who left Portland owing $21 for an advertisement, the *Alta California* called it a bad precedent.[42]

Layout and Copy

The inaugural issue of the *Californian* carried an official notice banning liquor sales in Monterey and one advertisement offering translation services. Before long, the *Californian* had added advertising for a restaurant, general merchandise, and groceries, as well as J. F. Romie's offer to provide fresh water from his well at the rate of two *reals* per week per family.[43] The *Columbian*, the pioneer newspaper in Washington Territory, ran small ads for an engineer, hotels, merchandise, help wanted, shipping, real estate, bakery, and an attorney in its first issue, a collection typical for the period.[44] This and most other early advertising was of the size and shape of a business card, but as a business community matured, so did its advertising. Nevertheless, for years columns of business cards continued to provide a core of advertising matter which many newspapers published on the front page. Lawyers' cards were the most prominent, but physicians, milliners, and other providers of services kept their names before the public in this inexpensive way.

Business cards aside, most advertising looked little different from twentieth-century classified advertising. Even late in the era advertising design relied largely on simple typographic devices in rarely successful attempts to make an ad stand out from its neighbors. Illustration was rare, with the exception of the patent-medicine and other national advertising that developed in the 1870s and 1880s. Promoters of traveling shows, such as circuses, also provided stereotyped plates as they moved from town to town.[45] The *Deseret News* carried some modest line drawings in the early 1850s, but the paper was nevertheless noticeably enlivened when its efforts in 1868 to attract more eastern advertising also brought more illustration.[46] Publishers could buy an assortment of general-purpose small drawings, engraved and ready for insertion. A shoe, hat, horse, stagecoach, and ever-present pointing finger appeared repeatedly.

Type, however, was the principal tool at the creative compositor's disposal. In the 1850s, papers like the *Oregon Statesman* had little more than basic body type to work with, but acquiring additional fonts was a high priority, and early profits often went toward new type. Printers learned to use their limited resources with considerable imagination. They varied type as much as they could, and mixed lines of all capital letters with others strictly lower case. Centering lines was a popular device, giving the ads a symmetrical look, and lines might be divided and spaced to form an hourglass shape. Stepped lines were unusual enough to stand out in a page, and an arch of type sometimes crowned the message. One-column width was standard but ads occasionally stretched across the page. Some merchants made effective use of white space to attract attention. An advertiser in the Stockton, California, *Independent* bought ten column-inches and inserted only his name, together with a note that he did not have time to write any copy. Others ran advertisements sideways or even upside down. The *Independent* once ran its entire front page of advertising upside down under the nameplate.[47]

Boxes within boxes or the use of a multiplicity of small letters to create a large letter relieved the usual grayness, but complicated typesetting took considerable time, skill, and patience on the part of the typesetter, and devices such as alphabetic designs could drain a type case of specific letters perhaps better employed elsewhere.

Like the layout, copy tended toward the conservative, with most advertising giving basic information of who was offering what product or service. Rarely did they include price; one historian has suggested that frontier residents cared more about availability than cost, but the common practice of barter may also have influenced the decision not to include prices.[48] However, advertisers occasionally announced discounts for cash.

Gentility was the keynote to the language, early on, at least. Advertisers announced or "respectfully" called readers' attention to the product or service, or held themselves in readiness to greet customers. "The undersigned begs leave to inform the citizens of Marysville and vicinity that he has opened a splendid stock of imported Havana and domestic cigars," advertised a smoke shop proprietor.[49] "The travelling public are respectfully informed that a house of entertainment has been opened," said another merchant.[50] An Oregon tonsorial saloon owner hoped "long experience will enable him to render satisfaction to such as may call upon him," while a neighboring merchant who had moved worried whether his customers would find his new location: "Don't make a Mistake And get in our old stand and spend all your money before you know it." He also welcomed new customers provided "it will not interfere with the trade of our neighbors."[51] Occasionally, a remarkable streak of honesty showed up in an advertisement:

EVERYBODY

KNOWS

Loutzenheiser's Establishment

HE NEEDS NO ADVERTISEMENT

But the Printer Wants to make a living.[52]

As the decades moved on, advertising design improved and claims became stronger, but the use of flamboyant language and style tended to have more to do with location—and probably personality of the publisher, or at least his compositors—than to development of the advertising business. For example, in the 1850s, the *Oregon Statesman*'s advertising columns could hardly be distinguished from legal advertising and "Rare chance for Bargains" was a strong sales message, yet the *Territorial Enterprise* was declaring "Eureka! Eureka!!" on behalf of the "very best" carriages and that "Startling Disclosures!" could be found in the New York *Ledger*.[53] In the 1880s when the relatively reserved "Ho! Ye Hungry, Go to the Railroad Depot

Lunch Counter" stood out in the pages of the Albuquerque *Daily Journal*, Los Angeles *Daily Times* readers perused claims that an "invincible mattress" cured all ills.[54]

Merchants took inspiration from current affairs for product messages. In Butte, Montana, an advertisement shouted:

WAR

Declared

Not only between Turkey

and Russia

-but by-

D. COHEN & BRO.

Against High Prices and the

CREDIT SYSTEM.[55]

They used testimonials: "I have cultivated the JAPANESE PEA the last year, and raised them at the rate of 200 bushels to the acre. The bloom excels buckwheat for bees."[56] And they indulged in eloquent but meaningless language. "A Big Little Thing!" said an ad in the Oakland *Tribune*. "The Complete Washer. EVERY Family should have one of these Little Wonders."[57]

Restaurants and hotels, in particular, practiced the art of hyperbole with monotonous regularity. Their meals, service, and facilities were always "unsurpassed" and compared favorably with San Francisco's eating houses. The Symposiac Chop House in remote Columbus, Nevada, added extra flair to its claims: "Game and poultry served daily, to order. The elegant style in which these delicacies are spread is not excelled in San Francisco, and excites the admiration of all who visit the house."[58] San Francisco restaurants, in turn, insisted they could match the quality of any establishment in the eastern states.

And, of course, the medicine men spared no adjectives in touting the wonders of their products and services. "Any intelligent man or woman who is suffering from CONSUMPTION, or any disease of the THROAT or LUNGS, and wishes to find the best remedy, will be amply repaid for attesting the efficacy of DR. HALL'S BALSAM, a remedy that has the sanction of scientific men," proclaimed a typical appeal.[59] A more flamboyant physician's advertisement said it was "well known" that he had "taken patients from the very verge of the grave, and restored them to perfect health."[60] Dr. Radway's Ready Relief promised to cure the worst pain in less than 20 minutes, his Sarsaparilian Resolvent performed astonishing cures, and his Perfect Pergative Pills took care of all digestive disorders.[61]

For a time verse was popular for advertising messages, particularly in San Francisco which harbored a considerable literary contingent, including an ample supply of bad poets. In 1865 the *Daily Dramatic Chronicle* introduced the San Francisco Business Directory, to be published every Saturday, with a double column of verse heralding advertisers. Some samples:

> A well made and well fitting shirt,
> To buy go straight to WARD;
> The price he'll charge you cannot hurt—
> 'Tis what all can afford.
> 'Oh, hang this aching tooth!' one cries,—
> No draw it; that's the cure;
> And he who C. E. DAVIS tries,
> Is satisfied, that's sure.
> ... And if perchance you should prefer
> Advertisements in rhyme,
> Allow me to inform you where
> You'll get the most sublime.
> Call on Clay street 4, 17—
> Enquire for the "poet,"
> We've got a patent rhyme machine,
> Can by the hour go it,
> Wholesale or retail, by the foot,
> Yard, perch, furlong, or mile,
> Our machine grinds it out to suit—
> It's running all the while.[62]

An Arizona bard showed that Californians had no monopoly on poor poetry:

> Economy is now the order of the day,—
> All you gents that want to look gay,

For the cheapest work it does not do.
I, T. Curry, that do address you,
I tell this without flattering you,
I can make old clothes look almost new,
I am a tailor and a renovator, too.
Do not peddle with me about the price,
Or I will shave you "like a mice."[63]

Whether advertising messages were organized in the columns depended on the inclination of the publisher. Some newspapers grouped advertisements under headings such as hotels, merchants, transportation; others did not. Most kept business cards and legal notices together under appropriate headings. Although sophisticated advertisers recognized the value in having their messages next to a story or at least not placed next to a competitor's advertisement, publishers could do little to accommodate them. When fifty or more advertisements had to be located in four pages, there was little room for such proprieties.

Advertising historians have said that the practice of putting advertisements on the front page of a newspaper died out with the Civil War because of the demand for news of that conflict, but western editors did not notice. Whether a newspaper had front-page advertising appeared to be as idiosyncratic as their choice of language. Many papers, even those in big cities, had anywhere from a column to a full page of ads decades after the war. In the 1880s the San Francisco *Chronicle* filled its front page with advertising; the Albuquerque *Journal* also ran commercial messages on page one.

Few publishers overtly censored their advertisers. The editor of the *Boulder County Pioneer* declared in 1869 that he would not accept "unsavory" advertising; "no whiskey, quack abortionist, lottery swindle, gambling device, or in fact any advertisement or announcement, large or small, whether it pays much or little, that savors in the least of the illegality or swindling, shall find a place in these columns while we control them."[64] His publisher, a Boulder liquor dealer, soon found a less righteous editor. This is not to say publishers adopted a strict "buyer beware" position. When fraud slipped into their advertising columns, they took pains to alert their readers—as well as other publishers who might also lose in fraudulent transactions. The Helena *Herald* discovered in 1871 that it had run a series of ads for a nonexistent New York insurance firm and quickly published a warning.[65] An Idaho paper told of an "accomplished scoundrel" who advertised that he would help people get divorces; he provided neither the divorce to people who answered the advertisement nor payment to publishers who ran his message.[66] Recognition that not all advertising was what it seemed may have prompted a clothing merchant to declare about his sale, "This is no humbug."[67] Still, raffle and lottery advertising that some publishers considered objectionable was a staple to others, particularly in cosmopolitan San Francisco.[68]

Legal notices played an important role in frontier newspapers, sometimes serving as justification for the newspaper's very existence. Such advertising often made the difference between survival and failure. Homesteads, mining, and timber all were affected by laws that required publication of notices through which an individual or company established claim to ownership. A Nevada publisher thought it worth noting in his diary that on one day he got four patent applications for mining claims at $50 each,[69] and the Washington Press Association credited the rapid growth in the number of newspapers in the 1880s to the revenue potential from notices of timber applications, proof of homesteads and claims of pre-emption.[70] Two young men established Washington's *Snohomish Eye* to take advantage of timber-notice revenue.[71] Nevada's *Ione Advertiser* was started as a vehicle for mining notices.[72]

Because of the requirement, attracting new settlers clearly meant opportunity beyond the commercial advertising that might result. In 1888 a Colorado correspondent accused booster publishers of having more in mind than community growth when they encouraged immigration. The urgings from the booster press should be footnoted, he wrote, "give us $5 for publishing your proof notice."[73] In cattle country, ranchers had to document their cattle brands by publishing them in the newspaper.[74]

Newspapers that depended heavily on legal advertising faced extra trouble when the mines closed, for example, or when the laws changed. The final issues of the Borax, Nevada, *Miner* were filled with delinquency notices as the mines closed.[75] If miners could not pay their other bills, they were not likely to have the resources to pay their newspaper accounts. Publishers in Santa Barbara, California, were among those hurt when local governments were allowed the option of posting, rather than publishing, their notices.[76] In 1887 one of the objectives of the new Montana Press Association was to persuade the legislature to pass a law requiring that all legal notices be published in a newspaper, to protect this important source of revenue.[77]

Advertising by Other Names

Not all advertising was clearly identifiable as such. In the most conservative papers, it was difficult to distinguish news stories from ads, but even after typographical display became popular, advertising mingled with news. In the local columns that virtually every newspaper ran, news, free publicity for advertisers, and reading notices (paid publicity) were indiscriminately mixed. Publishers knew that a kind word about an advertiser helped make him or her more amenable to continuing to buy space. At the same time, advertisers knew the value of editorial endorsement and were willing to pay for space that resembled it. The practice of giving reading notices as premiums to advertisers was common throughout the nation. Although the New York *Herald* declared in 1848 that it was stopping the practice, few other newspapers followed suit and they were still widely used in the latter half of the century, when a growing cadre of experts advised advertisers to buy such notices, especially if they were truly difficult to distinguish from the regular stories in the paper.[78]

Such notices appeared regularly in frontier papers. How many were paid for and how many were free is impossible to determine, but evidence of the practice is clear. A typical item: "Askew's restaurant, on the east side of Eddy street, is doing a smashing business in the boarding line, and is deservedly popular with its patrons. He patronizes the printer; that's why we take pleasure in directing attention to his business. See advertisement."[79] Or: "Remember that Mrs. Brown is getting new goods all the time."[80]

Another:

TROUT.—Every Thursday O. D. Lang of Lake Valley runs to the Genoa and Carson markets a big load of delicious Tahoe trout. Day before yesterday he came to town with several hundred pounds of fine fresh fellows, weighing all along from one-and-one-half to near twenty pounds, generously dropping at our door as he passed two most beautiful ones. Mr. L. finds ready sale for his fish at two bits per pound.[81]

Is this reciprocity for the fish he left as a gift or was the fish a direct exchange for the notice? We can only speculate. Similarly, publishers acknowledged news agents and express companies that provided them with newspapers, and it is not clear whether this was the result of formal agreements or frontier courtesy on both sides.

Sometimes those mentioned in the news columns advertised elsewhere in the paper, sometimes not. D. B. Starratt—"Go to Starratt's for the first quality coal oil," said the note in the locals column—had a regular two-inch advertisement in the *Reese River Reveille*,[82] but the promotion for "our business houses" in the *Arizona Miner* named some merchants who were not otherwise advertisers in the paper, at least for that issue.[83] An announcement of the arrival in town of an agent for a San Francisco doctor who had a "celebrated method for the radical cure of rupture" may have been paid advertising or it may have resulted from the work of a press agent or a visit from the good doctor himself.[84]

Sometimes, circumstances were clear. In 1874–75 the *Daily Independent* in Virginia City ran a column of editorial-style advertising including a half column for a department store that begins: "A Scene of Unrivaled Splendor.—Passing along the street last evening, our attention was attracted by the brilliance reflected from the Wade House. The store, as is well known, extends back from C to B streets, and the whole length thereof glistened and shone with all the splendor of a fairy hall." Although it reads like an item of local news, at the end was the same kind of notation used in the advertising columns: "no4-tf"—it started running November 4 and was to run until further notice.[85] National advertisers purchased mentions in the local column. George P. Rowell & Company, New York advertising agents, sent an insertion order to the Denver *Gazette* in 1868, directing that it appear as a local or editorial item once in the weekly edition and three times in the daily. Rowell also attached a two-line notice for magnolia water that was to run a full year. Total cost for the order was $80, payable quarterly.[86] The previous year, the same Denver publisher had received an insertion order for a patent medicine advertisement accompanied by the notation, "If not against your rules, I would be pleased to have you give me a short Editorial notice, calling attention to my advertisements, and send bill for same."[87]

Printing reading notices or editorial advertising in the news columns, however popular with advertisers, was marked by controversy within the newspaper fraternity; not all publishers were willing to run paid advertising in the editorial columns. In 1852, Asahel Bush declared in the *Oregon Statesman* that while he might voluntarily call attention to an advertisement, "We insert nothing in the editorial columns for pay, and receive no price for anything inserted there."[88] In contrast, at least one newspaper clearly had no objection to the practice; the Cheyenne *Leader* listed a special rate of 25 cents a line for the first insertion of advertising in its locals column and almost all items in the column came from advertisers.[89]

Advertising Sheets

Mitchell Stephens in his *History of News* says that more than half of early nineteenth-century city newspapers in the United States had "advertiser," "commercial," or "mercantile" in their titles.[90] Such names were rare on the frontier, but the concept of advertising as the driving force led several publishers to attempt to operate solely on its revenue, instead of the traditional subscriber support base. One of the West's leading newspapers, the San Francisco *Chronicle*, began in 1865 as a free, advertising-supported newspaper, and a few other publishers followed its example. In fact, the *Chronicle*'s success, together with its journalistic enterprise in covering Lincoln's assassination left traditional papers examining their options. Its presses in continuous operation the Monday after news of the President's death arrived, the *Chronicle* published three editions and distributed them at no charge. The *American Flag* and the *Bulletin* became so concerned about the competition that they, too, gave away some copies in an attempt to tempt readers from the *Chronicle*.[91]

Other papers also tried free distribution, some apparently hoping to succeed by advertising alone, others testing the waters and luring readers before establishing a subscription rate. The San Bernardino *Advertiser* operated for six months before it changed its name to *Times* and sold subscriptions.[92] For the *Times* and the Oakland *Tribune*, which also started as a giveaway, free distribution

TABLE 4.1

*Percent of Revenue from Advertising
in Relation to Subscriptions
Daily and Weekly Newspapers, 1880*

STATE	DAILY[a] (%)	WEEKLY[b] (%)
Arizona	64	60
California	60	44
Colorado	53	67
Idaho	n/a	51
Montana	46	48
Nevada	65	57
New Mexico	50	52
Oregon	46	50
Utah	47	42
Washington	57	55
Wyoming	72	63
WEST	58	50
UNITED STATES	49	39

Source: U.S. Census.
a. Includes weekly editions of daily newspapers.
b. Includes weeklies and all others.

relieved them of having to deal with subscribers until they had the rest of their operation running smoothly.[93] The Los Angeles *Weekly Mirror* also started as a free newspaper and later became a paid circulation paper.[94] In 1879 Congress distinguished between paid-circulation newspapers and those relying solely on advertising when it established the second-class mail category and made one of the requirements a legitimate list of paid subscribers.[95]

Meanwhile, revenue figures proved the West to be an advertising bonanza. By 1880, California, twenty-fourth in population, was the sixth highest of 48 states and territories in terms of estimated advertising receipts and third in terms of per capita expenditure on advertising. Colorado, thirty-fifth in population, was eighteenth in estimated receipts and second in per capita expenditures, and Nevada, forty-third in population was twenty-eighth and first, respectively. Smaller western states' receipts ranked in proportion to their populations but their per capita rates were high. In most western states, advertising outstripped circulation in producing revenue; in the region as a whole, daily newspaper advertising receipts were nearly 20 percent higher than those for circulation. In the nation

TABLE 4.2

Advertising Revenue 1880–1890

STATE	1880 ($)	1890 ($)	% CHANGE
Arizona	58,000	59,680	+ 3
California	2,150,238	3,099,453	+ 44
Colorado	567,442	1,125,534	+ 98
Idaho	19,190	67,060	+ 249
Montana	84,130	227,865	+ 171
Nevada	215,139	51,835	− 76
New Mexico	35,883	78,230	+ 118
Oregon	177,095	544,328	+ 207
Utah	81,270	271,770	+ 234
Washington	48,840	759,784	+1,456
Wyoming	32,950	61,214	+ 86
WEST	3,397,034	6,346,753	+ 87
UNITED STATES	39,136,306	71,243,361	+ 82

Source: U.S. Census.

as a whole, conditions were reversed, subscriptions accounting for more than half of the revenue (see table 4.1). By 1890, western advertising revenue exceeded subscription income by 36 percent, while nationally circulation still slightly surpassed advertising. As it did for circulation, the 1880s meant skyrocketing figures for advertising. The region as a whole increased its advertising revenue 87 percent from 1880 to 1890 (in contrast to a national increase of 82 percent), led by Washington's mammoth 1,456 percent (see table 4.2).

5

JOB PRINTING

If frontier publishers had been forced to survive solely on the income from advertising and subscriptions, the number of failed newspapers would no doubt have been significantly larger. Fortunately, their skills as printers were much in demand for job printing, and they were able to supplement their newspaper income by producing the multitude of printed items necessary for the functioning of social, commercial, and political enterprises.

The desire to put excess printing capacity to use has sometimes been given as a reason for starting a newspaper, suggesting that a printer set up his shop to print forms and stationery and only turned his hand to a newspaper when he had extra time. Western newspapers were rarely the by-product of a job-printing office, but it is almost a chicken-egg kind of question, so intricately were the two related. Publishers took it for granted they would do job printing as part of the routine work of their offices, and often they did not bother to keep separate accounts for job work and the newspaper, making it more difficult to learn how successful they were at one or the other.

To be sure, not all printers were newspaper publishers. Augustin V. Zamorano arranged for the first printing press in Monterey in 1834 to do job printing. He announced that he was available to anyone who wanted to hire him to print a newspaper, but there is no indication that he ever printed one.[1] When Colton and Semple resurrected Zamorano's press for the *Californian*, however, they set a pattern for western development. In 1870 only 32 (39 percent) of California's 82 printing offices were unconnected with a newspaper, and by 1890 even fewer (24 percent) of the printing offices concentrated only on job printing.

Although the newspaper generally came first in printing-office planning, it was not necessarily in operation first. A newspaper publisher might use his facilities for job printing while working to get his initial issue out. While racing the *Cherry Creek Pioneer* to be first in Denver, the *Rocky Mountain News* staff printed a handbill about a lost horse and dog.[2] Later, in Pueblo, Dr. Michael Beshoar welcomed the opportunity for his print shop to earn some money as it was being readied for the *Chieftain*.[3] But in both cases it was clear that the newspaper was no afterthought of an underutilized job shop; the Denver people had even brought two newspaper pages preprinted from Omaha.[4]

Ambitious publishers considered job printing needs when they purchased type and presses, sometimes trying to get equipment to do double duty, more often acquiring a small press specifically for handbills, stationery, and business cards. Frank A. Leach saw that the Napa, California, newspaper shops in which he worked were poorly equipped for job printing, so he arranged to lease the *Register* plant, add a job press, and go into business for himself. When Leach later moved to Vallejo to publish a newspaper, he again made sure his job office was equal to the demands that might be placed upon it. He had one of the few steam-powered presses outside San Francisco, three smaller job presses, and a bindery.[5]

Gold rush–era San Francisco presented particularly rich job-printing opportunities, and Jonas Winchester begged his brother Heman to help finance an office. In 1849 he noted that the *Alta* was operating with two hand presses, while another printer with but one press was so overwhelmed with work he had two crews running it night and day. "With a Napier Adams, two hand presses and card presses," Winchester wrote, "we could sweep the field and become the leading establishment in California, with branches at Sacramento City and Monterey."[6] He ordered a stock of cards of all sizes and directed that plant and materials be sent across the Isthmus, rather than around Cape Horn; the extra expense would allow them to start making money sooner. From across the continent, Heman apparently found it difficult to share Jonas's enthusiasm; although he eventually sent some materials, the supplies were both too little and too late for Jonas to make the fortune he anticipated.

In Salt Lake City the *Deseret News* developed its job office quickly in order to serve the needs of the LDS church; one of its early projects was the "Deseret Almanac." The *News* probably pioneered color printing in the Intermountain West, using colored inks and gold bronze in 1852 to print invitations for the first typographical festival in Utah.[7]

Binding was a particularly sought-after addition to facilities. A

Washington publisher in the 1860s hoped that by doing his own binding of the laws, he could salvage some of the profit lost by currency depreciation.[8] Eager to inaugurate his bindery, a Nevada publisher personally made a clamp to hold books while they were being stitched. He had, he said, a "big lot" of license and tax books to bind.[9] A Montana woman who helped in her husband's bindery bemoaned the difficulties of stitching with an awl and mallet.[10]

Publishers were called upon to bind more than their own printing output. A Washington resident inquired about binding his personal collection that included two sets of magazines, some poems and sermons, two encyclopedias, and two copies of William H. Prescott's *History of the Conquest of Peru.*[11]

Printing of Every Description

Publishers regularly promoted their printing facilities in their newspapers. Although they sometimes urged patronage of their job shops to encourage local industry, most framed their advertisements to show potential customers that they could meet their needs. If these ads are to be believed, there was nothing in the printing world they could not do. The Sacramento *Union* called its book- and job-printing facilities "unsurpassed" and promised they were "not to be outdone, either in cheapness or neatness."[12] A Nevada office advertised "plain and chromatic printing of every description,"[13] and another declared, "And in fact every description of PRINTING executed with neatness and dispatch, at the most REASONABLE TERMS."[14]

The shops had their limits, but they could, in fact, handle a wide range of projects and go a long way toward supplying the large amounts of printed paper that changed hands in a nineteenth-century town. They printed stock books, receipt books, bill heads, circulars, checks, ball tickets, cards, labels and posters, meal checks, subpoenas, way bills, letterheads, business cards, tax notices and petitions, license and tax books, city directories, and stock certificates. No job was too small. A shop might be asked to print 4 cards reading "Law Office," 50 copies of police regulations, or 1,000 business cards. Some jobs, however, could be too large. Although newspapers often produced city directories, among the most demanding of the commercial jobs, they subcontracted many of the avidly sought public-printing contracts, usually to eastern printers.

The job book for the Cheyenne *Leader* in 1868–1869 is particularly helpful in assessing the scope of a job shop's work.[15] In February 1868 that office printed more than 18,000 sheets of card or paper in 55 orders for 33 clients. Much of the *Leader*'s printing was entertainment-related, a classification that was a major factor in frontier job shops. Theater handbills and programs, tickets, and invitations provided steady work, at least during prosperous times. In the last week of February 1868, the *Leader* printed 1,300 tickets, 500 handbills, and 1,000 programs for theatrical events.

Traveling shows of various kinds—drama, music, circus—relied on local offices for much of their printing. Publishers insisted on payment in advance, well aware that impresarios might not stay around long after the last performance, and these jobs often provided cash when none other was forthcoming. Invitations and tickets required for local entertainments were more likely to be done on credit.

From February through April 1868, the *Leader* did $212 worth of printing clearly related to entertainment events; other printing, such as posters, may have also been for that purpose. The $212, about a fifth of the paper's job-work income for the period, totaled more than the printing for city, county, and federal governments combined.

In addition to meeting the multiplicity of printing requirements of frontier businesses, job shops published pamphlets for direct sale. In Utah, after LDS church members devised the Deseret alphabet to simplify reading and writing, the *News* office printed and sold a number of works using the alphabet.[16] Type set for newspaper articles was sometimes turned into pamphlets; the Los Angeles *Herald* reprinted its booster edition in pamphlet form.[17] Laws and political speeches printed in the newspapers were also frequently issued as pamphlets.

Large newspaper offices could earn extra income either helping a fellow publisher with temporary press problems or by contracting to print other papers on a regular basis. The publisher of the Cheney, Washington, newspaper printed the first issues of the Spokane *Review* when the latter's press failed to arrive on time, the Stockton *Times* printed the first issue of the Sonora *Herald*, and the Los Angeles *Mirror* printed the first issue of the Los Angeles *Times*.[18] The Seattle *Leader* had been printed by another office but in 1889 finally set up its own printing plant to avoid the problems of hiring press work done.[19] Other such arrangements were longer term. In the 1870s the *Commercial* in Los Angeles printed both the *Express* and the *Herald*; after the *Herald* installed steam presses, it printed other newspapers in the city.[20] The *Washington Standard* in Olympia set type for two newspapers besides its own, and its steam press printed a total of seven papers, including one published some miles up Puget Sound.[21] The *Deseret News* printed Utah's first foreign-language newspaper, *Utah Posten*, a Danish-Norwegian paper, as well as the *Woman's Exponent*, the second women's paper west of the Mississippi.[22]

Some offices also earned extra income by offering special items such as books and engravings for sale; at the height of Comstock interest in the Sutro Tunnel, Adolph Sutro's newspaper in Virginia City offered a "splendid pictorial" of the tunnel, together with a copy of a lecture by Sutro.[23]

Political Printing

Election years brought political printing to the job offices. Posters, handbills, banners, and lists of party candidates (the "ticket") were part of the election hoopla of the period that required the attention of the printer. Nevada's Alf Doten in 1876 printed 15,000 copies of the regular Republican ticket. Two years later he printed 30,000 copies but may have made little, if any, money on the job, because after he delivered them to the Republican committee, a name was discovered missing from the roster. He reprinted 7,500, then found another error, and with two job presses running all night printed still another 5,000. Doten also printed 20,000 copies of a speech by Nevada Senator John P. Jones, 6,000 of which were put on the overland train for the eastern part of the state.[24]

In theory, at least, political printing should have been remunerative for the print shop and in some cases no doubt it was. Political printing and advertising, like that of transients, was subject to payment in advance. A publisher too close to the party, however, might find himself prevailed upon to do the work at unprofitable rates "for the sake of the party," or worse, to extend credit, or even to do the work for nothing with the promise of a public-printing contract later, assuming his party won. Doten published at least one campaign supplement that he distributed free.[25] Although most frontier publishers were enthusiastic party men, they nevertheless must have railed at too many requests to do work for which they might not get paid.

A publisher had to weigh the benefits of party activism and decide how far his newspaper would go in a partisan cause. Some publishers decided they needed readers and advertisers of all political stripes if they were to survive, and they followed a moderate course. The purchaser of the Susanville, California, *Sage Brush* declared his newspaper to be independent politically because he said the county could not support two views.[26] When Charles Prosch started the *Puget Sound Herald* in Steilacoom, Washington, in 1858, he learned from his unsuccessful predecessors to minimize his Republican sympathies in the interests of gaining readers. A few years earlier the *Puget Sound Courier* had supported the Whigs, but the small Whig population could not return the favor, and local Democrats preferred their party paper in Olympia. Prosch, looking forward to a long life for his newspaper, determined to avoid dividing his audience.[27] Another Washington publisher, the owner of the *Bellingham Bay Mail*, a member of a Republican clique in the 1870s, also kept a relatively moderate political profile, thereby managing to avoid competition.[28] Even in a multi-newspaper town, a publisher often tried to avoid taking sides. In the 1850s the Sacramento *Daily Union* threw its support to different parties at different times as it tried to mediate community conflicts without unduly alienating advertisers or subscribers.[29]

The level of partisanship was decided for publishers who accepted financial backing from party stalwarts. Like town boosters, politicians provided funds for the purchase of press and material and sometimes subsidized the publisher with direct payments. Asahel Bush expected Oregon Democrats to help get subscribers and otherwise support the *Statesman*.[30]

Party-supported newspapers were of two basic kinds: those published for the duration of a campaign and those intended to become a permanent voice for the party, aided by public printing contracts. If the party lost, a newspaper usually closed, regardless of original intent; even strong party papers generally lasted only a year or two. Virginia City, Nevada, Democrats subscribed $3,000 in 1863 to start the *Daily Democratic Standard* to challenge the town's three Republican newspapers; the *Standard* lasted three months. A German-language paper, to which Democrats promised $500 but paid only $100, lasted seven months. The Virginia City *Union* survived fewer than five years as a partisan newspaper, three of them as a Republican organ, the remainder in the Democratic camp.[31]

In 1864 Washington Territory Democrats found themselves in need of a voice and called upon Urban East Hicks, well known in Oregon and Washington newspaper circles, to publish the *Washington Democrat*. After nine months Hicks said farewell. "We are determined to do the best and all we can to fulfill our contracts," he wrote, "but no consideration can or will induce us to jeopardize the roof that shelters our family, for the sake of keeping up a party paper."[32]

The Walla Walla *Union* proved a notable exception to the pattern of short-lived partisan papers. The original owners of the *Washington Statesman* in Walla Walla followed a moderate political line, but after the Civil War they sold to a Democrat who delighted in poking fun at the internal bickering of territory Republicans. To counter his influence, local Republicans put up $1,500 to buy a printing plant and start the *Union*. The newspaper became such an economic success that commercial interests purchased it from party members, although it continued to speak for the Republicans.[33]

In 1868 Thomas Fitch tried to buy the *Silver Bend Reporter* in Belmont, Nevada, in order to have an organ to support his candidacy for Republican nomination for Congress. The owner of the *Reporter*, a Democrat, would not give up his newspaper but sold Fitch surplus printing materials, enabling the politician to start the *Mountain Champion*. Fitch was successful not only in his campaign, but also in driving the *Reporter* out of business. He turned the *Champion* over to his editor who soon moved it from Belmont, but for commercial rather than political reasons.[34] Henry Pittock, who succeeded Dryer at the *Oregonian*, was more sensitive than the *Reporter* publisher to the threat of competition. He sold shares in the *Oregonian* to party men talking of starting their own paper, thereby diverting them from entering the market.[35]

Printing the opposition's campaign newspapers forestalled competition in several towns. In the 1856 campaign the *Old Mountaineer*, a Republican paper in Quincy, California, printed the *Plumas Democrat* and the *Fillmore Banner*, and an eastern Washington Democrat printed his Republican opposition.[36] Because the publishers of the Boise *News* avoided politics altogether, their job shop got business from both parties, printing campaign newspapers for both Democrats and Republicans, charging each party $200.[37]

Throughout the West newspapers were known to be in the control of a particular party or politician. James L. Collins of the Santa Fe

Gazette, sometime Superintendent of Indian Affairs for New Mexico, often took direction from the territory's power brokers, and Arizona's John C. Goodwin could not have won election as territorial delegate "without the help of Secretary [Richard C.] McCormick, whose newspaper, the *Arizona Miner,* molded public opinion in the territory."[38]

Few politicians were willing or able personally to subsidize a newspaper indefinitely, but arranged for public-printing contracts to serve that purpose. In the golden years of public printing—the 1850s and 1860s when there were few limits and little accountability—publishers started newspapers and joined battles to establish territorial and state capitals and county seats in hopes of being designated the official printer.

Asahel Bush established the *Oregon Statesman* after he was promised the territorial printing; the early issues of his paper testify to the rancor that Democratic-party support for his efforts aroused in other publishers.[39] A few years later, across the Columbia in Washington Territory, John Miller Murphy's Vancouver *Chronicle* was struggling, thanks to his partner's incompetence.[40] Murphy noted that Abraham Lincoln had a good chance of winning the 1860 presidential election, which meant Republicans would control territorial offices. Territorial Republicans, in turn, would select someone to print the laws, ballots, forms, and other official printing—and there was no Republican newspaper in Olympia. Returning to his boyhood home, on November 17, 1860, Murphy issued the *Washington Standard,* telling his readers that they "will be vastly benefitted by the opportunity to learn sentiments opposed to the dominant party," referring, of course, to the Democrats.[41]

Even with the advantage of being first, Murphy found the public printing more difficult to acquire than he had anticipated. The biennial appropriations for territorial printing ranged from $6,000 to $20,000, offering enough profit to ensure a contest among printers. Murphy had powerful political friends, but his bid for the public printing got caught up in higher level rivalries. He tried several times before he finally acquired a contract, and even then he had to use his brother-in-law's name in order to neutralize the opposition.[42]

California publisher Jonas Winchester was another eager seeker of public subsidy. Winchester wrote his wife, Susan, in May 1850 that as California state printer he could expect good patronage and prestige and would be able to make a "princely fortune." Advertising and job work were lucrative but "it is on the State work that we shall coin gold." His contract with the state was for $35,000 and it allowed him to print and sell extra copies of the state laws. He estimated that he could sell 1,000 copies in California at $30 each, plus another $20,000 worth to customers in the "old States." The job would cost him $15,000, leaving a profit of $70,000. He urged Susan to move to California to help him "count the money."[43]

As the months passed, however, Winchester's letters became less optimistic. By August he noted that he had to share the San Francisco printing with five other offices. Of more concern, he had finished the English edition of the laws and had the Spanish edition in progress, but the state treasury was empty because taxes had not been collected. He had not been paid and had to borrow $15,000 to cover his expenses.[44] A month later he estimated that he would eventually come out all right on the public printing, even though copies had been damaged by fire. He added that he was putting a bad public face on it to shame the legislature into doing well by him the next time. Still confident his fortune lay in California, he was further tested when water damaged most of the copies of the laws he had planned to sell on his own, costing him more than $13,000. Then the legislature decided to rewrite a number of laws, killing the market for the old edition.[45]

Winchester, who had become publisher of the Democratic San Jose *Argus*, remained ever the party loyalist. Even losing $50 a day, the *Argus*'s value to the party made the effort worthwhile, Winchester believed, particularly in view of future profit he still expected to make from the state printing. When he discovered the state would pay in warrants that fluctuated in value through the spring from 37 ½ cents to 70 cents on the dollar, he realized that he would be fortunate to make expenses.[46]

The discounting of government payment for the public printing concerned other publishers as well. A Washington man wrote, "I don't know how my printing investment is going to come out, in consequence of the great depreciation, on this coast, of the Government currency. Coin is our basis. One dollar in Government currency is worth but *fifty cents* here."[47]

Enthusiasm for the public printing varied. In the 1850s, John A. Lewis of Los Angeles lobbied to get the contract to print California laws in Spanish, promising to start a newspaper if the contract was forthcoming.[48] By contrast, Alf Doten published federal laws in 1872 and 1874 but in 1873 calculated that he would lose money and declined even to bid.[49]

In 1881 the federal government appropriated $3,000 for printing the Washington territorial code and, reportedly at the instigation of a San Francisco printer, decided to award the contract by bid rather than follow the usual practice of letting the territorial secretary select the printer. Olympia publisher Clarence Bagley investigated prices in San Francisco and estimated the Californian's bid would cover 4,000 copies for the $3,000; Bagley offered to print 4,135 copies for the same sum and won the contract.[50]

Winners of public-printing contracts did not necessarily do the printing themselves. Publishing sets of laws taxed the capacity of frontier shops, and many public printers subcontracted the work to out-of-state printers. Bush of the *Oregon Statesman* defended sending the printing to be done in New York because no Oregon printer was equipped to do it.[51] By the 1870s the *Statesman* office was well enough equipped to supply supplements containing the federal laws to a number of newspapers. In 1872 Doten collected $776 from the federal government for the Nevada edition of the laws and split the sum with the *Statesman*. Robert D. Armstrong, who has closely examined public printing practices in the West, suggests that Doten's receiving half of the fee seems excessive "unless, as seems probable, part of the arrangement was that Doten kick back a portion of his pay" to those who organized the deal.[52] Armstrong also observes that the public printing for the state of Nevada was not done in the state until about 1881.[53]

Doten was fortunate in receiving payment about a month after submitting his bill, but other publishers, like Winchester, had difficulty collecting what was due them, and the delays soured them on doing government work. In 1861 a Washington printer turned to an old friend, John G. Nicolay, private secretary to President Lincoln, to help him get payment for the printing.[54] Delays of six months to a year were common, but a San Francisco printer waited three years to be paid for printing the Idaho Territory laws of 1866.[55]

In some states and territories, the public printer was elected, in others appointed, either of which was highly politicized and subject to abuse. Henry R. Mighels, publisher of the Carson City *Appeal* and speaker of the Nevada Assembly, pushed through the 1877 legislature a bill to have all state printing put up for bid, a move intended to "make amends for his [Mighels's] legalized robberies" when he was public printer and to quell "the plundering of the Treasury" possible under the old law.[56]

Government officials did relatively little monitoring of the printer's work and rarely insisted on measures to economize. In 1869 Washington Territory governor Alvan Flanders vetoed a series of minor amendments to the laws that would have meant little to anyone but the public printer who got to reprint them, but Flanders's watchfulness was unusual.[57] A committee that was supposed to check the quality of Nevada public printing in the early 1870s apparently never noticed that the size of type was not the same as that prescribed by law, nor did the state printer recognize that his San Francisco subcontractor was charging for one size type but printing in another.[58] In 1878 an Oregon public printer was accused of expanding one page of matter over four pages, counting one ream of paper as four, and charging five times what the job was worth.[59] A California publisher commented that because there was too much work for one printing office, a group commonly backed one of their number for state printer and then divided the work. He condemned the practice as costly and subject to corruption.[60]

Newspapers also competed feverishly for county printing and complained as bitterly about the mishandling of the process. The *Columbia Chronicle* in Dayton, Washington, charged that county commissioners had failed to advertise the county printing contract so they could award the job to the rival publisher, the Dayton *News*. Learning about the contract at the last minute, the *Chronicle* put in a bid of 75 cents a square, equal to an inch and an eighth; the *News* bid 90 cents, but, according to the *Chronicle*, the *News*'s square grew mysteriously from one inch at the beginning of the bid process to one and a half inches, guaranteeing the *News* the contract.[61]

Public printers were responsible for producing the bound copies of the laws and documents, but other newspapers might be made official papers of record, which assured them not only the income from legal advertising but also from publication in their newspapers of the laws and notices. These papers carried a label such as "official paper of the territory" under their name on the front page, and sometimes laws and advertising were about the only content.

TABLE 5.1

*Job Printing as Percent of Total Product
Revenue Newspaper Job Shops, 1890*

STATE	PERCENT
Arizona	25
California	12
Colorado	17
Idaho	25
Montana	24
Nevada	12
New Mexico	15
Oregon	15
Utah	16
Washington	17
Wyoming	21
WEST	15
UNITED STATES	18

Source: U.S. Census.

Value of Job Printing

Job printing is generally assumed to have kept frontier newspapers afloat, if not actually solvent; firm figures are elusive, however. The Cheyenne *Leader*'s job book showed $387.50 in income for February 1868; for a three-month period, February to April, the total was $1,036. It would appear that the *Leader* had job-printing income of about $300 a month, or $3,600 annually, although there is no assurance the level of business held steady through the year. The census of 1890 showed western newspaper offices averaging about $1,500 a year from job printing. The value of book and job printing amounted to about 15 percent of total production. In states far from major centers—Idaho, Montana, Wyoming, and Arizona—job printing represented a higher proportion of total value, 21 to 25 percent, largely because there were no separate job shops to compete with the newspapers. Only 12 percent of the product value from California newspaper offices was attributed to job printing, thanks largely to the concentration of specialized printing services in San Francisco (see table 5.1).

The number of people employed also indicates the relative importance of job printing to newspaper budgets. In California in 1870, newspapers employed 65 percent of all printing-industry workers and paid 68 percent of the wage. They also accounted for 61 percent of the printing offices in the state. Wages for job shop printers were inferior to those paid by newspapers, $805 to $958. By 1890, 376 California newspapers employed 73 percent of the state's printers and paid 77 percent of the wages. Colorado's 159 newspapers employed 85 percent of the printers and paid 86 percent of the wages.

Collecting payment for job printing presented a challenge similar to that for subscriptions and advertising, but local business requirements for forms and cards may have resulted in more conscientious attention to payment. The restaurateur who failed to pay for his printed meal tickets, for example, might not get any more from the printer, and lack of tickets could hinder his ability to keep track of his business. In contrast, a merchant whose advertising was removed from the newspaper for nonpayment might consider it merely an inconvenience. Like advertisers and subscribers, printing customers probably also frequently paid in kind, and printers may have eaten well at the restaurateur's table.

Publishers' insistence that transient customers pay cash would have helped balance accounts. About 45 percent of the jobs recorded in the Cheyenne *Leader* job book were cash transactions, particularly the tickets and programs for entertainers.

PART III

Expenses

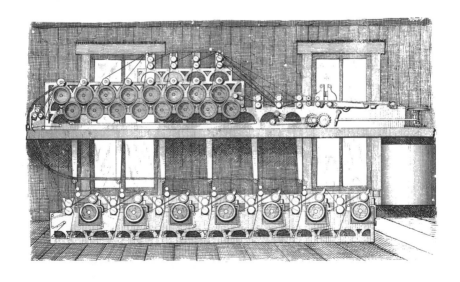

6

SETTING UP SHOP

The first expense a publisher had to consider was his equipment. He needed a press, type, rollers, material for spacing (leads) and making lines (rules), and tables and cabinets to hold everything. He also needed a building in which to put his press and office. In setting up his facilities, he could travel economy or deluxe class, depending on what his budget would bear.

The image of the frontier printer roaming the West toting his press and a shirttail of type, like so many other western images, is overly romanticized. Few printers fit the image for one very practical reason: printing materials are heavy, not the kind of load a wanderer puts in his knapsack.

A hand press was the staple of the frontier newspaper and although small and initially made mostly of wood with a minimum of iron, even a modest hand press could weigh several hundred pounds. In the late 1860s a Washington hand press large enough to print a 15-by-21-inch page weighed about 1,500 pounds, so, together with frames, type, and other necessary materials, the equipment needed to set up a print shop would weigh more than a ton, hardly a portable load.[1]

Still, frontier presses often seemed featherweight and well traveled. One press in California printed four different newspapers in two years.[2] An Arizona press served six newspapers in four years.[3] The Ramage press used for the *Californian* was secondhand when the Spaniards brought it from Boston to Monterey in 1834. The Americans who printed the *Californian* said even then that it was "old enough to be preserved as a curiosity."[4] Nevertheless, it later was used in the *Alta California* office in San Francisco, then for papers in Sacramento, Stockton, Sonora, and finally Columbia, California, where it was burned by vandals as it awaited transportation to still another location.[5] Jack Merrick, who planned to publish the *Cherry Creek Pioneer* until he lost the race to be first to William Byers and the *Rocky Mountain News*, carried to Denver a press that formerly belonged to the Mormons; an anti-Mormon mob had thrown it into the Missouri River in 1833; years later it was recovered to print the *Gazette* in St. Joseph, Missouri, where Merrick acquired it.[6]

With rare exceptions, presses used in western America were built on the East Coast and the earliest were transported around Cape Horn to the West. After the development of the Isthmus passage, some presses followed that passage, and it is questionable which was the more hazardous journey. The publisher of the San Diego *Herald* bought his printing outfit in New Orleans, but lost parts of it in the Chagres River in Panama.[7] Presses for inland locations could travel by sea or the Isthmus to the Pacific Coast and thence inland, or they could be hauled across the Great Plains. The Mormons carried theirs to Salt Lake City from Missouri, and the Helena *Herald*'s press arrived via the Missouri River route.[8] Meanwhile, the Boise *News* was started on a press which probably had come via San Francisco and the Columbia River to Walla Walla to serve first the Whitman Mission and later the Walla Walla *Watchman*.[9]

At least two publishers managed temporarily on presses built by local craftsmen. In Oregon a wooden press was constructed for the *Free Press* in Oregon City, and its builder claimed that it would "tell the truth quite as well as an iron one."[10] The St. George, Utah, *Enterprise* also had a homemade press.[11]

Frontier newspapers generally started in primitive facilities with secondhand material, and worn, used type and presses forced publishers to be inventive. Walter Colton recalled that the type with which he and Robert Baylor Semple printed the *Californian* was rusty and "pied" (a printer's term meaning the letters are jumbled): "It was only by scouring that the letters could be made to show their faces." Nor was it sufficient for their needs. They had no rules or leads, so "a sheet or two of tin was procured, and these, with a jackknife were cut into rules and leads."[12]

In addition, the letter "w," not part of the Spanish alphabet, was largely missing from the fonts found with the old press, so the American publishers improvised by using two v's side by side; when they ran out of v's, they turned to u's.[13] Material purchased from Pacific Northwest missionaries for use in Oregon's *Free Press* also lacked w's, so the publisher had the missing letters carved from wood.[14] Printers at the *Placer Times* at Sutter's Fort in 1849 modified o's to make c's, and the first issue of the *Rocky Mountain News* in 1859 was short of periods and lower-case k's.[15]

Publishers met other printing needs with available items. The imposing stone (on which the pages were put together) at the *Territorial Enterprise* is said to have doubled for a dinner table.[16] The printers who set up shop in Idaho City in 1863 for the *Boise News* bought an incomplete outfit in Walla Walla, and made their own composing sticks—which held the letters as the printer selected them from the type case—from a tobacco box, covered a slab of pine with iron to serve as an imposing stone, and shaped a chase—the frame that holds a page of type—from horseshoe iron.[17]

When they exhausted their resources and ingenuity, publishers borrowed or bought supplies from nearby colleagues. The first issue of the *Territorial Enterprise* was delayed when the proprietors ran out of letters and had to send to Placerville for a loan of more.[18] At the inaugural of the *Yakima Record* in 1879, the publisher discovered column rules had been omitted from the shipment of materials, so he borrowed some from an Ellensburg office.[19]

Publishers were craftsmen enough to be embarrassed when their limited resources yielded poor results. "We are not fond of making apologies," the publishers of the *Californian* said, "but at present beg leave to inform our readers that the materials on which the Californian is printed, was found in the public buildings here, and have been used for the Spanish language, and in deed has been much injured by neglect. Many of the letters have been wasted or mislaid, and the whole very much out of order, so that, in fact, we have made our first number almost from chaos."[20]

Colton and Semple chanced upon the material for the *Californian* and decided to take advantage of the opportunity that presented itself, but most newspapermen planned their enterprise and assembled the best equipment they could find and afford. They also expanded as quickly as possible, not always for the sake of their newspapers, but often to enhance their job printing capabilities. Posters, flyers, and other specialty printing required more than a small press and a font or two of type.

By the time it was a year old, the *Alta California* had a steam press and a large assortment of type; soon its owner felt justified in calling it "one of the most complete establishments in the United States."[21] In 1859 *El Clamor Público* in Los Angeles had a Washington press, and about 750 pounds of different kinds of type, including accents of all kinds suitable for any language.[22] When owners of the *Overland Press* in Washington advertised the sale of their plant in 1863, they listed Washington and Ramage hand presses, 1,000 pounds of primer type, 500 pounds of minion type, 300 pounds of new small pica type, a large assortment of wood and metal job type, and nearly 100 fonts of card, advertising, and other type sufficient to print two or three newspapers and do territorial job printing.[23]

Limited equipment both aided and constrained the development of the frontier press. Small-town publishers favored the hand press because it was relatively inexpensive and quick to set up, but it was also slow to operate. It had a sheet platen that the printer screwed or levered down onto a frame full of type which had been inked and on which a sheet of paper was laid. The type sat on a bed that could be moved under the platen and out again for placement of the paper. Only one side of a sheet—usually two pages—could be done at a time; while the printers finished printing all the sheets on one side, the ink dried and the sheets were ready for printing on the other side.

The output of the typical hand press depended to a degree on the skill of the pressmen, but fifty to sixty completed papers an hour seems to be about par, assuming two pages printed at the same time.[24] In all, it could take all day to print a four-page weekly with 500 circulation, and it was hard work. A printer who operated the *Californian*'s old-style Ramage described it as "about the size of a Yankee cider press, of the tub pattern, and of iron. When the lever was drawn forward, it took considerable force to push it back."[25] The effort required to operate the Ramage led printers to call it the "man killer."[26]

The hand press best suited a weekly newspaper, but even dailies were sometimes printed on them. The daily Portland *Oregonian* in 1861 and the Los Angeles *Daily Express* in 1871 were started on hand presses because their owners wanted to forestall competition, but they quickly turned to steam power to meet the requirements of daily production.[27] Steam had been applied to printing presses for several decades, and newspapers took advantage of it as soon as circulation and job work warranted the extra speed and justified the investment. The *Oregon Statesman* started using steam in 1859 and the *Territorial Enterprise* in the 1860s.[28] In 1873 the Los Angeles *Herald* was the first newspaper in Southern California to print with steam; use began in Walla Walla in 1880.[29]

Steam power greatly increased the capacity of the press. A basic power press could print the typical weekly's requirements in an hour or so. In the 1880s an Oakland newspaper acquired a double-acting single cylinder press that could handle 3,000 copies an hour, the fastest the publisher had ever seen and one which "gave us much trouble keeping it fastened to the floor."[30] About the same time the *Oregonian* acquired a continuous web press—using paper on rolls instead of individual sheets—capable of printing 12,000 pages an hour.[31] By 1890 presses were spitting out 48,000 copies an hour with more pages, but western papers outside of San Francisco generally did not have such large production needs.[32]

Owning a press that *could* be powered by steam did not necessarily mean that it was. The press itself was a large expenditure, the steam engine another, and some publishers could not afford both at the same time. When a Vallejo publisher bought a Hoe cylinder press in the 1860s—the $1,500 to $2,000 price "seemed like a large investment, although the paper required it"—steam was too costly and not readily available.[33] He initially hired a big Chinese man to turn the handle, but soon spent another $1,200 for a boiler and steam engine. Publishers in Spokane, Boise, and New Mexico also employed strong men to turn their cylinder presses for a time in the absence of steam.[34]

Having a steam-powered press not only increased capacity, it served as a symbol of a lively, progressive enterprise, and publishers promoted it as such. At the same time, steam power meant more things could go wrong, compared to hand-operated presses. The publisher of the *Daily Avalanche* in Idaho installed steam in February 1875. In October it broke down with "a terrible crash, as if the entire building were coming down."[35] The cast-iron rocker level that propelled the bed on which the type lay had broken. It took five days to get it fixed; in the meantime the paper was printed in a smaller form. The Gold Hills *News* in Nevada introduced steam power in June 1876. It, too, needed repairs a few months later. The repairs were done quickly but improperly, forcing the pressmen to print the day's edition very slowly. Next, the main drive shaft broke; foundry workers mended it within hours, but it broke again, and again was fixed, just in time for the *News* to meet most of its mail deadlines.[36]

Water power was sometimes used but it could offer a different set of problems. The Times Mirror Company in Los Angeles had a Taylor cylinder press operated by a Pelton water motor which sometimes stopped when a fish got caught in it.[37] Uncertain water conditions could affect printing schedules. In 1882 daytime garden watering by Reno residents so reduced the flow of the Truckee River that the Reno *Gazette*, an evening paper, did not have enough water to power its press. When residents ignored a request to refrain from watering during the afternoon, the *Gazette* switched to steam power. Meanwhile, the rival *Nevada State Journal* changed from steam to water; a morning paper, it printed at night when residents had finished their watering.[38]

Throughout the frontier period, indeed into the twentieth century for many small newspapers, type was set by hand, selected letter by tiny letter from cases where each letter had its own box. A compositor's speed depended partly on his knowing where each letter was located in the case and on being able to rely on letters being in their designated places. He did not have time to check whether a letter was a p, q, b, or d. After printing was completed, type was distributed back into the case.

A dropped type case or a chase full of type meant "pied" type— letters so mixed up each one had to be examined as it was returned to the case, a slow process considering the thousands of letters involved. When the *Territorial Enterprise* moved from Genoa to Carson City— its first shift before finally settling in Virginia City where it became famous—a type cabinet containing twenty trays was tipped over and the type pied, resulting in a production delay.[39] On another occasion, the *Enterprise* came out with its center pages blank because the type had been dropped and printers did not have time to restore the page. The neighboring Gold Hill *News* reported that an old drunk, Dufferdink, took a look at the blank page, declared, "I'm struck stone blind," and passed out.[40] At another newspaper, a compositor handling a page containing eight columns of small type for the Nevada constitution inserted too much spacing and caused the type to bulge and spill onto the floor. The paper's printer's devil spent two months sorting the jumbled letters.[41] Printers at the Calico, California, *Print* had to redistribute type pied in shipping before they could produce the first issue of the newspaper.[42]

Typesetting was mechanized much later than printing. The first typesetting machines, available commercially in the late 1880s, did not appear in the West until the following decade. Not only were they too expensive for the typical western newspaper, their capacity—

one estimate was ten times that of a hand compositor—far exceeded the needs of the typical four-page weekly or even small daily. City dailies were quicker to take advantage of the innovation; producing eight or more pages on a regular basis, they welcomed any labor-saving devices. Nevertheless, the first western newspaper to acquire a Linotype, the Mergenthaler Company's typesetting machine invented by Ottmar Merganthaler, was not in San Francisco as might be expected, but in Helena, Montana, in November 1891.[43]

Similarly, stereotyping, which came into general use among eastern city papers around 1861, was not a realistic tool across most of the frontier.[44] Stereotyping—an impression of a newspaper page or other typeset or engraved material molded on a metal plate—was particularly useful when newspapers had multiple presses operating or needed curved plates for type-revolving presses where the type needed to fit around a cylinder. Few frontier newspapers had either of these requirements. However, business demands in major centers, particularly from customers who wanted to distribute advertisements to other newspapers, justified the necessary investment. The *Deseret News* installed stereotyping equipment in 1878, the San Bernardino *Times* was equipped by 1883, and the *Rocky Mountain News* by 1886.[45]

An essential piece of equipment frontier printers often made themselves was the ink roller. Colonial printers inked their type with leather balls, but by the time of the frontier newspaper, the composition roller was in use. To make a roller, printers boiled glue and a substance such as glycerine or treacle or molasses, until the mixture was as tough as rubber. They then poured it into a special mold around an iron core.[46] The resulting roller, highly effective in optimum circumstances, did not stand up well in extreme weather conditions. Byers in Denver complained that the dry climate was "death on rollers" when he wrote a Chicago friend to send him a 24-inch brass roller mold to replace one broken by a helper.[47] The *Arizona Miner* reported that the hot summer sun had melted its roller, and printers in Sacramento tried burying a new roller in the ground in an unsuccessful attempt to keep it away from the heat.[48] The Yakima, Washington, *Record* also lost a roller to heat and had to have it recast at The Dalles, Oregon.[49]

Because of their ingredients, rollers had a sweet taste that led to other complications. In Seattle an Indian boy nibbled on a discarded roller, decided it tasted like an Indian pudding, and ate it.[50] In another Washington town, the publishers called for a law to control the town's hogs after they saw "to our horror, a fierce-looking old sow, just swallowing the last morsel of our composition roller, which cost $3 to replace, and was quietly picking her teeth with the core."[51]

A Roof Over the Press

Frontier newspapers typically started in rickety wooden structures or tents that kept out few of the elements. Hot in summer, they were freezing in winter; one publisher complained that his office was so drafty the frost even solidified his ink, and publishers sometimes begged readers to pay their bills with wood.[52] Extreme temperatures competed with rain and snow in creating uncomfortable surroundings. Roofs often leaked. Printers setting type for the *Rocky Mountain News* in Denver in April 1859 rigged a tarpaulin over the press to protect the paper from the melting snow that dripped through the roof.[53] In Virginia City, printers struggled to keep their fingers limber as they worked their type cases in icy weather, and when it rained, they attached strings to the ceiling to divert the water. "At times there were so many strings that the ceiling of the office resembled a huge cobweb."[54]

Sometimes the primitive facilities resulted from the publisher's higher priorities—any shelter would do so long as the paper got printed. Sometimes they were the result of circumstances; John P. Clum could not get construction materials during Tombstone's building boom in 1881 and resorted to stretching a temporary canvas on a frame to shelter the *Epitaph*.[55] Sacramento's first newspaper occupied a similar structure.[56] San Francisco's *California Star* was housed in temporary quarters above a grist mill, and the *Californian* started its San Francisco days in an adobe house.[57]

Printers frequently lived in the building that housed the print shop. Single men bunked near their work; the publisher and his family, if he had one, might have an apartment behind or over the shop. When the *Californian* and the *California Star* combined, the staff moved into a small one-story building that served as office, print shop, and lodging for the editor and printer.[58] The Los Angeles *Star* plant occupied the ground floor of a two-story building; the proprietor and printers lived upstairs.[59] In the early years of the *Territorial Enterprise* all operations and living arrangements centered in one room.[60]

Having a proper home for their newspapers was a matter of pride to publishers. As they developed their production facilities, they also improved their quarters whenever they were financially able. The prosperous *Alta California*, which grew out of the *Star* and the *Californian*, by 1850 occupied a brick building valued at around $30,000; its editorial rooms were termed "luxurious."[61] Two decades later across San Francisco Bay, the Oakland *Tribune* bragged about moving to "the coziest suit [sic.] of elegantly furnished rooms we have ever seen occupied by journalists this side of the bay."[62] A new fireproof brick building particularly provided evidence of a newspaper's prosperity.

In spite of the weight of presses and type, publishers often located their newspapers on the second floor of buildings. The *Rocky Mountain News*, for example, started above a store-saloon.[63] One publisher, who built his own building in the 1870s, offered the lower floor for rent, and found that saloon owners were the main applicants for the space—although he finally rented it to the postmaster.[64] A Washington publisher who had bitterly attacked railroad interests in his Tacoma newspaper became their landlord after he moved to Spokane and rented the lower floor of his newspaper office to the Northern Pacific.[65]

More prosperous papers tended to retain the ground floor for business offices which provided for better public access; situating production upstairs helped discourage unwanted visitors. Publishers complained about hangers-on hindering printers at work and creating confusion in the shop. In 1850 the *Deseret News* told readers that "No Admittance" meant what it said and people should keep out of the print shop.[66] A California mining-camp publisher issued a similar message:

NOTICE EXTRAORDINARY.—Certain of our friends will save themselves the humiliation of being individually addressed on the subject, if they will heed this notice and not meddle with copy-hooks, files, pigeon-holes, &c., in this office. This injunction will be enforced and the next man who trespasses will be properly rebuked.[67]

A frustrated Utah publisher summed up a similar litany of complaints with what he called a Quaker printer's proverb: "Neither do thou loaf about, asking questions, or knock down type, or the boys will love thee like they do shade trees—when thou leafeth."[68]

Until they got their own brick buildings, some newspapers changed quarters often, not always by choice. The Los Angeles *Express* moved at least five times between 1871 and 1897, apparently more or less willingly with a view to improving conditions, but other frontier newspapers were forced from their homes at various times by fire, flood, or earthquake.[69] The year after the *Alta California* moved into a new brick building, its luxurious accommodations burned, and in 1850–51, San Francisco's *Pacific News*, California's first Democratic organ, was damaged by fire several times.[70] One of the many early fires in San Francisco also damaged the *Courier, Herald, Standard, Picayune, Eureka*, and *Public Balance*; the *Alta*'s escape from this particular conflagration gave it an economic edge on its rivals. Fire destroyed most of Virginia City in 1875, including the plants of the *Territorial Enterprise* and the *Virginia Evening Chronicle*; in 1889 major fires swept through both Seattle and Spokane, damaging newspaper plants in its path. After the Seattle fire, the *Morning Journal*, appearing in reduced size, reported, "There is not a cylinder press left in the city, and the newspapers are among the heavy losers by the fire."[71]

Although fire meant the end for some papers, frontier publishers showed a remarkable resilience in the face of catastrophe. After an 1873 fire did an estimated $12,000 in uninsured damage to a Nevada paper, the publisher telegraphed for new material which arrived quickly from San Francisco, and publication resumed. Two years later the same paper was damaged by flood and in 1879 by another fire, but it continued to publish.[72]

In some locations water posed as much danger as fire. To maximize his business potential, the founder of the *Rocky Mountain News* appealed to residents of both Cherry Creek and Auralia, which lined either side of Cherry Creek, by building his office on an island in the middle of the creek. The inevitable happened in 1864. May rains and melting snow flooded the creek and washed away the office. It was back in business in a few days, but the original press used to start the newspaper was lost until 1899 when pieces of it were dug out of the sand well downstream.[73]

Publishers in Olympia, Washington, and Stanislaus County, California, also made injudicious choices of location, initially sitting their newspapers in swampy areas almost impossible to reach during the rainy season. The Olympia paper soon moved to higher ground, but the California paper apparently managed without serious flood problems.[74]

The experience of the *Reese River Reveille* in Austin, Nevada, shows the resignation and even humor that helped frontier publishers cope with disaster. Austin, a mining center from the early 1860s, was built in a steep canyon. Because the relatively barren hillsides held few trees for fuel or construction, most of the buildings were of brick and stone, making fire a minor worry to the early settlers. However, Nevada canyons are prone to gully-washing rains. In 1878, the *Reveille* staff had almost completed the Thursday, August 14, edition when a cloudburst unleashed floodwaters on the town. The brick newspaper office, which had withstood a similar flash flood in 1874, was the first building swept from its foundations. Employees managed to get out the back door, but when the publisher did not appear, townspeople assumed he had gone down with the building. He claimed later that onlookers cheered his demise and were disappointed when they learned he survived, having been at a local hotel from which he was able to escape to higher ground.[75]

Some type, including most of the advertising that had been ready to go into the pages, was somehow salvaged from the newspaper office, but resumption of the *Reveille* was delayed until the following Monday, August 19. In the meantime, two newspapers in nearby Eureka, as well as the Carson *Appeal*, wired offers of help, and two San Francisco printing-supply firms telegraphed that anything the *Reveille* needed would be shipped at once.

"The *Reveille* got knocked end-wise in the flood, but we ain't dead yet," the two-page *Reveille* said in its abbreviated Monday edition. "We have saved enough from the wreck, with which—with some type borrowed from Eureka—to issue this small sheet." The publisher asked readers to ignore errors because the proof press was gone, and to avoid the office until the damage was cleared away. The Monday paper printed a column of news rescued from the debris "as a memento as it were of what would have been Thursday's paper if the cloudburst had held off for about half an hour." Gradually getting back to normal, on August 21 the paper filled three pages but did not have enough type for a fourth. Throughout it all, the publisher treated his situation almost as though a major flood was just an everyday problem.

Earthquakes must have shaken many a California office, but only one complaint of serious damage has been located. In 1868, an earthquake that shook Pacheco forced emergency removal of the press and type from the second floor of a brick building to the ground floor of a vacant frame structure nearby.[76]

Disaster brought out the camaraderie of the printing fraternity and publishers rallied to help afflicted brethren, as in the Austin flood, by lending material and production facilities, and sometimes letting the staff of another newspaper move in temporarily. When fire destroyed the San Francisco *Call* in the late 1850s, the newspaper missed only one day's edition because the publisher was able to scrounge bits of type and materials from other offices around the city. Loans were floated and in five months the paper had new presses.[77] When the *Territorial Enterprise* office was destroyed in the Virginia City fire of 1875, the publisher set up shop in the nearby Gold Hill *News* plant, and never missed an issue. The *News* accommodated the *Territorial Enterprise* for about two months, as well as the Virginia *Evening Chronicle* for a few days.[78]

Few frontier newspapers escaped disaster entirely, and for some, fire or flood was a permanent setback. At least thirty Pacific Northwest newspapers are known to have been destroyed by fire.[79] The damage to the newspaper could extend well beyond the confines of its office. The Montana *Post* survived a fire in Helena in 1869, only to succumb because the rest of the business community was also burned and the newspaper was unable to collect for subscriptions or advertising.[80]

Bigger Is Better

The newspapers that were produced in western plants fit no single model. The size of the press and available paper stock largely determined dimensions. Three-column papers, such as the earliest in California, likely developed on presses primarily intended for job-shop work. The size of its existing paper supply caused the *Arizona Miner* to shift from a six-column format to five columns when its order of newsprint did not arrive.[81]

Presses—and paper—came in a great range of sizes, from about 5 by 7 inches to what were sometimes called "blanket sheets" of 22 by 34 inches. The early *Deseret News* measured somewhat less than 8 by 10 inches; the *Idaho Statesman* was 10 by 16. The *Alta California* started at 18 by 22 inches and over the next year enlarged several times to 20 by 26.[82] In 1866 R. Hoe & Company advertised a Washington hand press and suggested a popular size was the Imperial Number 1, which had a page size of 15 by 21 inches.[83]

Publishers adhered to the notion that bigger newspapers were better newspapers, an attitude that put smaller papers on the defensive. The Ione *Advertiser* apologized about its small size, which it blamed on economic depression,[84] while another publisher wrote, "And yet there are men who take such contracted views of this matter, that unless they are getting as many square inches of reading matter in their home papers as they do in a city, they think they are not getting the worth of their money."[85] "Much ridicule usually attaches to a small sheet, contemptuously characterized as a 'seven-by-nine concern,'" a writer commented, "but it has been remarked that the Reese River Reveille, in its prime, removed the stigma and prejudice against small papers."[86] Meanwhile the publisher of the Gold Hill *News* boasted when his paper became an inch wider than the *Territorial Enterprise*, and when the *Daily Inland Empire* in Nevada enlarged to 20½ by 28 inches, its publisher declared it a first-class paper because it was the size of the Sacramento *Union*, the leading blanket sheet of its day.[87]

Some newspapers frequently changed size. The *Territorial Enterprise* started as 21 by 28 inches (five columns to a page) in 1859, four years later enlarged to seven columns in a sheet size of 22 by 32 inches; nine months later it measured 28 by 42 inches, with nine columns, and returned to its original dimensions in 1866 (but with six columns); later that same year it enlarged again to 24 by 36 inches (eight columns). In 1876 the *Enterprise* it had nine columns and dimensions of 27 by 42 inches; two years later it had changed to 24 by 36 inches (eight columns).[88]

Publishers did not worry unduly about consistency in size or appearance or even in the name of the paper. On one occasion the nameplate of the newspaper might be engraved with the town name in front of "Times" or "News"; the next time it might not. The *Owyhee Avalanche* became the *Idaho Avalanche*, perhaps because the publisher thought the latter better identified its locale. In any case, the cavalier approach to names sometimes makes tracing a newspaper's lineage difficult.[89]

Regardless of overall dimensions, four pages were standard for early frontier papers, although the Ione *Advertiser* made its debut with a single small page, and initially the *Deseret News* had eight pages in a magazine format. *Deseret News* publishers numbered pages consecutively over the course of a volume, with a size and format to accommodate binding of issues because publishers anticipated readers would want to keep the history of Joseph Smith, tabernacle sermons, and other church-related information that they published.[90]

The appearance of the frontier newspaper matched the simplicity of its production facilities. Initially, stories and advertising were generally limited to single-column width and it was difficult to tell them apart; later, double-column advertising became more common, although rarely the rule. Handling two columns of type in a compositor's stick and on the press required extra care, but it was by no means beyond the skill of most printers. Some printers may have avoided multi-column setting because they lacked type large enough to be aesthetically pleasing in the wider space, but probably habit—the sense that a newspaper was supposed to look a certain way—played the greatest role in the prevalence of single-column material.

Pages were almost solid type, relieved occasionally in the news columns by capital letters and sometimes italic or bold type, and in the advertising columns by as much variety of type faces and sizes as facilities allowed. Headlines were either nonexistent—perhaps in all capital letters at the start of a story—or merely labels. City papers eventually adopted the eastern practice of setting apart the first lines of the story in special type, but away from the major centers, papers seldom used anything more than a label for a headline. They nevertheless tried to call attention to special stories. In Arizona in 1867, the *Miner* used all capital letters in the regular small body type to construct a headline in the shape of an inverted pyramid, to tell of "Exciting News," the latest "outrage" by the Indians.[91]

Illustration in the news columns was almost unknown and in the advertising columns more common in some newspapers than others. Most newspapers relied on a stock of standard pictures, but engraving services were available in big cities and occasionally even country papers arranged for special artwork. An engraving signed by a San Francisco craftsman appeared in Stockton's *San Joaquin Republican* in 1854.[92] The same year, during the campaign to move the seat of Eldorado County to Placerville, the *Mountain Democrat* printed a county map across the top half of the front page; three years later another California paper ran a half-page map showing proposed immigrant roads.[93] A number of quite elaborate engravings of the Centennial Exhibition buildings in Philadelphia appeared in an Idaho paper in 1876.[94]

Publishers sent to San Francisco or other cities for specially engraved nameplates. The *Enterprise* in Oxford, Idaho, had an unusually elaborate nameplate that had figures of men reading newspapers draped among the letters.[95] Another paper used specialty type that resembled pieces of wood, a little rough around the edges.[96] Some newspapers promoting local development—and perhaps reflecting a subsidy—had trains in their nameplates.[97]

The multitude of legal advertisements did not enhance the appearance of the page. Then, as today, publishers tended to set them in small type, adding to the grayness of the columns. But to the nineteenth-century newspaper printer, it was often enough to have a clean-appearing page, free from typographical errors, broken type, and smudged ink. Competition was played out in forms other than a handsome appearance.

7

STAFFING THE NEWSPAPER

Modern newspaper employees work in five basic areas: news-editorial, business, advertising, production, and circulation. The smaller the newspaper, the more duties overlap, but the labor is still essentially specialized. Frontier newspapermen wore several hats, and personnel generally fell into only two categories: those who were printers and those who were not.

The smallest newspapers tended to have publishers determined to produce their newspapers single-handedly, perhaps employing a strong-armed boy to help with the press. More often, thanks in part to the job-printing business, a publisher found it advisable to hire assistance, usually looking for people to complement whichever skills he best contributed to the enterprise. As a newspaper grew and overall management responsibilities expanded, or as he found himself involved in other businesses or community affairs, a publisher increasingly depended on hired help.

The gold rush that brought the frontier's future publishers to the West also attracted the labor that helped staff the newspapers and job shops. The excitement of Sutter's Mill produced a sudden influx of men with the skills to produce a newspaper, but the various discoveries of gold, silver, and other metals that marked the West through the frontier period had a mixed impact on the western labor market. The West might be full of printers, but if they were in the mines instead of the printing offices, they were of little value to the publisher trying to produce his newspaper. The labor supply often depended on the proximity of the nearest mines and how well they were producing. In 1848 the fledgling San Francisco newspapers, the *Californian* and the *Star*, suspended publication when the printers took off for the goldfields. Warning of the probable suspension, the *California Star* moaned, "already our 'divil' has rebelled, our pressman, (poor fellow!) last seen of him was in search of a pickaxe."[1] Similarly, the Oregon City *Spectator* lost its printer to the diggings and was forced to stop publishing for about a month.² On one occasion the entire staff of the Gunnison, Colorado, *Daily News* went prospecting, and the publisher called on local volunteers—including a minister and a dance-hall girl—to help print the paper.³ One writer commented that compared to gold fever "cholera is a mere bungler in the way of depopulating towns."⁴

On the other hand, the willingness of men to chase the gold bug could have a positive effect on the labor supply. San Francisco's listless economy benefited when the city's unemployed responded to gold discoveries on the Kern River in northern California in 1855 and on the Fraser River in British Columbia in 1858.⁵ New finds also helped distribute the labor pool throughout the West, many men electing to stay in new territories instead of returning to California or to homes in the East.

The more remote, poor, and undeveloped a community, however, the less likely it would attract printers. A Washington publisher apologized to his readers for the small amount of reading matter, but he said printers were difficult to find.⁶ Rural Utah newspapers struggled to retain printers, the Salt Lake *Tribune* said, because "typos become starved out."⁷ One southern Utah man took leave to build himself a house, disrupting publication because no other printers were available to take his place.⁸

Mining-camp newspapers generally had access to a sufficient labor pool, even when printers were in short supply in other communities. Publishers of the *Rocky Mountain News* had only to announce a need for printers to immediately be rewarded with assistance.⁹ The publishers of the Boise *News* found they had worried needlessly about getting skilled help, subsequently writing:

The advent of the Boise News into the basin seems to have resurrected all of the typos who have been buried since old Dr. Faust's league with the devil, and turned them loose, without any money, on the southern slope of the Salmon River Mountains. These specimens of human clay, done up in old flour sacks and gum-boots, are alive, however, to the necessity of their winter's rations of sowbelly and beans as they've been flocking around the *News* office the past week thick as flies about a meat market, gallinipers along the Snake—aye, or office-seekers in Idaho! The office has been so crowded at times, that the editor has not had room to stick the point of a pen, except in a keyhole.[10]

In addition, the legendary journeyman printers who wandered from place to place—"birds of passage" they were sometimes called—provided competent, if irregular, staff. Nevadan Alf Doten told of a tramp printer named Hazlett who traveled around the country, mostly on foot. He appeared in the Virginia City area about once a year, stayed a few days to "accept little jobs from his kindly printer brothers."[11]

Occasionally, publishers pressed other able-bodied men into service. The *Bellingham Bay Mail* in northwestern Washington had its office in the old courthouse which also housed the jail, and prisoners sometimes helped run the press.[12] Soldiers performed similar work in some locations.

In the early years, the number of printers in the West grew rapidly, particularly in California. In 1850, before California felt the full impact of the gold rush, the state supported seven newspapers, staffed by probably fewer than fifty printers.[13] A decade later, 621 people, not counting all publisher-printers, reported their occupation as printer. The increase in printers was nearly four times that of the increase in California's total population (1,142 percent compared to 310 percent).

Most weeklies managed with one or two hired journeyman-level printers, depending on the skills the publisher brought to the operation and the amount of job work. In 1867 the publisher of the *Weekly Silver Bend Reporter* in Belmont, Nevada, was such a jack-of-all-trades that he coped virtually alone, assisted only by a boy, and the founder of the Fresno *Times* usually operated with just one assistant.[14] In general, however, a staff of three full-time people appears to have been common on weeklies: a journalist and two printers, plus the printers' "devil"—the "go-fer," clean-up person who might be either a young apprentice or low-paid unskilled laborer. Since newspaper offices invariably did job printing, thriving communities usually produced enough work to justify another printer or two, who could also serve the newspaper when needed. The Placerville, California, directory in 1862 listed three employees and a publisher for each of the town's four newspapers.[15] The directory for Helena, Montana, in 1868 listed an average of one editor and five printers for each of the three newspapers published there.[16] Print shops in

California in 1880 averaged about seven people each. Differences between papers could be substantial. The San Francisco *Bulletin* had about forty printers in 1856, and the *Territorial Enterprise* employed more than twenty typesetters during its heyday in the 1860s.[17] The production crew of the Calico, California, *Print* in the 1880s consisted of a printer, two typesetters, and two pressmen.[18]

Journeymen printers who staffed newspapers in the early years received their training in formal apprenticeship programs on newspapers in the East and Midwest. On the frontier, however, training programs were often casual and a number of pioneer printer-publishers did not serve formal apprenticeships. Washington publisher Clarence Bagley learned to "stick type" in the Olympia *Territorial Republican* office, hanging around until the printers gave him something to do. And Ike Hall, the attorney who published newspapers in Seattle off and on during his legal career, also frequented the *Republican* printshop.[19] Californian Frank Leach originally planned to enter an apprenticeship as a machinist, but agreed to work temporarily for the Napa *Register* where, without benefit of a formal agreement, he was taught the "mysteries of the printing business, the lay of the case, how to 'roll' for a hand press, and was called the 'devil,'" and was launched into a newspaper career.[20]

At the same time, western printshops welcomed apprentices, and tried to treat them according to tradition even though agreements did not always conform to the national standard. Elsewhere in the nation, a youngster typically started an apprenticeship at age 15, and stayed six years, the employer providing room, board, and/or a small wage.[21] In the West's expanding economy other employment opportunities made stringent requirements unattractive. A Washington publisher took on an apprentice in 1873, agreeing to provide his board for the first six months, board and clothing the second six months, pay of $50 the second year, and $100 the third year.[22] About the same time a Nevadan paid his apprentice $6 a week.[23] The *Deseret News* offered a strong incentive to the apprentice to learn quickly. The first year the apprentice received $312; for the remaining years he got a portion of the income from work he did for the office.[24] Advancement could be rapid; a young man started an apprenticeship at the Antioch *Ledger* about 1879; three years later he was editor.[25]

In 1874, the Belmont, Nevada, *Courier* bragged about 14-year-old Charley Rood who asked for instruction in typesetting, learned the placement of the type in the case in half an hour, and quickly built up speed. The lad worked after school, the *Courier* said, could "get up one column a day," and was considered the "little star type-setter" of the Pacific Coast.[26]

Publishers recognized the importance of bringing young people into the craft and of honoring its traditions. In 1880, Doten wrote encouragement to the printer's devil at the Gold Hill *News*:

> ### To a Young Printer
>
> Be yours within the book of life
> A record clear, of honest measure,
> Imprinted there in well-set form,
> That all may read with solid pleasure.
> Your stand be firm in every case
> Where right should bear no imposition,
> And give clean proof that manhood's type
> Is registered in your composition.
> And when at last your form is laid
> Awaiting final distribution,
> May you a hopeful parting take,
> And leave behind a good impression.[27]

Although frontier publishers managed to assemble sufficient numbers of skilled craftsmen to print their newspapers, labor was not so plentiful that it was cheap. Indeed, in the 1850s and 1860s pay for western printers was substantially higher than for their eastern counterparts. When printers in eastern centers earned 30 cents per 1,000 ems of type set, printers on the West Coast received $1.50 or more.[28] A good compositor could set 1,200 ems an hour.[29] If he could maintain that speed nine hours a day for six days a week, at $1.50 per thousand, he could make nearly $100 a week. Not many achieved that level of income, largely because of the irregular nature of the work, but in San Francisco in the early 1850s when labor was at a premium because of the exodus to the mines, printers could make $12 to $16 a day when they worked, while other trades earned only $4 to $7. Meanwhile, the price of meals at a boardinghouse ranged from $20 to $80 a week and hotel rooms $25 to $100 a week; a shave and haircut cost $4, and eggs sold for 75 cents to $1 a piece.[30]

Difficult economic times after the initial rush led publishers to cut wages, which in turn resulted not only in labor unrest (see chapter 11) but also in the establishment of one of the period's premier newspapers. When several printers in Sacramento were asked in 1851 to take a 25 percent cut in wages, they decided instead to pool their resources and started the Sacramento *Daily Union*.[31]

Even with cuts, a report in the *Alta California* in 1853 showed printers and pressmen still earning about $10 a day, a good wage compared with shipwrights, carpenters, and machinists at $7 a day, wagonmakers and coopers at $4 to $6 a day, and common laborers at $4 a day. Enthusiastic reports from the goldfields claimed some men made $500 a day, but realistically, miners panning gold could expect from $10 to $30 a day—if they were lucky; if they were not— the majority—a dollar or two a day was more likely.[32]

High piece rates to compositors became a matter of argument when territorial printers handed federal government bureaucrats their bills for public printing. Asahel Bush, public printer in the Oregon Territory in 1852, stated that even if he charged the government $2.50 per 1,000 ems, he would lose money on the public printing because he had to pay type setters at least half that amount. At that rate, Oregon compositors earned about three times that paid in the eastern states.[33]

In the 1860s, wages continued substantially higher than in the rest of the country. Reports of $10 to $15 a week were common, about twice that paid on average to printers in Wisconsin, for example.[34] Even in Olympia, Washington, a town not as prosperous as the mining camps, a printer could expect to make $50 a month.[35] A Napa, California, printer, offered an $18-a-week job at the San Francisco *Chronicle* in 1868, considered it insufficient improvement in his situation and turned it down.[36]

Depressions in the 1870s brought a decline in the piece rate, but some printers still fared fairly well. A foreman, whose job was more secure than that of a casual employee, could earn $30 to $50 a week, depending on the prosperity of the job shop. The mining areas of the Comstock continued to prosper and in mid-decade one publisher's payroll included $30 a week for each of four printers and $36 for his foreman.[37] Tucson newspapers paid $40 for foremen, and $10 to $25 for other employees.[38] However, printers without steady work found the 1870s hard. Fremont Older, subsequently editor of the San Francisco *Call*, worked as a compositor on the *Territorial Enterprise* in 1873 for $40 a week, then moved to San Francisco. In the depressed

California job market he sometimes only worked one day a week. He rejoiced when he finally found steady employment with a new Redwood City newspaper even though it paid only $12 a week. He soon became part owner of the paper, with an income of $18 a week—still a considerable cut in income.[39]

The 1880s continued the pattern of the seventies. Weekly pay for regular work was $20 to $30, but the piece rate fell to 40 cents a thousand, and printers had difficulty making ends meet. The annual wage per newspaper employee (including editorial employees who accounted for about a fourth of the staff) was less than $600 a year. In 1885 California printers earned about the same amount as their counterparts in New York, $13 a week. They had lost ground in comparison to other West Coast tradesmen, some of whom still maintained a high differential from New York rates. For example, a California bricklayer made $30 a week, a New Yorker, $20; California baker, $18, New Yorker, $7; California teamster, $15, New Yorker, $10.[40]

At some newspapers, where printers slept in the office and paid rent for space on the floor, part of the wages immediately returned to the publisher.[41]

When fully employed, printers worked long hours. Nine- or ten-hour working days were standard. A Washington publisher recalled that it was not unusual for men to work eighty and even ninety hours per week. "I had one man who worked on the laws for me several winters who sometimes was paid for over one hundred hours per week, which meant about ninety hours actual labor, as all over sixty hours was paid at the rate of one and one half times for each hour."[42]

Although in the 1860s California legislators raised the possibility of an eight-hour day (a bill even passed the state assembly only to be defeated in the senate), labor made little demand for a shorter work day. In 1884 James H. Barry, a prominent member of the typographical union, was probably the first printer-publisher to establish an eight-hour day for his employees.[43]

Printers were expected to be available when needed. Employees on the tri-weekly *Idaho Statesman* worked three nights a week after the arrival of the mail in order to rush the news to the mines, and they put in long hours to fill job-printing orders.[44] Jonas Winchester on the *Pacific News* regularly worked until after midnight while the paper was still a weekly; he anticipated a "laborious life" when it expanded.[45] Indeed, a small daily may well have offered the most onerous working conditions because it rarely had resources much beyond those of a weekly, yet its commitments were substantially greater. The proprietors of a Nevada daily complained that they had damaged their health in getting the paper out without assistance.[46] A California publisher described life on his new daily as an ordeal until he established a routine and had a supply of advertising already set.[47]

Printers' willingness to work almost anytime extended to Sundays, and the publication of Monday morning papers or even Sunday morning papers was apparently not hindered by lack of labor. Printers seemed to have few scruples about working on the Sabbath. Washington's Clarence Bagley, writing to his minister father about job prospects, explained that he could work Sunday after church.[48]

Printers, as a group, were not thought to be particularly religious. One publisher recalled that when a compositor won a bet that he could set up the Lord's Prayer in the dark without error, observers claimed to be surprised that the man even knew the prayer.[49] But publishers of the Butte *Miner* one Christmastime told readers it was a misconception that newspapermen were "destitute of religious sentiment." Indeed, said the *Miner*, Christmas was dear to them, especially the dances; in fact they liked it so well they were skipping an issue in order to enjoy the holiday.[50] Although morning papers might publish on a holiday such as Christmas, New Year, or Thanksgiving, schedules generally allowed them to skip the next day so that, like Sunday, there was little if any work on the holiday itself. Evening papers did not publish on Sundays or holidays.

Some publishers solved the inevitable labor problems by involving family members in the enterprise. John Miller Murphy, founder of the *Washington Standard* in Olympia in 1860 had his two sons and two daughters helping stick type, and Caroline Gale Budlong, the typesetting daughter of a newspaperman, said her stepmother had a type case at home.[51] In Oregon, the daughter of one of the most prominent pioneers married a printer who taught her to set type and made her Oregon's first woman typesetter, and the publisher of the *Daily Avalanche* called his wife "Mrs. Avalanche," because of her intimate involvement with the paper.[52] When all of his regular help left, a southern Utah publisher employed his 14-year-old daughter and apprenticed his sons, aged 11 and 15.[53] The sheets of the *Deseret News* were folded by the editor's daughter.[54]

Wives and daughters were not the only women hired to work in printing offices. In 1880 about 7 percent of the production staffs of western newspapers were women, and it is likely that this was in addition to many female relatives who helped out sporadically. About 1870, the *Deseret News* started to employ women typesetters, "called" to the vocation by LDS President Brigham Young, and throughout Utah women helped produce newspapers.[55] One Utah paper advertised specifically for "two girls to learn the noble art of typesetting."[56] Two young Nevada women (one of them in her late 20s), apprenticed themselves to the newspaper in their hometown in 1882, and the *Wallowa Chieftain* in Oregon listed a woman compositor.[57]

In the 1860s, when printers struck the San Francisco *Call* for better pay, the publisher, Loring Pickering hired women and taught them typesetting. The union printers courted the women and, Pickering complained later, "The 'Call' office became a matrimonial agency. Every woman we had got married."[58] Pickering gave in and paid the higher wages the men demanded.

The Journalists

A different kind of skill, a facility with words, was required of a journalist/editor. Some printers were also successful writers—setting type for articles and books could provide a good education—but not all printers were interested in the news and editorial functions of the newspaper. Just as journalist-proprietors found it necessary to hire printers, printer-proprietors found it necessary to hire journalists.

The supply of experienced journalists was supplemented by people whose primary vocation involved words and writing. As we have seen in connection with publishers, lawyers and teachers, in particular, tended to gravitate toward newspapers. O. J. Goldrick, Denver superintendent of schools in 1861, wrote for the *Rocky Mountain News* as well, meeting the stagecoach to get the latest news from the driver and guards.[59] An Oakland attorney who was persuaded to write for the Oakland *Enquirer* soon gave up his law practice to devote full time to journalism.[60]

Many journalists started in the business by writing about their towns for newspapers in larger centers. Mark Twain began with the *Territorial Enterprise* as a correspondent from Aurora, a mining town some 90 miles south of Virginia City. He impressed publisher Joe Goodman who, when he needed a local editor, the person responsible for going about town collecting local news, offered Twain the job.[61]

Newspapers employed relatively few staff journalists—smaller papers rarely had more than the local editor—and relied on correspondents, who were paid by the story, to fill the columns. The *Deseret News* had a built-in corps of correspondents in the missionaries the Mormon church sent abroad.[62]

Most correspondence was local or regional, but city publishers, at least, knew the importance of news from the nation's capital and made an effort to ensure a representative in Washington, D.C. The San Francisco *Bulletin*, an early leader in news gathering, had regular correspondents in Washington, New York, New Orleans, Panama, and London in the late 1850s, as well as occasional writers such as the Springfield, Illinois, resident who sent stories about Lincoln and Douglas.[63] New Orleans was so important as the last eastern point before steamers departed for Panama that even a remote eastern Washington newspaper claimed a correspondent there.[64]

Although journalism required no formal training, many journalists brought special backgrounds as well as writing experience to their positions. According to one early editor, the gold rush brought to San Francisco an "overflowing of college trained men, not a few of whom when they were 'down on their luck' showed an inclination for journalism rather than dishwashing or waiting on the table, occupations which men of education when their resources were low found much easier than manual labor, which was much better remunerated than writing for the press."[65] As with printers, advancement could be rapid. Harvey Scott went to work for the *Oregonian* part-time in 1864 as an editorial writer and librarian; eight months later he was editor.[66]

Some publishers, like Joseph Goodman at the *Territorial Enterprise*, had definite ideas about how their reporters should go about their work. Anticipating by a century the debate over confidential sources, Goodman took care to give Mark Twain guidance on how to prepare stories. According to Twain, Goodman told him: "Never say 'We learn' so-and-so, or 'It is reported,' or 'It is rumored,' or 'We understand,' but go to headquarters and get the absolute facts, and then speak out and say 'It *is* so-and-so.' Otherwise, people will not put confidence in your news."[67] Few other editors worried about confidential sources undermining public confidence, and such anonymity was common. Nevertheless, publishers were concerned about how the public perceived their efforts. An eastern Oregon newspaperman told his readers he would attempt to give them the "exact truth," but "It must be remembered that commonly the itemizer is not the maker of the item; he merely presents it just as he sees and feels it."[68]

Publishers also urged readers in general to submit articles or at least provide the editor with information. A Colorado publisher took such pleas one step further when he established a volunteer editorial board, and invited several of his town's best-educated men to write for his paper.[69]

Editors of this period frequently referred to their work as a task involving pen and scissors, and much early western journalism was accomplished in the newspaper office with the printer-editor-publisher accepting correspondence and the news that townsfolk brought to him, and clipping stories from other newspapers. As late as 1886 Doten thought it worth remarking that he had written everything that he put into the *Territorial Enterprise*, boasting, "I did not use any scissors."[70]

The level of journalistic enterprise varied from editors who waited for news to come to them at the office to those who actively collected information for stories, like two young California newspapermen in the 1860s. The journalist of the pair "would make the rounds of the principal streets once or twice a day for local news and to interview friends, upon whom we depended for information of the occurrence of anything worthy of notice," but both partners were sensitive to the need for local news: "No time was lost or wasted by us, for when we went out for meals or any other purpose we were alert for news items and discussion of subjects of local interest."[71]

Where staffs were large enough, reporters searched their towns for stories, contacting their "regulars"—routine sources of news such as the courts and other official agencies. Twain and reporters for other Virginia City newspapers exchanged items from the regulars in order to economize on the work and cover more territory.[72] Reporters went to fires and accidents. An early San Francisco newspaperman spent the evening after a steamboat explosion collecting information, and the rest of the night putting out the paper.[73] When the Yellow Jacket Mine burned in the Comstock in 1873, killing six miners, Doten noted in his diary, "I was on hand & saw all the items—Wrote up account of it—got out "extra" at PM—sold about 300 extras."[74]

The larger the staff, the more enterprising a newspaper could be. In the Comstock's prosperous 1870s the Gold Hill *News* sent one reporter to Carson City to get the governor's message regarding a veto, another to Steamboat Springs to interview the Emperor of Brazil on his way to California, and assigned "beat" reporters, one to cover Virginia City and Gold Hill, another to Carson City and Reno.[75] San Francisco journalists covered the Modoc Indian campaign in northern California, one of them witnessing the capture of Captain Jack, the Modoc leader.[76] Frank J. Parker, future editor of the Walla Walla *Statesman*, reported the campaign against the Nez Percé for the San Francisco *Chronicle*.[77]

Just as women staffed print shops, so, too, women wrote for newspapers. Wives of country editors contributed homemaking columns and fiction to their husbands' newspapers. In the cities, many women journalists wrote for specialized publications. Flora Haines Loughead said she thought she was the first woman general reporter in San Francisco when she started part-time work in 1879. Mrs. Loughead's first assignment was to investigate a San Francisco baby-selling scandal. Her completion of the disagreeable and somewhat dangerous assignment helped her gain acceptance from men in local newsrooms. Willing to cover almost any kind of a story, she drew the line at going where there was swearing, drinking, or low women. A "careworn young mother," she sometimes took a child with her when she delivered her work to the office.[78]

Writers had an advantage printers lacked; they could effectively be in more than one place at a time and be paid for it. Thus a journalist could write not only for his own paper, but also send the story to other newspapers. Twain and Doten corresponded for California newspapers at various times while working for Nevada newspapers. Some writers sent letters for publication in newspapers in their eastern hometowns, and western journalists advertised in New York that they were available as correspondents.

In 1866 Twain persuaded the Sacramento *Union* to buy correspondence from him when he went to Hawaii. While there, he beat San Francisco reporters to the story of survivors of a wrecked clipper ship, much to the delight of the *Union*. When he returned to the mainland

and presented his special account for the survivor story—three columns of copy at a hundred dollars a column—the publishers called it robbery but appreciated the grand scoop enough to tell the bookkeeper to pay him. Responded Twain, "The best men that ever owned a newspaper."[79]

Because journalists did not organize to demand standard wages, as printers did, the amounts paid to them are difficult to pinpoint. In 1850 the *Pacific News* in San Francisco hired an editor at $500 a month; the Los Angeles *Star* paid $50 a week.[80] On the Comstock in the 1860s a chief editor could earn $300 to $500 a month; reporters collected $40 to $60 a week, about the same as printers. In the 1870s millionaire William Sharon is said to have paid his *Territorial Enterprise* editor as much as $250 a week.[81]

Not all newspapers were in mining boomtowns and able to afford such pay scales, and salaries of $30 to $35 a week were more common through much of the frontier period. Comstock journalist Doten received about $30 a week through most of his twenty-year career, although in one depressed period he was offered a job for as little as $40 a month.[82] An editor particularly valued for his astuteness and editorial-writing ability might get $40, especially if he also supervised other writers, but in a depressed area he might get only $20. The *Deseret News* hired a locals editor in the 1870s at only $1,000 a year, or $20 a week, and Edgar Wilson Nye, better known as humorist Bill Nye, recalled that he was paid $12 a week in 1876 to edit the Cheyenne *Daily Sentinel*.[83] These salaries compared with about $20 a week for a writer in New York in the mid-1880s.[84]

Pay for correspondence varied also, but a hardworking writer who corresponded for several papers could do well. Doten commonly charged $20 for stories he wrote for California or other Nevada newspapers. In addition, a journalist could make extra money writing advertising and what would today be considered press releases. Doten was paid $25 for writing a long response for a doctor defending himself against charges of malpractice; on several occasions he mentions writing advertising copy for which he was probably paid.[85]

In the volatile environment of a gold or silver boom, journalists found other opportunities to increase their incomes. Twain's pay on the *Enterprise* started at $25 a week. After six months or so, it was increased to $40, but Twain claimed he rarely collected it. "Reporting was lucrative," he wrote, "and every man in town was lavish with his money and his 'feet.'"[86] Twain said that when miners took up a claim, they went straight to the newspaper offices and gave the reporter 40 or 50 "feet," or stock, in the claim in return for doing a story on it. Reporters received "feet" every day and sold it when they needed money or when it increased in value—if it did. Sometimes, when mining was particularly prosperous, stock was given simply as a gift, for friendship or in recognition of past or future favors. Twain admitted that reporters paid for the stock with kind words. If a mine looked promising, they "frothed at the mouth as if a very marvel in silver discoveries had transpired."[87] Even when they thought the miner exaggerated his find, the reporters always found something to praise.

Doten supported the notion that journalists benefited from the generosity of mining-camp residents. On one occasion he recorded receiving $10 from a woman who had been arrested for keeping a brothel, presumably to give her sympathetic coverage, although he is not specific on that point.[88] Another time, Nevada senator James G. Fair gave Doten a $50 greenback to show that he appreciated the "courtesies in the paper."[89] A Vallejo editor received 100 shares of stock in the Sutro Tunnel after printing a story complimenting Adolph Sutro on his vision; he eventually sold the shares for $500.[90] Local contacts also put journalists in proximity to investment opportunities. In 1871 Doten turned down a job offer from the San Francisco *Chronicle*, apparently because he felt he could better keep a lookout for mining-stock opportunities if he stayed in the Comstock.[91] Journalists covering state legislatures sometimes received special state appropriations to supplement their income.[92]

Small newspapers rarely had a business manager as such. The publisher commonly took care of the accounts, but business managers were valued, if faceless, members of larger newspaper staffs. According to Nevada publisher Sam Davis, "In journalism almost anybody can run the brain box of a newspaper, but it takes the smartest man in the establishment to run the cashbox and keep the creditors of the sheet paid up."[93] Early San Francisco papers employed business managers, as did the *Territorial Enterprise*.[94] The *Oregonian*'s Dryer, much too trusting to be a business success, finally hired 18-year-old Henry Pittock to help straighten out the newspaper's accounts.[95] Another Portland newspaper, the *Northwest News*, bragged about its "counting-room" with "gentlemanly clerks" and the "accomplished and polite young man" from California who supervised the subscription books.[96]

Lifestyle

For newspapermen, being promised a decent wage and collecting it were not necessarily the same thing. For the publisher, payroll was a drain on his cash resources and covering the cost of paper and ink could have more urgency. When the Gold Hill *News* fell behind in wages, the union chapel set a deadline for payment; the publisher borrowed the necessary money and the men were paid.[97] But a reporter for the *Deseret News* in the 1850s worked for so little pay he once had nothing to give his sick wife but bread and water, and an employee of the Salt Lake *Telegraph* remembered six consecutive Saturdays when there was no money to pay him.[98]

Publishers shared with employees the food and other items they received as payment for both advertising and subscriptions. To meet severe food or fuel shortages, they asked specifically for in-kind payments. Even in the late 1870s, *Deseret News* employees were still being paid in produce and tithing scrip.[99] A newspaperman's survival was aided by sympathetic townspeople who extended credit and sent food to newspaper offices even when they did not owe money. Staff usually ate well on holidays. A Virginia City woman who obviously knew something about printing terms, sent the *Territorial Enterprise* a Christmas pie with this note: "To the Members of the Press: I wish you all a merry Christmas; and please except [sic] this Pie, hoping you may have the pleasure of knocking the same into pi at your discretion." The *Enterprise* responded with thanks, adding, "You would have been amused, no doubt, to have seen with what gusto and indiscretion we knocked it into pi."[100] Two young California men starting a newspaper had insufficient cash for room and board after paying their initial expenses. Too proud to ask for credit, they tried to get a hotelier to let them have a room only, intending to prepare their meals at the office. When the hotelier pressed for a reason, they admitted their poverty and accepted his offer to carry them on credit.[101]

Local taverns tended to be generous to printers, perhaps because printers tended to be good customers. One Nevada newspaper thanked a local establishment for remembering the "weary printer last night, when, wan and faint, he was ready to close his typal form. The music of the presses resounded to the gurgling of the joyous throats, made glad by the Hamilton Exchange."[102] After another tavern made a similar gift to its local newspaper, the editor wrote, "The typos say it [whiskey punch] can't be beat and their opinion is worth something on the liquor question. One of the boys is off to-day, but of course the punch had nothing to do with it."[103] A wedding was always occasion for cake and libation, the nuptial notice matching in extravagance the treat to the newspapermen.

References to alcohol are common in frontier newspaper records. Both journalist and printer ranks had considerable turnover because of the drinking habits of some members, in spite of publishers' considerable tolerance. Doten frequently noted that he filled in for someone temporarily incapacitated by drink or worked a longer term when an extended spree cost a newspaperman his job, and many of Doten's own problems resulted from a liking of liquor.

Newspapermen did not lack for entertainment. Theater passes were common; Doten frequented the theater several times a week, and during prosperous periods was rarely in bed before midnight. He also expected circus passes as a matter of course and once sent back a state fair pass, complaining that he wanted passes for all his family—or none at all.[104] Newspapermen also regularly expected and received railroad passes.

8

NEWS ACROSS THE MILES

The tremendous distances that characterize western America inhibited, but by no means halted, communication. The very existence of so many newspapers provides evidence that channels remained open because the newspaper required contacts beyond its immediate surroundings. Roads, railroads, mail and freight services, and eventually the telegraph were integral to a newspaper's success. The frontier publisher needed to be able to get himself and his equipment to his chosen location and be assured that future supplies would reach him. He needed a service—mail or express or telegraph—that would bring the news, either as letters or dispatches or in the form of other publications, the "exchanges." He needed a means of delivering the newspaper to his customers, whether across the county or across the country.

Weather, as might be expected, played havoc with the wagon trails that connected western towns, especially in winter and spring when, despite the West's overall reputation for aridity, much of the region was plagued by snow and rain. Poor road access hindered delivery of both supplies and mail. In 1852 Sierra storms delayed the April mail to Salt Lake City from the Pacific Coast for nearly two months, while floods stalled deliveries from the East.[1] Thornton McElroy complained to his wife in January 1853 that Olympia had no mail for six weeks because of three feet of snow, followed by rain and flooding which made the route from Portland impassable.[2] Storms were blamed for "an intolerable state of things" that left Prescott, Arizona, without mail for forty days, "impracticable roads" that held up delivery of vital supplies to eastern Nevada, and "almost impossible" travel in Montana.[3]

Rutted byways made hauling presses and type a challenge. William Byers started for Denver on March 8, 1859, but almost immediately his oxcart bogged down in the mudholes that passed for streets in Omaha. Twice he had to unload the wagons so the oxen could pull them from the mire. En route to Colorado, the oxen had to swim flood waters, cross makeshift bridges, and negotiate icy trails. "I think," Byers' partner John Dailey commented later, "our printing press particularly resented the bath, for it accumulated considerable rust as a result of the experience. However, it was that method or wait several days, and neither Byers nor myself cared to sit in a drowning wilderness to wait for an uncertain turn of the flood."[4]

In 1864 John Buchanan loaded his press in St. Louis and headed for Montana, expecting to reach Fort Benton in 50 days. En route on the Missouri River, his boat grounded on a sandbar and the journey took him nearly twice as long. From Fort Benton, he still had some 280 miles to reach his final destination, Virginia City. Travel was also expensive; Buchanan calculated that transportation nearly doubled the cost of his equipment.[5] The passage of time did not necessarily improve the roads. Fifteen years later, sixteen horses drawing two wagons took six days to carry Francis Cook's printing gear 79 miles from Colfax, Washington, to Spokane.[6] The next year, of two parties with presses destined for what is now Sun Valley in central Idaho, one stalled in snow, the other in mud.[7] In June 1889 a Wyoming publisher got stuck trying to drive through a creek with his printing outfit; it took him four hours to carry his equipment piece by piece across the creek, wallowing through mud to his knees.[8] Even summer travel could test one's stamina. McElroy explained that he had to take a steamer from Portland to the mouth of the Cowlitz River, paddle in an Indian canoe up the Cowlitz to Warbassport, and then ride horseback the remaining 40-odd, often muddy miles to reach Olympia.[9]

Yet travel they did. We have already seen the mobility of printers and presses; at times the mining boom created its version of bumper-to-bumper traffic. In the 1860s, for example, a traveler observed 274 freight teams, 19 passenger wagons, three pack trains, 69 horsemen, and 31 walkers on a 180-mile stretch through central Nevada.[10]

Westerners repeatedly demanded a railroad to ease their transportation problems. "Give us a railroad!" begged one newspaper. "Though it be a rawhide one with open passenger cars and a sheet iron boiler; anything on wheels drawn by an iron horse! But give us a railroad!"[11] The Union Pacific and Central Pacific linked East and West in 1869, the Southern Pacific connected with eastern lines in Arizona in 1881, the Northern Pacific completed its line to Puget

Sound in 1883, and the Great Northern reached the Pacific Northwest in 1889. The much-anticipated iron horse failed to guarantee regular service when it arrived, however, as winter storms frequently upset train schedules, and mail and freight continued to be delayed.

Publishers tried to lay in sufficient supplies of paper and other consumables to see them through the winter, but inadequate foresight or an extended bad season could exhaust their stores. In 1859 the *Territorial Enterprise*, out of newsprint, lauded John A. Trumbo for his "toil over the snowclad summit of the mountains with the paper on his back—to peril his own life," and frequently relied upon Trumbo and another mountain expressman, John "Snow Shoe" Thompson, to bring mail and supplies when snow filled the Sierra passes.[12] Even so, the newspaper occasionally skipped issues because it lacked paper.

Even when freight and mail services were more or less reliable, they were often slow and infrequent. In 1841 it took three months and twenty days for news of the death of President William Henry Harrison to reach Los Angeles. Oregonians learned of John Quincy Adams's death in 1848 four months after the fact.[13] By about 1850, largely in response to demand for better connections with the gold regions, the time for messages to move from East to West Coast had been reduced to less than a month. However, the sea route led directly to San Francisco, and other centers experienced further delays. In 1853 news reached San Francisco in about a month, including a fifteen-day steamer trip from Panama. The steamer did not stop in Southern California on its way north, and residents there had to wait for the coastal ships that traveled between San Francisco and Los Angeles only every two to three weeks.[14] The Los Angeles *Star* of May 17, 1851, carried two-week-old news of a major fire in San Francisco, as well as New York news more than six weeks old. Inland centers waited even longer for news.

Relying on the Mails

Transportation routes were critical because they were necessary for postal service. In 1859, when Denver's *Rocky Mountain News* was first pulled from the press, the nearest post office was 220 miles away at Fort Laramie. Most newspapers, however, were started in towns that already had post offices.[15]

A post office promised service, not necessarily reliable or efficient service. Publishers complained about schedules and pressed for more frequent and regular deliveries. In the 1850s Salt Lake City got mail from east and from west about once a month if all went well; in the fall of 1854 thirteen sacks of mail arrived at the *Deseret News* office, some of it two years old.[16] Other centers were more fortunate; in 1857 Genoa, Nevada, had stages three times a week over the Sierra, a service that connected eastward with Salt Lake City. When prospectors discovered silver in Nevada's Comstock region, communications with the Pacific Coast improved rapidly. In 1864, mail moved daily from Virginia City to Sacramento in less than thirteen hours.[17] Other mining areas, such as the Idaho diggings, also benefited from improved services in response to population growth and the need to exchange economic information.[18]

Publishers relied on the mails both for delivery of their newspapers to out-of-town subscribers and for news, both of which led them to set press times and frequency according to mail schedules. The Aurora, Nevada, *Daily Times* issued an evening paper to ensure that it was as up-to-date as possible for the express that left early the next morning, and the Carson *Daily Independent* published a morning paper in order to catch the afternoon express. The San Francisco *Chronicle* expanded in 1868 to issue both a morning edition for city readers and a 3:00 P.M. edition to go inland for distribution the next day.[19] The *Idaho Statesman* started as a tri-weekly in order to take advantage of the tri-weekly mail service to Boise,[20] and in 1865 the *Deseret News* started a semi-weekly, scheduling it for Wednesday and Sunday to coincide with mail schedules. A year later the *News* moved production forward a day when the postal schedule changed.[21] John Dailey at the *Rocky Mountain News* noted in his diary that he was "hurried to death to get the paper out" because it was so important to make the mail.[22] The publisher of the Butte *Miner* blamed the mail service for his decision to cut back to weekly from tri-weekly, claiming that too many potential readers had only weekly mail, eliminating the value of more frequent publication.[23]

Publishers expressed frustration and anger when, despite their efforts to have the papers ready for the mails, deliveries to subscribers were not made on schedule. A mail clerk's failure to put the *Oregon Statesman* on the stage provoked its irritated publisher to comment that "such blunders are vexatious both to our readers and ourself."[24]

Richard Kielbowicz, who has examined the relationship of the mails and newspapers, has shown that government postal policy has generally favored newspapers, in terms of both rates and services. The principle of special privileges for newspapers was embodied in the first important postal act in 1792. Over the years rules varied according to Congress's concerns. Sometimes newspapers could circulate free within the county of origin; at other times, the service was free within thirty miles of the office of publication; rates were low even when the post office charged for delivery.[25]

Reliable mail service ensured delivery to subscribers, but publishers also counted on the mails to bring news. The western press devoted a substantial amount of its space to local happenings, but publishers knew that readers relied on their newspapers for news of people and places they had left behind when they came west. The exchange of newspapers helped fill this need by serving as a national news service in the pre-telegraph era. Western newspapermen exchanged papers with their eastern counterparts, and each clipped and freely reprinted stories.

Editing with Scissors

Nineteenth-century editors were valued as much for their judicious wielding of scissors as for their writing abilities. Walter Colton, recalling the inaugural of the *Californian*, wrote, "Who would think . . . of issuing a weekly journal . . . without a solitary exchange paper."[26] When a flood severely damaged the *Reese River Reveille* in central Nevada, the editor noted that townspeople were coping without asking for relief; "The Reveille, however, wants relief." His "cherished scissors" were washed away in the flood. "We cannot conduct the Reveille successfully as a first class family journal without scissors."[27] A few days later the *Reveille* acknowledged receipt of a pair of scissors—a rusty pair, not the silver blades with gold handles and diamond monogram for which the editor had hoped: "But this is a world full of disappointments."[28]

From the exchanges, a New York story might be picked up by a St. Louis newspaper, which in turn was read by an Arizona editor who might credit both newspapers—or neither—when he reprinted the item. Still another paper might copy the story from the Arizona paper.

The system facilitated the movement not only of news but also of misinformation and outright hoaxes. In 1884, John H. Dennis, publisher of the Tuscarora, Nevada, *Times-Review*, respected by contemporaries for his wit and humor, published a story about a tree that he said emitted enough light to read by. Describing the phenomenon in convincing detail, he suggested that scientists should investigate. Soon, doubtless prompted by the exchanges, inquiries from scientists and other individuals from all over the nation started arriving in his office, requesting more information and asking for seeds or samples of the leaves. Dennis continued the game for awhile. After four months he tired of the hoax and sent the tree up in literary flames, telling his readers that it was burned by Indians who thought it had evil spirits.[29]

The exchanges provided the foundation for the booster press, publishers hoping that stories they printed about their locales would end up in another publisher's columns. They also used the exchanges to convey specific, utilitarian information. Occasionally, for example, when printing a death notice, an editor would add, "Wisconsin [or Ohio, or wherever] papers, please copy" as a means of letting the hometown of the deceased know about the death. The *Reese River Reveille* lost not only its scissors in the flood but also its subscription lists, so it printed a story asking subscribers to contact the office and requested state exchanges to copy the story to carry the word to mail subscribers.[30] A writer to the *Placer Times* hoping for wide dissemination of his letter about transportation problems added: "The San Francisco press is respectfully requested to consider the above as being addressed to all the Editors in the State."[31]

Exchanging newspapers entailed a certain responsibility to one's fellow journalists. When a publisher sent papers, he expected recipients to reciprocate. One Nevada newspaper, slow to start publication, expressed appreciation to the newspapers that mailed copies even though it had sent nothing in return.[32] Another Nevada newspaper, noting that it had sent out more than twenty exchanges, threatened to drop newspapers from its mailing list if they failed to forward papers.[33]

Publishers looked to friends or travelers to bring them news. Emigrants arriving in Salt Lake City often carried eastern papers. Once, when the mail brought no news, the *Deseret News* borrowed a Salt Lake City resident's copy of the New York *Herald* and found a story about the bill to establish Utah Territory.[34] Publishers tried to prepare for occasions when the mail failed to get through. An Idaho newspaperman kept a copy of a Greek mythology handy, and examination of almost any western newspaper's content suggests they used whatever they could find to fill their columns.[35] At the same time, publishers' reliance on exchanges did not necessarily cloud their news judgment. The Sacramento *Union*, after acknowledging the freight agent that provided San Francisco newspapers, commented succinctly, "They contain nothing of importance."[36]

Magazines and big-city newspapers would not exchange with every little paper in the country, so publishers subscribed to some publications and received others as a courtesy from local news agents, steamer captains, or freight agents, who could count on a "thank you" in the newspaper. In 1863, the *Carson Daily Independent* acknowledged receipt of, among others, the Louisville, Kentucky, *Journal*, *Missouri Republican*, and *Godey's Ladies' Book* from a local news agent.[37] Availability largely determined which exchanges a publisher credited most. In California the *Placer Press* liked the New Orleans *Picayune*; the Butte *Record* frequently credited the Toledo *Blade*; the *Trinity Journal*, *Knickerbocker Magazine*; the *Empire County Argus*, *Gleason's Pictorial*.[38] Montana's Butte *Miner*, which scanned the exchanges especially for mining news, drew heavily from Comstock camp newspapers.

Most publishers considered their news columns inadequate if they carried no regional or national information. Noting on one occasion that it received only a few exchanges, the *Deseret News* bemoaned getting "only an occasional link in the chain of history circumscribing the earth."[39] By the 1870s the telegraph had reduced the importance of the free exchange between newspapers and the privilege was eliminated in the Postal Act of 1873, but the practice of clipping stories from other newspapers continued.

Ponies and Wires

Both the U.S. government and private concerns tried to respond to the pressure from westerners for better communication with the East, and in 1860 one private firm started a service that would not only show that mail delivery could be counted in days rather than weeks, but would capture the imagination of the nation. This, of course, was the famed Pony Express, a service intended for businesses, because it was too expensive for the average letter writer—and very much used by the newspaper business.

The first trip of the Pony Express from St. Joseph, Missouri, to California—1,966 miles—took ten days; many later trips took only nine, an impressive time when regular mail still required three weeks at best, more often longer.[40] California newspapers, the primary journalistic users of the service, arranged for news to be telegraphed to St. Joseph where it was copied onto tissue paper so the rider could carry as many messages as possible within the 20-pound limit. Generally the news dispatches were delivered to the Sacramento *Union*, which in turn telegraphed them to the San Francisco *Bulletin* and the *Alta California*, its partners in a news consortium.[41]

At least one paper started with the intention of capitalizing on the Pony Express. The *Overland Press* in Olympia, using dispatches relayed from California, cut Puget Sounders' wait for information to three weeks instead of six.[42] Other papers, like the *Deseret News* which was on the main route, printed extras when the Pony Express arrived. The *News* issued its initial "Pony Dispatch" when the first rider reached Salt Lake City on April 7, 1860, only four days out of St. Joseph. Later that year, thanks to the service, Salt Lake City readers learned of Lincoln's election only eight days after the voting.[43]

The Pony Express was as exciting as it was welcome, but it was also expensive. When it began, senders paid $5 in advance per half ounce; shortly before the service ended eighteen months later, the cost had dropped to $1. After the start of the Civil War, a rider could expect bonuses for speed, in addition to his $120-a-month salary. The rider who carried news of Antietam in 1861 received an extra $300 for his efforts when he arrived in California.[44] Initially, the *Deseret News* had access to the service because church leaders were willing to pay for it, but they soon found it too expensive, and the newspaper began to charge a dime for each dispatch issued as an extra.[45]

The expense meant the Pony Express was suited only for short dispatches; the exchanges, with their fuller accounts of happenings, remained the primary source of news and these still came by slower routes such as steamer via Panama. Except in the most competitive situations, western publishers resigned themselves to old news. On September 1, 1863, the *Carson Daily Independent* printed European news from London dated July 25, a Civil War story from the Rich-mond *Enquirer* dated August 1, and an item from The Dalles, Oregon, *Mountaineer* from August 18, as well as a San Francisco story as recent as August 31, thanks to the local telegraph line.

The telegraph significantly improved the timeliness of news, and local lines quickly cobwebbed the West. Marysville and San Fran-cisco were linked in 1853 and the wires reached Yreka, near the California-Oregon border, in 1858.[46] The latter year a line was also completed between Placerville and Virginia City.[47] San Francisco and Los Angeles were joined in 1860.[48] Then in October 1861, building from the West, the California Telegraph Company met the Pacific Telegraph Company, coming from the East, in Salt Lake City, provid-ing full transcontinental service.[49] Now news of a battle in the Civil War could be on the West Coast the day it happened.

Other cities tied into lines as quickly as possible. The telegraph reached Denver in 1863, Portland in 1864, Seattle a few months later.[50] In Utah, in 1865, the Mormons built a line from Logan in the north of the state to St. George in the south.[51] Eureka, California, got its first service in 1873, Silver City, Idaho, in 1874.[52]

Publishers and other businessmen who were not on the Pony Ex-press or telegraph lines developed supplemental connecting services to speed the news. William N. Byers and other businessmen of Den-ver supported a trader who agreed to run a regular express line to Fort Laramie to pick up the mail. It, too, was costly. When the first express, carrying some 1,500 letters and many newspapers, arrived from Laramie in time for the second issue of his *Rocky Mountain News*, Byers noted that the charges of 50 cents per letter and 10 cents per paper were "a heavy tax, yet we were glad to get them at any price."[53] The arrival of a new express service from Fort Leavenworth, Kansas, which took only a week to reach Denver, occasioned an extra from the *News*. The *News* arranged to get telegraph news as early as 1860, even though it had to hire a courier to ride from the nearest terminal, 500 miles away.[54]

In Nevada, an express rider left Carson City for San Francisco at 4:30 P.M. every day except Saturday,[55] and still another traversed an easterly route. "It becomes the duty of every one living here to patron-ize the Pony, in order that it may be kept up," a Nevada newspaper intoned.[56]

As the telegraph line inched northward toward Oregon, the *Ore-*

gonian arranged for a courier to collect news at Redding, California, or however far the line had reached, and carry it to the stage at Jacksonville, Oregon, which carried it on to Portland.[57] In Nevada in the late 1860s, telegraph dispatches received at Jacob's Wells were delivered via Pony Telegraph Express to the *Daily Inland Empire* at Hamilton.[58]

Although the telegraph's principal benefit was in long-distance communication, some publishers also used local lines to advantage. Newsmen telegraphed a report of a Virginia City torchlight political parade to nearby Carson City, sent the story of a fire from one end of the Comstock to the other,[59] and forwarded dispatches about the Nez Percé Indian wars throughout the region.[60]

Stealing the News

Although newspapers tried to ensure that they received the most important telegraph news, dispatches were expensive for day-to-day use. In addition, some towns had no direct service. A common approach to obtaining news was to treat telegraph news as part of the exchanges and take it from another newspaper. Publishers voiced little overt objection to the practice as long as the newspapers were not direct competitors. Idaho papers waited for Salt Lake City papers, inland Nevada papers for the Comstock or California press, and then copied the telegraph reports, as well as other items of interest. Wyoming's first newspaper, the *Daily Telegraph*, was started in 1863 by the Fort Bridger telegraph operator who eavesdropped on war news being transmitted across the continent.[61]

But in towns where daily competition was fierce, publishers complained of theft when newspapers waited for their more prosperous rivals to print telegraphed news, then rushed their own editions onto the street. Said one Virginia City paper about another:

It is an interesting sight in passing by the Chronicle office to see the editor-?-in-chief, with scissors in hand, lacerating the Enterprise in his search for telegraphic news with which to fill the columns of his sheet. Anyone making a comparison between the two papers, will be astonished to notice the similarity between the two reports. The matter being almost verbatim. Well, frauds must be exposed.[62]

The *Rocky Mountain News* accused a Denver competitor of having the "impudence of highway men" in stealing news "they have neither the industry nor the brains to procure otherwise."[63] A Montana paper charged that the only arrangement its rival had made to get timely news was to steal it and "make its readers think they are getting the latest dispatches."[64]

For a time in California, a select group of papers had such a stranglehold on the telegraph service that theft was the only way other journalists could obtain information. The San Francisco *Bulletin*, the *Alta California*, and the Sacramento *Union* were particularly aggressive news gatherers. When the transcontinental line was completed, they first relied on the telegraph operator at St. Louis to compile news but soon hired their own correspondent to prepare dispatches. The *Bulletin* and the *Union* also helped finance completion of the Atlantic and Pacific Telegraph Company by paying a rumored $500 a month in exchange for preferential rights to transmit news.[65]

Connections with the telegraph companies gave the *Bulletin* and the *Union* a virtual monopoly on the wire services, frustrating other California newspapers, like the *Alta*. After futile attempts to get the California legislature to break the news monopoly—the *Bulletin* insisting that the arrangement was "in the interests of the people"—the *Alta* counterattacked by forming its own association, the Pacific Associated Press. The effort nettled the monopolists, but the *Alta* still found it necessary to steal news by waiting for the *Union* to publish and then telegraphing the *Union*'s stories to San Francisco.[66]

When new owners of the Atlantic and Pacific telegraph line expanded access, the *Bulletin* and *Union* withdrew their financial backing from the service. As a result, the *Alta* group obtained the news, but had to carry the full burden of support. On April 24, 1860, the *Alta* claimed the service had cost $14,000 since the first of the year. By this time, however, the *Alta*, which had invested in the Placerville and Humboldt Telegraph Company and planned to develop an exclusive service in conjunction with the Pony Express, had changed sides and joined with the *Bulletin* and the *Union* to create the California Associated Press. The Pacific Associated Press, handicapped without the *Alta*, managed to limp along for awhile, while the CAP quickly became the stronger of the two services and the better able to deal with the telegraph companies. It pressured Missouri telegraphers to refuse or at least delay news for the PAP papers, and persuaded

Nevada operators, too, to give preference to the CAP when relaying items. It was more than a coincidence that the Nevada line often broke down after CAP dispatches were sent. When the overland line was completed in October 1861, Missouri operators refused to let the PAP correspondent send messages collect. He had no funds to prepay charges, but CAP papers ensured that their man had the necessary fees. The CAP also developed an exclusive arrangement with the New York Associated Press that strengthened members' control over news into California.[67]

Under intense political pressure, the CAP finally agreed to sell news to nonmember papers, demanding such a high premium that poorer papers still found the dispatches beyond their financial means. San Francisco papers like the *Herald* and the *Call* had to be content with taking stories from the CAP papers after they were published.[68] But political pressure against the monopoly continued to grow. In 1864 one politician complained, "The result is, they have, over a line subsidized by the General Government and the State of California, the entire control of all this great war news, and everything that excites the world, for the benefit of their papers, and thus they crush every other paper that attempts to come into competition with them."[69] The National Typographical Union joined the fight by calling the New York Associated Press a "direct infringement on the liberty of the press."[70]

At the heart of the furor stood James W. Simonton, owner of the San Francisco *Bulletin* (and later the *Call*, as well). Simonton, who was also general agent of the New York Associated Press and who used his position to protect his California papers, managed to deny AP news to the San Francisco *Chronicle* until 1876. Eventually the Associated Press could no longer ignore the paper's importance, and the New York partners agreed to supply the *Chronicle* with a special report.[71] Further efforts eased the grip of the CAP, which admitted other newspapers to the association, but the Republican publishers in control consistently denied membership to Democratic newspapers.[72]

In other parts of the West, as long as few papers and small circulations were involved, both the New York Associated Press and the Western Associated Press, headquartered in Chicago, were content to let Western Union deliver the news, but when an area grew large enough to make a news service profitable, the various professional providers scrapped for the contracts.[73]

Initially, like the Pony Express, telegraph service was costly. When the transcontinental connection was completed in 1861, transmitting ten words from California to New York cost $7.50.[74] During wartime most publishers ignored the cost or recouped it with special charges so they could meet the demand for war reports. The publishers of the *Southern News* in Los Angeles managed to publish war news three times a week, and the *Deseret News* issued extras almost daily.[75] *Deseret News* extras also circulated in the Boise Basin where they sold for a dollar each until the Boise *News* started publication and issued its own extras—based on the *Deseret News*. The Idaho paper relied on the Utah and California exchanges for news, but it was fresh to local miners, and the publisher claimed he sold $500 worth of papers after each major battle.[76]

Rates declined and by 1880 ten words could be sent across the continent for $1.50, but regular telegraph service remained prohibitively expensive for small newspapers. In the 1880s one Nevada newspaper noted regretfully—probably because it was copying dispatches—that another had canceled its Associated Press service "on account of the dull [economic] times,"[77] and when the Portland *Standard* discontinued AP service, the Spokane Falls *Evening Review* commented: "The fact is that the charges are so high for dispatches that only a favored few are able to use them at all."[78] Before long, however, *Review* publisher Frank M. Dallam decided that the charges were not as great as the threat of another daily being started in Spokane and moved quickly to secure the Associated Press franchise at a cost of $5,000.[79] Dallam got a bargain. Only five years later a Denver newspaperman offered to sell his unused AP franchise for $100,000.[80] In New Mexico some dailies found the telegraph essential for competitive reasons, but few papers used it regularly until after 1890.[81]

People accustomed to waiting weeks or months for news responded gratefully and enthusiastically to publications made possible by speedier transmission—at least until asked to pay for them. When the telegraph reached Seattle in 1865, J. R. Watson, publisher of the weekly Seattle *Gazette*, issued first the *Citizen's Dispatch* and then the *People's Telegram* to convey the latest telegraphic news. To pay for the dispatches, Watson established a sliding subscription scale. If 100 subscribers paid 25 cents a week, the sheet would be weekly; 200 subscribers would result in twice-weekly publication; 400 subscribers would cut the cost in half. The experiment failed after four issues.[82]

However much it improved communication overall, telegraph service, too, could be unreliable. Heavy snow not only stopped trains and stagecoaches, it brought down telegraph lines. Wires for Bee's Grapevine, as Colonel F. A. Bee's Placerville and Humboldt Telegraph Company was called, were hung on trees through the Sierra, and lines could be out of commission for months because of weather or because wagon drivers used the wires to mend wheels.[83] The transcontinental telegraph was once interrupted when emigrants seeking warmth reportedly burned the poles on which the wires were strung.[84]

Publishers who depended on telegraph dispatches to fill a daily newspaper on occasion found themselves scrambling for copy. In December 1876 Alf Doten at the Gold Hill *News* canceled his arrangement with the San Francisco *Chronicle* for eastern telegraphic news because of unpredictable service and returned to the Associated Press. A month later he noted that the weather had stopped all dispatches anyway except those from nearby Carson City and the San Francisco stock report.[85] The Seattle *Morning Dispatch* blamed downed wires for its heavy reliance at times on local news.[86] The St. George, Utah, *Evening Telegram*, trusting "the like will not happen again," apologized for the lack of dispatches.[87] Irregularity of service contributed to a nine-month suspension of the Spokane *Times* in 1882.[88]

Publishers greeted the telegraph with mixed feelings. A Colorado publisher bragged that because of the telegraph his was the only county journal that published nothing secondhand; the same publisher was, however, accused of borrowing without giving credit.[89] Another regretted that the telegraphic dispatches took up so much space, while still another made a virtue of promising never to use them, probably because he hoped to avoid the cost.[90]

An early Oregon editor expressed reservations about the reliability of telegraphed news. M. H. Abbot, who started the *Oregon Herald*, said his paper would carry telegraphic news but could not guarantee its accuracy: "We shall be dependent upon persons hundreds, and sometimes thousands, of miles distant, for statements which they may, from day to day, embody. We shall give them to our readers as we get them . . . Our telegraphic reports will cost us not less than One Hundred Dollars per week, and it will be no fault of ours if at times they will be incorrect."[91]

Availability of telegraphic news was generally a prerequisite for a daily newspaper although a few early dailies were started without it. Several daily papers, including the *Alta California* in San Francisco, the Sacramento *Union*, and the Portland *Oregonian*, started with only local telegraph service. Significant expansion of daily publication came after telegraph lines reached throughout the West. The *Owyhee Avalanche* in Idaho became daily after a line reached Silver City from Winnemucca, Nevada, in 1874, and the *Humboldt Times* in Eureka, California, became a daily in 1873 a few months after the telegraph arrived.[92] The Spokane *Daily Review* started as an experiment after the arrival of the telegraph, "an expensive luxury run on the most economical basis."[93]

As Seattle's Watson found, the ability to print telegraphed news did not assure success; a number of newspapers alternated between daily and less frequent publication before settling on a permanent periodicity—or closing. The *Avalanche* returned to weekly publication in 1876. Washington Territory's first daily, the *Puget Sound Daily Gazette* in Seattle, lasted but a few months before its publisher concentrated his efforts on his weekly.

Daily newspapers almost always had a companion weekly, and some, like the Pendleton *East Oregonian* and the Helena *Herald*, published on three different schedules each week. In publishing multiple editions they followed the practice of the large eastern newspapers whose weekly editions circulated in the West. Daily editions were intended for distribution in town, and selected news was transferred to the weekly and mailed to subscribers in the surrounding countryside. Weekly or daily were most common frequencies, but a few publishers opted for two or three times a week. Most gave the mail schedules as their rationale but when the Butte *Miner* started, it claimed to have selected tri-weekly for the convenience of its readers. Weeklies take a long time to read, the *Miner* said, whereas "a fresh, crisp little tri-weekly with a half-hour's interesting reading in it, is just what a man wants after a day's work."[94] The *Miner* seems to have ignored the fact that the typical four-page weekly was no larger than the typical four-page tri-weekly. More likely, the *Miner*'s publishers hoped that tri-weekly would make them competitive with the Helena dailies. It did not. Butte was not ready to support its own daily, so the *Miner* shifted to weekly after three months.[95]

As postal service improved and subscribers had more ready access to the daily press, interest among daily papers in publishing weekly editions declined. In the 1880s the *Deseret News* transformed its weekly edition into a magazine that emphasized original material, although it continued to use some articles from the daily edition.[96]

Extra! Extra!

Regardless of their regular frequency, most western newspapers issued extras at the slightest encouragement. As already noted, the arrival of a bulletin via telegraph often resulted in an extra, but any important news could prompt a special issue. Extras were seldom full-sized newspapers. Rather, they were single sheets, sometimes quite small. A Nevada publisher described his Fourth of July 1878 extras as "about a couple of inches square."[97] The Los Angeles *Star* called its small extras "slips."[98] The *Deseret News* issued a 48-page pamphlet on polygamy that it called an extra but more commonly published one- or two-page sheets.[99]

Almost anything might be a subject for an extra. The Gold Hill *News* issued two extras after receiving news of a train crash in California in which a Nevada judge was killed. The *News* also delayed its regular edition in order to include more telegraphic news about the crash.[100] Napoleon's surrender, a vigilante hanging, mine fires, election campaigns, Indian attacks, and polygamy provided just a few excuses for printers to drop other duties to set type and print a special issue. Simply the arrival of long-delayed mail could call for an extra.

Extras were particularly common during the Civil War. In Colorado, quartz-mill operators blew the whistles to stop work upon the arrival of an extra carrier so that the dispatches could be read to the men.[101] Demand for news was especially heavy when news of Lincoln's assassination reached a town. Nevada journalist Alf Doten said he "never saw such a stir in the 'extra' line" as for the extras issued by the *Territorial Enterprise* and the Virginia City *Union*.[102] In Idaho, where it took eleven days for the news of the President's death to arrive, miners eagerly awaited the extras.[103]

News of the war reached Oregon via Pony Express to Sacramento, telegraph to Yreka, California, then by stage or courier to Jacksonville, Salem, and Portland; the short telegraph line between Sacramento and Yreka saved about three days over conventional channels. When the publisher of the weekly Jacksonville *Sentinel* realized he was issuing an extra every time a dispatch was received, he changed to semi-weekly publication, which he felt would be more convenient and economical. After the telegraph reached Jacksonville in 1864, the paper arranged to publish extras every day except Sunday. Customers were asked to pay 75 cents a week or 25 cents a copy, enough to cover the cost of the telegraphed news, ink, and paper. The publisher insisted that he only sought enough to make expenses; apparently the effort failed to cover costs because the *Sentinel* did not publish as many extras as planned.[104]

Not all extras were printed by the issuing newspaper. Less timely items, such as presidential addresses, were sometimes printed in cities and shipped to other centers. Oregon papers purchased extras printed in San Francisco, and vied to see who could be first to distribute them. In 1860 the Jacksonville *Sentinel* claimed it had beaten the Corvallis *Oregon Weekly Union* with President Buchanan's annual message; both distributed preprinted copies. The Eugene *Review* apparently bought extras from the *Statesman* in an attempt to stay ahead of the *Oregonian*.[105]

One kind of extra became routine in some parts of the West. The departure of a steamer from San Francisco to Panama had special significance to westerners because it meant a closing of deals and accounts so that money could be sent to head offices in the East. One day as a steamer was scheduled to leave, Edward Kemble issued an extra he called a "Steamer Edition." The idea of observing Steamer Day caught on and persisted even after steamers were no longer in use.[106] Many California papers also issued extras on the *arrival* of a steamer in order to rush the news it brought to their waiting readers.

Publishers were strongly influenced by the mails in their selection of publication times but also responded to other considerations including competition. *Southern Vineyard* in Los Angeles chose middle-of-the-week publication so it would not conflict with the *Star* or *El Clamor Público* which came out on Saturdays.[107] Another publisher shifted his daily from morning to evening publication because he found it easier to produce a newspaper during the day than overnight.[108]

9

SUPPLIES AND SERVICES

Just as the frontier newspaper developed in response to the needs of communities, so, too, other businesses developed to meet the needs of newspapers. By creating a market for these businesses—paper manufacturers, type foundries, advertising agents, and others—the newspaper industry compounded its impact on the economic development of the West. By 1890 western newspaper offices held more than $4 million in machinery, tools, and equipment, and used $440,000 in raw materials, much of which was acquired locally. Although the manufacture of presses centered in the East, type foundries, paper manufacturers, and suppliers of other goods and services to the industry rapidly set up operations in the West. Within a decade after the people of Monterey greeted their first newspaper, the *Californian*, which was printed on cigar wrappers, paper mills had been established in an attempt to meet the chronic shortage of newsprint. By the mid-1850s wholesalers of other printing supplies had opened offices on the coast.

Of all the supply problems, paper proved most frustrating to publishers. The lack of newsprint on which to print the *Californian* symbolized the problems publishers had as they attempted to set their news product before an eager public. While erratic mail service might mean no news for their columns, they could always turn to the classics for copy. Coal dust and lamp black could suffice for ink. They could even whittle type or build a press if they had to. But they had to have something to print on and making paper required specialized skills generally beyond even creative newspapermen.

They were indeed creative when they ran out of newsprint, as they so frequently did. Despite efforts to stockpile enough paper to see them through seasons of impassable roads, most publishers, at one time or another, printed on wrapping paper, wallpaper, tissue, or whatever usable medium they could acquire to keep publishing. Alternatively, they changed the size of the newspaper to take advantage of any kind of paper they had on hand, reduced frequency, or interrupted publishing altogether, sometimes for weeks at a time.

In 1850 the first issue of the Stockton, California, *Times* appeared on paper normally reserved for lawyers' briefs.[1] The young Los Angeles *Star* printed on half-size sheets for more than a month and sometimes resorted to brown or blue stock or cigar paper while waiting for supplies to arrive.[2] A San Francisco correspondent wrote in 1852:

> Newspaper in this city is not to be had for love or money. Our papers still appear in all kinds of quaint disguises. At times they are seen this large, and then, again, small—now in brown wrapping, and then in yellow, and again in deep blue that won't bear reading at all, and then in light green that can be read both sides at once. Middle-aged gentlemen who wear glasses are in great distress, therefore. They can't read, and no one has time to read to them.[3]

Publishers rarely went to the extreme of completely shutting down, but the *Deseret News* changed from weekly to fortnightly because the publisher feared a paper shortage and sometimes skipped issues when fears were realized.[4] The *Daily Inland Empire* in Nevada started in a smaller format than planned because of concern that weather would interrupt the supply of larger sheets.[5]

The Civil War disrupted supplies of all kinds, and a publisher's politics could aggravate his problems. Paper intended for the pro-South Mesilla, New Mexico, *Times* was turned back by a blockade at a Texas port. The publisher scurried around town and discovered that a Mesilla merchant had a ream of foolscap, but the latter refused to sell it, fearing charges of treason if he supplied a Secessionist newspaper.[6] Even as late as the 1880s, the San Francisco *Examiner* canceled a planned special edition when local mills could not provide paper, and the San Diego *Union* resorted to wrapping paper at least once.[7]

Publishers helped one another when paper shortages arose, selling or lending supplies. In 1852 the Los Angeles *Star* thanked the *Alta California* for a stock of white paper, and the *Deseret News* made paper available even to the anti-Mormon *Valley Tan*.[8]

In the 1840s and 1850s almost all newsprint came from the East Coast, although inland cities like Salt Lake City, Denver, and Santa Fe may have received stock from Wisconsin which started producing paper in 1848.[9] Paper shipped from the East had a long ride in the hold of a ship where it was subject to water damage, or in a wagon, also at risk of water, as well as snow and ice and attacks from Indians. The publisher of the *Arizona Miner* once printed on Manila paper "of rather a sombre hue" because his new supply was held up by "the infernals, who are the dread of all travelers. The last we heard of our stock of paper, was this side of La Paz, the teamsters coming to a stop, waiting for a guard through the Apache country."[10]

Because of the great distances to many points in the West, freighting costs substantially increased the overall cost of supplies like paper. In 1850 the *Deseret News* told its readers that it had to pay $18 to $20 for a ream of paper that cost $3 to $4 in the states. It is not surprising that the thrifty Mormons, who knew the value of being as self-sufficient as possible, started the first paper mill in the West. Determined to issue their newspaper regularly, the Mormons early made preparations for a paper mill. "Save your rags," the *Deseret News* urged soon after its introduction in 1850, "everybody in Deseret save your rags; old wagon covers, tents, quilts, shirts, etc., etc., are wanted for paper."[11]

Paper-mill construction was repeatedly delayed, but in 1851 an experienced papermaker arrived in Salt Lake City from Great Britain, and, together with a sawmill builder, developed plans for a mill in the Salt Lake Valley. For the next three years, the *News* published erratically because of paper shortages, while the Mormons pursued other priorities. Finally, in 1854, the papermaker, Thomas Howard, persuaded Brigham Young to allow him to convert a sugar mill to a papermaking facility. Advertisements again urged the brethren to save their rags and waste paper, which were pulverized in a grinder originally used for sugar beets. The hand-made, sun-dried paper was thick and gray, but it was paper. However, as soon as the *Deseret News* acquired a year's stock of newsprint from its regular supplier, the mill closed.[12]

Paper supply problems continued. In 1860 the *News* again published irregularly, so President Young ordered a papermaking machine from Philadelphia; the machine was placed in the Sugar House, a six-year-old building in which dark molasses had been produced. Another appeal went out to the faithful for rags, and on July 24, 1861, the first paper issued from the machine. Initially too brown for newspaper use, by September the color had lightened enough for printing.

The paper was "thick and rather misty, but on the whole it was like satin compared with some of the homemade sheets" of seven years earlier.[13]

The first production supplied the *News* for a month, and the church stepped up its appeal for rags. Farmers were encouraged to plant flax and hemp. As inducements to save cast-off linen and cotton clothing, wagon-covers, and sheets, women were offered peppermint oil, hatchet handles, beeswax, buckskin needles, camomile flowers, and similar items in exchange for the rags. A special agent appointed by Young collected 20,000 pounds of rags in ten months. Paper produced during this period varied in thickness and in color, and the waterwheel that powered the mill froze in winter and ran dry in the summer, but the supply helped the *News* continue publishing.[14]

Over the next two decades, the Mormons improved the mill so that its waterwheel was no longer subject to the vagaries of the stream, and purchased new machinery. Church leaders turned the Sugar House mill over to the *News*, and from 1868 to 1875 it produced newsprint valued at $57,068.40, and wrapping paper worth $8,405.10. In 1877 its daily output of newsprint and wrapping paper amounted to 800 pounds. By 1880 the mill could not fill increased publishing needs, and authorization was given for a new plant on Big Cottonwood Creek. Three years under construction, the finished mill had a capacity of five tons a day.[15] The *News* sold the mill to a group of businessmen in 1892. The following year fire destroyed the mill, and it was never replaced.[16]

Other Utah papers benefited from the Mormon paper mill. Papers such as *Our Dixie Times* and the *Union* in southern Utah and the Manti *Home Sentinel* used the locally made stock, but there is no indication the *News* tried to market the paper beyond Utah boundaries.[17]

Meanwhile, the paper industry had been established in northern California and the Pacific Northwest. In the early 1850s, George K. Fitch, publisher of the San Francisco *Bulletin*, frustrated by recurring paper shortages, is said to have arrived in the office of Samuel P. Taylor, a flour miller in Taylorville north of San Francisco, emptied a stovepipe hat full of gold dust and $50 gold slugs on the table, and begged Taylor to make some newsprint. Taylor responded by producing his first rag newsprint in November 1856, and he ran a mostly successful operation until the panic of 1893.[18] Other paper mills followed, although not all of them produced newsprint. Santa Cruz had a mill in 1865, Oregon City in 1866, Mendocino in 1868, Stockton in 1873, and Agnew in 1878.[19] Most of these plants lasted only a year or two before being destroyed by fire, debt, or general business problems.

Publishers coped not only with irregular supplies but also with fluctuating prices for their principal consumable. In general, over the decades both the cost of the material and the expense of shipping declined, thanks to new technology and improved transportation. Even so, in 1880, prices charged Utah papers increased by about a third, leading the *Deseret News* to predict, "We presume many of our cotemporaries will have to 'go under' entirely, if the present state of things endures much longer."[20]

The industry variously measured paper in reams or pounds as measures in reference to cost, and because paper came in different sizes and weights, the number of pounds per ream could vary. These variations make cost and usage comparisons difficult. Assuming for the sake of comparison that newspapers used a standard ream weighing 40 pounds, in the antebellum years the Sacramento *Union* reported paying $50 a ream, or $1.25 a pound for paper, while in Salt Lake City, the *Deseret News* paid 60 cents a pound, and in New York the *Tribune* paid 8.3 cents.[21] Prices rose during the Civil War when shortages forced most newspapers to limit size but by the late 1860s started a steady decline. In 1867 a Washington Territory publisher paid 21 cents, compared to the New York *Tribune*'s 14.6 cents.[22]

In 1866–1867 paper made from wood pulp by a process invented in Germany was introduced in the United States, and by 1879 the technology reached the western states. R. B. Lane, of Stockton, a producer of straw and rag paper, was eager to move into wood-pulp technology. He contracted with the San Francisco *Chronicle* for a three-month supply of newsprint at 6.5 cents a pound. He also signed the San Francisco *Call* and the *Bulletin*, and with these guarantees purchased the necessary Fourdrinier equipment. In his first year he produced 225 tons of newsprint.[23]

Even having its own paper mills did not relieve the West of its reliance on the world economy, however. When Lane could not get enough wood chips locally, he imported them from Maine, New York, and Europe. He also had to get chemicals from Liverpool, England.[24] Partly for these reasons, and partly because labor costs were higher in the West, prices for local newsprint were barely competitive with eastern rates. In the early 1880s, regional prices were slightly higher than eastern prices, even after shipping costs were added. Western newsprint cost 8.5 to 9.5 cents a pound, eastern newsprint about a penny less, delivered. Still, Lane supplied many papers throughout the West, appealing to papers to practice what they preached to their communities: support local enterprise.[25]

In the late 1880s Lane's California Paper Company began getting wood pulp from Oregon and decided to establish an Oregon mill, the Willamette Pulp and Paper Company, in competition with Oregonians already in the newsprint business.[26] H. L. Pittock, publisher of the Portland *Oregonian*, had joined other Oregon businessmen to establish H. L. Pittock and Company, and later, the Clackamas Paper Manufacturing Company. These early plants produced paper from rags and straw. In 1883 Pittock and J. K. Gill started construction on a mill at Camas, Washington, that could handle both wood pulp and rag paper; the first paper came from the machines on May 5, 1885. Fire destroyed the plant in November 1886, at a loss of $150,000, but its owners had it rebuilt by the spring of 1888, with a new 86-inch Fourdrinier machine which could turn out eight tons of newsprint a day.[27]

Readyprint

Production of blank newsprint was one of the principal industries developed to serve the newspapers of the West; preprinted newsprint was another. Purchase of newsprint sheets with one side already printed meant that only two pages needed to be set in type, and for the publisher in remote communities where labor was not readily available, this could be a considerable saving in time and cost.

The preprinted pages, commonly called patent 'sides—the "'sides" being either the outside pages one and four, or the inside two and three—were first produced in England and distributed in the United States early in the nineteenth century. U.S. printers started selling their own preprints during the Mexican War of the 1840s, but their popularity basically grew out of the Civil War when so many printers were summoned for military service. What started as a necessity to meet a labor shortage developed into a way of keeping labor costs relatively low. Ansel N. Kellogg, publisher of the Baraboa, Wisconsin, *Republic*, promoted the readyprints among his fellow Wisconsin publishers so successfully that in 1865 he moved to Chicago and arranged to provide the pages on a large scale.[28]

Kellogg started with eight customers, but the number grew rapidly and within weeks he had more than fifty. Initially all customers received the same pages, but Kellogg soon offered a variety of page sizes, various numbers of columns, and content with specified political direction and proportion of advertising. Kellogg built a profitable national advertising clientele that helped pay for the sheets and reduced the cost to publishers. He could also accommodate publishers who wanted to control the advertising that went into their papers by giving them adless sheets. In 1872 he advertised:

Insides, Outsides, Exteriors and Supplements.

Republican, Neutral and Democratic.

Six, Seven, Eight and Nine Column Folios.

Headings changed free. No interferences.

Thirty-six Regular Editions Weekly.

Save a Thousand Dollars a Year.[29]

The use of patent 'sides spread rapidly in the 1870s and by 1880 it was estimated that Kellogg and his imitators served more than 3,000 of the nation's 8,600 weeklies.[30] Co-operative papers, as the preprints were also sometimes called, gave western publishers fast starts and quick profit, and aided the spread of weekly newspapers throughout the West. The 1880 census counted 94 co-operative papers in the region, 14 percent of the total.

Because preprint providers could customize their papers to include a client's local advertising, the use of patent 'sides is not always obvious. Sometimes preprints in the frontier press can be identified because they differed in type size, style, or spacing from the rest of the paper; preprinted pages sometimes were more neatly done than the local pages. The complete lack of anything local—including advertising—in two adjacent pages over a period of time is another clue to identifying them, although not a definitive one because of publishers' heavy reliance on exchanges and the amount of out-of-town advertising many papers carried. Some publishers acknowledged using preprints, and rivals often pointed them out. Suspect pages can sometimes be verified by an advertisement for a company supplying newsprint, type, and other printing supplies; this company probably provided the preprints. But a casual reader of the frontier press would not necessarily notice that the paper was not an entirely local production.

Publishers turned to patent 'sides most typically to help them get started with basic four-page weeklies. The owners of the *Palouse Gazette* in eastern Washington in 1877 used preprints; one of the *Gazette* owners started a companion newspaper in Moscow, Idaho, in 1882, again with preprints.[31] The San Bernardino *Index* and the Riverside *Press* in Southern California; the Vancouver, Washington, *Register*, and *Carson Valley News* in Nevada in the 1870s; the Gunnison, Colorado, *News*; the Beaver, Utah, *Utonian*; and the Anacortes, Washington, *Progress* in the 1880s were a few of the many newspapers that used patent 'sides.[32]

Occasionally, preprints facilitated larger newspapers. In 1875 six of The Dalles *Itemizer*'s eight pages were printed in Chicago, and the Yakima *Signal* in 1883 published an eight-page paper, four of them patent.[33] A Portland publisher determined that he could afford to issue a Sunday paper by buying a four-page news edition from a Chicago patent supplier; the other four pages would carry advertising and stories from his daily paper.[34]

Although patent enthusiasts argued that the experienced patent editor could produce a better product because he had access to more and better material than the typical country editor, use of patent 'sides was an economic not a quality measure. "To publish a paper entirely of home print, entails more than twice the expense of a patent outside," commented one publisher who refused to use them, promising his readers the "choicest miscellany" and "nothing but the very latest news" in his all-home paper.[35]

The principal appeal of the readyprints was cost. Kellogg and his imitators offered publishers a bargain because they operated with substantial economies of scale. Preprint providers could buy paper in bulk and, by using the same typesetting for a number of papers, greatly reduced the unit cost. By selling advertising, they could lower their price to publishers even more. From the publisher's perspective, preprints not only saved labor costs, they also cut production time in half, leaving the shop's typesetters and printers free to work on job printing; they also reduced editing and writing requirements, and left the publisher free to canvass for advertising and subscribers or pursue political objectives. Preprints usually cost the publisher somewhat more than plain paper but the savings in labor could more than make up the difference.

In 1868 Kellogg, then printing 16 editions a week, offered a Denver publisher preprinted pages of 7 columns, in quantities of 20 quires (a ream) at 36 cents per quire. (This equals about 18 cents a pound, only 3.4 cents more than the cost of plain paper in New York and less than the 21 cents a Washington Territory publisher paid for paper.) In his offer Kellogg reserved two columns for advertising, but said that if he sold more advertising, he would credit $50 per column per year to the newspaper's account.[36]

Preprint publishers worked hard to accommodate their clients. At a time when publishers played circulation games with advertising agents, inflating readership, at least one Chicago company promised to protect his clients by keeping circulation figures confidential.[37]

In resorting to preprints, publishers risked disapproval of their peers, so they rarely flaunted their use of the 'sides or promoted them as a benefit worth subscribing for. Journalists saw something undesirable about using less than all home print. A New Mexico newspaper described competitors that used patent 'sides as "emasculated humbugs,"[38] and when a Nevada newspaper died, one of its contemporaries remarked that the paper "was a patent-outside, weakly, milk-and-water sort of weekly, and its death creates no aching void in the journalism of Nevada."[39] The failure of the Yakima *Signal* to publish one weekend because its patent insides had not arrived prompted its competitor to remark, "This is only one of the many evils arising from the use of 'patents',"[40] and after the Port Townsend *Argus* doubled the number of its pages with the help of a four-page patent inside, another publisher urged, "Throw away the patent part, *it will pay*."[41] Another Washington publisher criticized competitors' use of preprints because it meant less work for local compositors and more money leaving the territory.[42]

National attitudes no doubt influenced local publishers. A trade publication, *The Journalist*, called the use of patent 'sides "antediluvian" and said they should be generally discarded because of worthless stories and advertisements that ruined the look of the paper.

They were, said *The Journalist*, a "fraud on the reader," although the magazine voiced no objection to other kinds of prepared content.[43] A census report that called the preprints "discreditable" also said they were better than no paper at all and blamed their use on too much advertising; the saving grace was that newspapers tended to outgrow them.[44] Indeed, when they felt they could afford to drop the preprints, most publishers did so. The *Palouse Gazette* and the *Columbia Chronicle* stopped using them because publishers said they had an obligation to subscribers to use as much locally selected material as possible.[45] A Tacoma publisher, who had himself once used patent 'sides, later insisted readers should support his paper because it was entirely produced at home while his competitors used preprints.[46]

Patent 'sides became a big business, with at least 21 companies in the United States providing service. The total value of preprints produced in 1880 was more than $1 million and they saved publishers an estimated $2 million. Western companies quickly exploited the potential market and soon competed with Kellogg. He had branch offices around the country, but apparently none in the West, serving his western clients from Chicago.[47] Palmer and Rey—type founders in San Francisco—and the San Francisco Newspaper Union were among the early western suppliers. Palmer and Rey and American Typefounders also supplied clients from Portland.[48] The Northern Newspaper Union, owned by American Typefounders Company, provided preprints from Spokane.[49] Inland papers, such as those in Wyoming, Utah, and Colorado, looked to cities like Chicago, Omaha, and St. Louis for their preprints, although the Salt Lake *Tribune* apparently tried selling them at one time.[50]

Preprinted pages gradually gave way to stereotypes or "boilerplate." Instead of getting a pair of pages printed, a publisher might subscribe to a service that gave him metal plates, pre-cast with stories or advertising or illustrations, that he could affix to a wooden base and include in his page. Sometimes material was put on both sides of the plate to economize. National advertisers such as patent-medicine firms regularly used the plates, sending their flamboyant copy to papers all over the nation. Other advertisers, as well as services providing the kinds of news and feature material common to the preprints, also adopted this means of delivery. Boilerplate suppliers such as the American Press Association from New York opened West Coast offices. At 15 cents per 1,000 ems (New York price, freight presumably extra), boilerplate, too, opened an avenue for publishers to save money.[51]

Stereotype services were much like the syndicate services most newspapers subscribe to today to enhance their content, but publishers who did not like readyprint, did not like stereotype plates either. "Boilerplate" had derogatory connotations, and editors who used the plates, cutting them to fit space, "were said to edit their papers with a saw."[52]

Publishers welcomed the establishment of western suppliers. Service from New York or Boston was slow; in the 1850s it sometimes took as much as a year for a shipment to arrive. Jonas Winchester begged his brother with considerable urgency to send printing equipment so that he could take advantage of San Francisco's booming conditions.[53] If his brother sent the material at all, it did not arrive quickly enough for Jonas to secure the corner on the market that he anticipated.

Rapid market growth made San Francisco the hub for western printing, as well as for many other industries. From the Golden Gate city, but later also from other major centers such as Denver, Salt Lake City, and Portland, companies supplied the Washington hand presses so popular in frontier towns, and more advanced power presses as they became available. William Faulkner and Son, San Francisco printing supply agent, probably provided much of the equipment with which the *Arizona Miner* was first printed.[54] In 1865, William P. Harrison Printer's Warehouse, on Clay Street in San Francisco, advertised itself as agent for Bruce's type, Gordon's and Hoe's presses, Mather's black and colored inks, and paper and card stock.[55] In Denver, Stebbins and Porter was agent for Washington presses and other supplies in the 1860s.[56]

Most supplies came from manufacturers in the East; the distance and hazards of transportation meant unreliable stocks. However, western suppliers soon built inventories so that by 1871, a northern California newspaper that burned in a fire reportedly had a complete new outfit in 48 hours.[57]

When they started casting type and manufacturing other materials on the West Coast is uncertain. Type foundries there early on could provide types and other material. The San Francisco office of the Chicago Type Foundry advertised in 1876 that it had started to cast type, but other foundries, such as Palmer and Rey, probably preceded it.[58] In Utah, the self-sufficient Mormons, having brought type matrices with them across the plains, started casting type in 1854.[59]

The amount produced by local type foundries was still too small to warrant reporting in the 1890 census, but the paper, stereotyping, and engraving industries in California valued their products at more than $700,000.

Part IV

The Balance Sheet

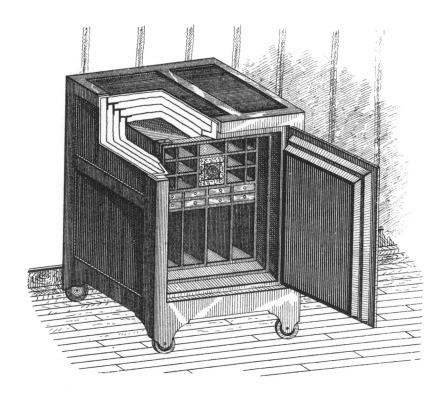

10

PRESSURES ON THE PRESS

Frontier publishers, like newspapermen in any era, had to cope with pressures from readers, advertisers, labor, special interests, politicians, and almost anyone else with whom they came into contact. Then, as now, everyone was an expert on what should go into the paper. Some were more expert than others, having the ability to exercise fiscal influence on the paper, and publishers knew that printing—or on occasion not printing—some kinds of things could benefit them economically. They responded to pressure in different ways, some honoring the finest traditions of independent journalism, some bowing to the almighty dollar, most trying to navigate through the best of both worlds.

Frontier publishers seeking business catered to what they perceived to be the special interests of their readers. Clearly readers wanted local news. It has been suggested that until about the 1860s newspapers generally ignored local news, either because they lacked interest or skill in reporting, or because they believed that news of local interest had already circulated by word of mouth.[1] But western newspapers carried columns of local news from the beginning. The *California Star* told of the discovery of gold at Sutter's Fort in 1848 and of California's agricultural attributes. The first issue of the Sacramento *Daily Union* in 1851 carried "locals," the generally short items that made up the local news columns of the frontier press, as did the *Puget Sound Courier* in 1855. Frontier newspapermen generally shared an Idaho publisher's view that local news came first with his readers and that interest generally declined in proportion to distance from the event.[2]

Even during the Civil War, when concern for national news ran high, one publisher found it advantageous to pledge to cover local news and another to apologize because a list of letters at the post office and lengthy election endorsements had forced the abbreviation of the day's local items.[3] Regretting that the telegraphic dispatches took up so much space, another publisher wrote that nevertheless "our local columns will be found replete with matters of immediate home interest."[4]

Local news meant births, deaths, marriages, meetings, formation of fire departments, parties, theater, mineral discoveries—whatever came to hand that publishers thought would interest their readers. They printed speeches and sermons. The *Deseret News* paid particular attention to sermons as part of its history of the Mormon church, and sermons are said to have boosted circulation for at least one southern Utah paper.[5] In Montana, a prominent citizen even delivered to the paper copies of his speeches, complete with notations indicating applause and cheers.[6] Not everyone considered speeches and sermons appropriate newspaper fare, however. The *Oregonian*'s Thomas Jefferson Dryer believed poetry readings and talks of any kind before local groups lacked interest for the bulk of his readers and insisted that the societies that wanted to see them in print pay for the space. "We cannot afford to, neither will we, print for nothing," he wrote.[7] Implementing a similar policy, the Butte *Miner* listed charges for publication of obituary remarks and poetry.[8]

Publishers were sensitive, as well, to the particular news biases of their communities. Mining-camp papers made an effort to keep readers up to date with new discoveries, stock issues, and other relevant news. An Idaho mining-camp paper pledged to publish the history of local prospectors.[9] The Butte *Miner* added to its local mining reports by selecting mining articles from the exchanges it received from Nevada's Comstock and other active mining areas. Newspapers in agricultural areas were similarly selective in their choice of copy. As one historian noted, "The newspapers, which certainly knew what their readers wanted, often gave more space to a new flume or a success with a new crop than they did to a case of assault."[10]

This is not to say they ignored the assault. Publishers also knew that sensationalism and controversy sold newspapers. Stories about deaths, violent or otherwise, crime, Indian raids, and allegations of corruption did not get big headlines because nothing got big headlines, but they mingled with items about visitors to town and plans for the library and provided the reader with both information and titillation. Most of the local news in the early issues of the Los Angeles *Star* had to do with crime and arrests. We have already seen how publishers catered to the desire for news of the Civil War, subscribing to expensive telegraph and express services and publishing extras. The Lewiston, Idaho, *Teller*'s reports during the Nez Percé Indian wars in 1877 were reprinted in many western papers.

Although not as common as Mark Twain's stories might suggest, the practice of embellishing articles to enhance otherwise dull reading was not limited to the *Territorial Enterprise*. One Montana writer, for example, admitted to sometimes making mountains out of molehills, "dressed up to the best of my ability in attractive phrases."[11]

Although they recognized the financial potential of sensationalism, most did not exploit it for its own sake. They were cautious about spreading sensational rumors that might cause alarm among locals as well as frighten away potential immigrants. The *Reveille* chided the *Lander Free Press* for reporting a case of smallpox that did not exist: "It is not good policy to get up a scare of this sort, and especially where there is no foundation for the report."[12] The San Francisco *Chronicle* rebuked the *Alta* for referring to a man as a "murderer" before his trial and declared that no one who read the *Alta*'s story should be on the jury.[13] An Idaho publisher, who declared he did not like printing false material, asked a man to prove his claim that soldiers had stolen from him.[14]

Editors enjoyed needling one another in print to provoke interest in their communities. Usually conducted as part of a good-natured rivalry, these exchanges sometimes had substance. From his first day as publisher of the *Oregon Statesman*, Asahel "Ass-of-Hell" Bush battled verbally and nastily with other publishers. Defending his acquisition of the public-printing contract, he assailed his detractors' printing competence and repeatedly reminded readers of a competitor's limited education.[15] Many newspapermen held strong convictions, and not every barb aimed at another publisher or politician was simply to attract readership, but if it helped circulation, too, so be it. A Nevada publisher even created a fictional newspaper whose vitriolic editorials he could reprint, thereby expressing his personal views with less danger to himself.[16]

Involvement in local controversies generally went hand-in-hand with newspapering, but issues could raise tempers and put a newspaper that supported the "wrong" side in a precarious, if not fatal, financial position. In Yakima, debate over the relocation of the city to accommodate the railroad turned violent after the publisher of the Yakima *Signal* decided to transfer to the new town site. The newspaper office was on jacks, ready for the move, when an explosion tore the side out of the building and scattered type in the bushes. What was left was moved anyhow and, with the help of other local publishers, the *Signal* continued to publish.[17]

Publishers also catered to readers' taste in humor, although the image of the frontier press as full of wonderful tall tales is overblown. Accomplished humorists such as Twain and his Comstock cohorts and Bill Nye in Laramie were rare, and although the typical frontier paper might clip and reprint other well-known humorists of the day such as Mr. Dooley, newspaper humor generally took the form of puns or jokes as filler items. Some samples suggest the vaudeville nature of their funny bone:

> Uneasy is the woman's head that wears a bonnet; unhappy is the Czar, whose clothing is made of metal and fastened on with rivets; but the unhappiest of all men is he whose suspenders break while he is waltzing.[18]

Or:

> Almost every young lady is public spirited enough to have her father's house used as a court house.[19]

Selling News Space

In addition to money undoubtedly changing hands to put advertising in the news columns—the reading notices discussed in chapter 4— newspapers may have been paid for printing stories for clients. In the 1850s, Californian Jonas Winchester accepted real estate bribes to promote a number of towns in the region.[20] According to Alf Doten, on at least one occasion the *Territorial Enterprise* required payment before printing an article. He said the *Enterprise* received $20 from an Austin man to print his letter on the Silver Question. Doten, who edited the communication, also wrote a notice for the local column calling attention to the article.[21] In 1884, when former Nevada Senator William Sharon was in a San Francisco court over claims from a woman who said she was his wife, a San Francisco correspondent said Sharon supplied the principal morning papers with a transcript of some of the courtroom testimony and paid them $200 a column to publish it. Sharon had, the writer said, paid out more than $12,000 to get coverage of his side of the dispute.[22]

Meanwhile, some publishers reportedly sought and accepted money to keep things out of the paper. The *Virginia Chronicle* has been called "little more than a blackmailing operation" as its publisher tried to extort money from the Virginia and Truckee Railroad, asking the railroad to buy him out at a "fantastic" $50,000. Instead the railroad offered him $150 a month to stop the attacks. He settled for the equivalent in advertising, plus free passes, and eventually sold the paper for $500.[23] The editor of the Tombstone *Epitaph*, J. O. Dunbar, claimed his counterpart at the *Prospector*, James J. Nash, blackmailed a local citizen by putting items in the paper hinting at revelations to come. Nash supposedly refused $25 to stop the innuendos, holding out for $100. Nash denied the accusations, retorting that they had been conceived and written by a drunkard.[24]

Frontier publishers brought to town at the instigation of local businessmen and land developers took seriously their booster commitments, but even those who were not specifically beholden promoted their locales. After all, if indeed they were to build their own markets, it was obviously in their interest to help promote growth. Frontier newspapers carried lengthy stories about the local district, its history, the level of business activity and similar information; a content analysis of selected Washington Territory dailies showed that in 1889 they devoted nearly half of their stories to economic development.[25]

Historians have called booster publishers servile and accused them of filling columns with exaggerated claims for their town while ignoring news that might reflect poorly on local prospects. Nineteenth-century readers looked at it differently. Townsfolk in Colfax, Washington, welcomed their new, admittedly booster, paper with a celebration and a monogrammed cake.[26] A Nevada woman wrote to her newly established local newspaper:

> I have been rejoicing at the thought of having a village paper, not because I am disposed to occupy a newspaper with my

notion of 'men and things'—I mean men, women and things—
but because it will become a medium through which the whole
community may become extensively and properly known.[27]

Nor was servility necessarily evident in the pages of the papers.
Despite the desire to attract settlers, the commitment to boosterism
did not mean the papers carried only positive stories. True, booster
publishers might be accused of exaggerating the fertility of the land
or the benefits of the climate or the value of gold veins, but whether
regular news coverage made a bad impression on potential settlers
seemed of little concern. Papers printed stories of violence, complained about the weather, and castigated their political opponents.
For example, the *Reese River Reveille* made no effort to bury the
negative image of Nevada when it reported, with little comment, that
the Washington, D.C., *Star* had said the state's mines were played
out and its population declining, and had called Nevada "confessedly
nothing more than a 'rotten borough' politically."[28]

Favorable local stories usually satisfied the local constituency, but
backers of the Los Angeles *Herald* hired a new editor in 1874 after the
old one filled the paper with clipped material instead of the booster
stories they wanted.[29] In Spokane, town founders quarreled with
Francis Cook, publisher of the Spokan *Times* over whether the town's
name should be spelled with the final "e;" the result was the establishment of a rival, the Spokane *Chronicle*.[30] Colonel W. R. Wallace,
founder of Wallace, Idaho, promised six months' free office rent and
guaranteed $1,800 in revenue for those six months to whoever would
start a newspaper to help him profit from land sales. Wallace later
claimed that the two printers who took him up on the offer broke the
agreement by printing an item questioning his property titles. The
printers, formerly generous with praise for Wallace, denied that they
were under obligation to him, and he, not they, eventually left town.[31]

Other special interests sought to influence the content of newspapers. The Catholic church was strong in New Mexico and Southern
California, and in Utah the Mormons were a dominant influence.
New Mexican Catholics for years fought the establishment of public
schools, contributing to the territory's low literacy rate.[32] This in turn
affected newspaper circulation and advertising, merchants seeing no
point in advertising to people unable to read.[33] In Santa Barbara,
California, the Catholic Spanish aristocracy considered positions

taken by the *Gazette* offensive to the church, and persuaded the state legislature to allow posting instead of publication of legal notices. This led to the demise of the *Gazette* which depended on revenue from publishing the notices.[34]

In Utah, the *Deseret News* was, of course, a Mormon newspaper, but it was not a typical "religious" newspaper, most of which were poorly funded and short-lived. The *News* at times was surely poorly funded, but otherwise hardly typical of religious publications, serving, as it did, community as well as spiritual needs. Although Brigham Young claimed he had no direct involvement in the *News*, the paper followed the instructions of the church.[35] While the Mormons tried to avoid undue attention during the height of the church's conflict with the United States in the 1850s, the paper stopped publishing sermons because leaders feared the opposition might find useful ammunition in their words.[36] On orders from church leaders who did not want an influx of non-Mormon miners, the *Deseret News* also tried to kill rumors of gold in the region. "We can think of no labor that is not positively dishonorable, the effects of which are more degrading than gold digging," the *News* wrote, in an attempt to discourage miners.[37]

In spite of its influence on Utah development, the church's imprimatur did not ensure a newspaper's success. In Provo, local businessmen started a paper with Young's express approval, but it failed to get the support of local residents.[38] At the same time, although enterprises with the church's blessing had a better chance of success than those outside the fold, neither Utah in general nor Salt Lake City in particular was such a monolithic Mormon community to totally preclude opposing ideas. The Salt Lake City *Tribune*, for example, had a checkered history of accommodation with the church. Started as a relatively mild protest vehicle against the church hierarchy, the *Tribune* went on the attack in the 1870s after the city council banned a reporter from its deliberations, then returned to a more cooperative posture in the 1880s when Charles C. Goodwin became an owner.[39] For non-Mormon papers, the church's authority was at least a convenient excuse for their problems. One editor complained that she was falsely accused of being anti-Mormon and not given customary complimentary tickets to the Opera House Company.[40] In contrast, the *Deseret News* was known to assist even virulently anti-Mormon competitors. When the Salt Lake *Evening Chronicle* had press problems, the *News* helped by printing a few editions, and on occasion it made paper available to the *Valley Tan*.[41]

Major business interests—railroads, mines, timber, ranching, depending on the location—put varying degrees of pressure on the press, owning some, influencing others. Transportation baron Ben Holladay started the *Oregon Bulletin* in 1870, pouring some $200,000 into it in five years.[42] Whatever the formal association between the Northern Pacific and the Kalama *Beacon*, located at the railroad's Columbia River construction headquarters, the newspaper promised that "the great and important enterprise inaugurated and already in rapid process of construction by the North Pacific Railroad Company, will receive from us the attention the magnitude of the undertaking demands."[43] The *Beacon* attacked those who attacked the railroad and when the railroad finally settled on Tacoma for its Pacific terminus, the *Beacon*'s proprietors relocated. In Tacoma they apparently published an issue or two of the *North Pacific Times*, doing so, according to a rival newspaper, at the instigation of the Oregon Steam Navigation, Northern Pacific, and Tacoma Land companies which "infused the first filthy breath of life into the disreputable sheet."[44]

In Sacramento, the *Union*, initially almost as friendly to railroad interests as the *Beacon*, turned on the Central Pacific and drew the wrath of its owners. An exasperated Collis P. Huntington, one of the railroad's "Big Four," wrote a friend, the "*Union* hurts us very much. . . . If I owned the paper I would burn it."[45] Instead, the Central Pacific banned the newspaper from its cars and boats, and increased pressures on advertisers. The publishers are said to have lost $150,000 each before the paper went on the auction block in 1874, proving that the pen was not necessarily mightier than the balance sheet.[46]

Huntington, in the nation's capital to lobby for the railroad when he expressed his unhappiness with the irksome newspaper, also wondered whether he could control the agent for the Associated Press in San Francisco because of dispatches that damaged the railroad's cause in the capital.[47] Later, a quarrel between Huntington and one of his partners, Leland Stanford, created an awkward situation for editors who did the railroad's bidding in exchange for support. "Most of them played safe and either ignored the situation or quoted minor railroad officials as deprecating the unfortunate misunderstanding."[48] Elsewhere, when the Union Pacific railroad arrived in

Santa Fe, it bought a share of the *New Mexican* to ensure the right kind of publicity.[49]

Adolph Sutro, San Francisco entrepreneur, mayor, and developer of the Sutro Tunnel, a project designed to keep water from flooding his Comstock mine, started the Sutro *Independent* to promote the tunnel after newspapermen like Alf Doten turned against him.[50] Montana copper king William Clark owned part of the Butte *Miner*, and Arizona's Pinkney Randolph Tully, freighter, merchant, banker, and investor in mines and ranches, helped found the *Arizona Weekly Star*.[51] While the owners probably hoped the newspapers would be good investments, their primary objective was to protect other interests. Clearly, Tacoma vice lord Harry Morgan supported a paper in order to defend his principal business activities from attacks by the anti-vice movement.[52] The *Kern County Courier* in Bakersfield in the 1870s was owned first by a company formed by a San Francisco drug wholesaler and a Kern County investor, then by the California Cotton Growers and Manufacturers Association, which was also connected with the drug wholesaler.[53]

Politics also had impact on content and economics. We have seen the importance publishers placed on the public printing contracts that could result from enthusiastic partisanship. But party promotion could also hurt circulation. The first newspaper in Washington Territory, the *Columbian*, avoided party politics because its backer, a Whig, saw little point in antagonizing the Democrats who were sure to govern the new territory.[54] When the *Alta California* became a tri-weekly late in 1849, it noted that none of California's other newspapers took partisan positions, so it did not plan to either.[55] In 1868 the new owner of the *Sage Brush* in Susanville, California, decided that because the county couldn't support two papers, he would follow a neutral political course.[56]

Nevertheless, few newspapermen could resist the prospect of pulling political strings, and as soon as one newspaper spoke with a partisan voice, opposition politicians felt the need for their own organ. Many western communities, at one time or another, boasted at least two newspapers. Party papers were particularly popular around election time when political leaders reached to fund necessary promotional activities. As the founder of the *Columbian* had anticipated, Democrats controlled the politics of the new Washington Territory and they soon purchased the newspaper from him, turning it into a highly political publication.[57] The establishment of the Whig *Puget Sound Courier* in nearby Steilacoom came as a direct political challenge to the Democrats. The *Courier*'s publishers started enthusiastically: "It is folly to tell us that the Whig party is dead. Not dead but sleepeth."[58] Enthusiasm waned quickly. Few Whigs came to the publishers' aid after they antagonized the Democratic territorial governor. When Indian troubles disturbed the settlement, the newspaper folded.

The threat of competition, both political and economic, influenced many decisions, including the sale of the Boise *News* by its founders who, as an election approached, explained, "The time has arrived when in order to further succeed in publishing a newspaper it is necessary to drive, or be driven, into politics, an employment that the undersigned have no relish for."[59] The economically and politically astute Henry L. Pittock sold an interest in the *Oregonian* to a senate candidate to prevent his starting his own newspaper; Pittock repurchased the share when the campaign was over.[60] Stratton suggests that New Mexican publishers adhered to party lines because it was so easy for politicians to start rival newspapers, but publishers recognized that partisanship had disadvantages.[61] Newspapers started with party funding from the party could easily fail if politicians removed their support before the paper developed a stable circulation and advertising base, a difficult task in the throes of a heated political campaign. Idahoan Frank Kenyon was persuaded to stay in Lewiston by a territorial governor who did not want to move the capital to Boise. Given an appointment as census taker and promised the public printing, Kenyon even increased the frequency of the *Golden Age* to twice a week. However, when the legislature voted to move to Boise after all, the governor signed the bill, and Kenyon was left in a declining town.[62]

Playing politics posed other hazards for publishers. The Las Vegas, New Mexico, *Weekly Mail* fought the powerful Santa Fe Ring which finally forced the paper out of business.[63] The *Arizonian*'s publisher Pierson W. Dooner, after supporting politician Richard McCormick for a number of years, switched his allegiance to McCormick's opposition, so McCormick and his supporters simply repossessed the press they had bought for Dooner's use.[64] Backers of the Oregon *Spectator* fired an editor for failing to look after their political interests.[65] When the *Territorial Enterprise* attacked William Sharon's candidacy for the United States Senate, Sharon and a group of friends bought the paper.[66] Publishers of the *California Statesman* sued a politician they said had broken his promise to pay them $2,500 and deliver the government printing in exchange for their support. The court dismissed the suit on the grounds that such a contract would be contrary to public policy.[67]

Debt increased publishers' susceptibility to political influence. Frank Leach bought the Oakland *Enquirer* from a gubernatorial candidate who, when Leach refused to support him, called in his note. As Leach scrambled for funds to pay the debt, an acquaintance walked into the office and offered to lend him the money. Leach later discovered that another politician had actually provided the necessary sum.[68] Washington Republican Allen Weir confided to a colleague, "I think a few more weeks will let Frank Meyers and the 'Democratic Press' out. His creditors are pushing hard, and he thinks of 'deserting the ship.' I think I can get hold of the mortgage at a discount of about $100. If so, I will put the clamps on and squeeze them out of journalistic existence."[69] Denver's Byers helped silence a local confederate newspaper when he bought it soon after the Civil War began.[70] Radical Montana Republicans, angered by attacks from the moderate Helena *Herald*, bought the *Herald*'s mortgage and tried to foreclose. Publisher Robert E. Fisk fought back successfully through the courts even though, as his wife, skeptical about the honesty of the judge, wrote, "We don't have much law out here."[71]

Most political rivalry was conducted in the pages of the newspapers or in the counting rooms of the banks, but opponents were not above physical sabotage of a partisan newspaper. A Nevada publisher who sought election as state assemblyman launched an attack on his opponent, whose friends retaliated by stealing the lever to the printing press. The publisher managed to construct a substitute and continue the attacks, but lost the election nevertheless.[72] Shots fired at Helena's Fisk and his partner probably stemmed from their fight with the radicals.[73]

The most systematic destruction, both physical and economic, of partisan newspapers came during the Civil War, particularly after the assassination of President Lincoln. The West was by no means united in its view of the conflict, and supported numerous Democratic newspapers sympathetic to the South—"Secesh" papers. The more scathing their attacks on Lincoln, the more they invited trouble.

As early as 1861 a "Secesh" paper in southern Oregon was refused admission to the mails.[74] Republican newspapers in San Francisco regularly condemned the anti-Lincoln *Democratic Press*, despite a warning from a Nevada contemporary: "Persecution is a dangerous weapon, and very often recoils upon those who use it."[75]

When news of Lincoln's assassination spread through San Francisco, the *Democratic Press* experienced the fury of the mob. The *Press*, the *News Letter*, the *Occidental*, the religious *Monitor*, the *L'Union Franco Americaine*, the *Irish News*, and *Voz de Méjico* were all ransacked, the latter four only because they happened to be in the way. Officials called in the Army and the mob dispersed, but the publishers of the affected newspapers sued the city for failing to protect their property and eventually collected sums ranging from $300 to $10,000.[76]

Meanwhile Major General Irvin McDowell, local commandant for the U.S. Army, declared that any newspaper expressing approval of the assassination of the president would be seized and suppressed. While pro-Union San Francisco newspapers frothed patriotically and urged McDowell to carry out his edict, the *Chronicle* suggested that their motives had less to do with politics than economics. The *Chronicle* publishers said they, too, would like McDowell "to suppress all those treasonable sheets that are interfering with our business by getting more advertisements than we do."[77] The mob relieved McDowell of having to deal with San Francisco secessionist newspapers, but the general moved against the *Amador Dispatch* a mining-camp newspaper that had supported the Confederacy. He arrested the *Dispatch*'s publishers who spent several weeks at Fort Alcatraz before being allowed to resume publication.[78]

New Mexico had strong Southern sympathies. When Mesilla residents learned in the fall of 1861 that Union Army Colonel Edward R. S. Canby was on the march toward their town, the pro-slavery Mesilla *Times* suspended publication for six weeks and moved its plant across the border into Mexico. The anticipated invasion did not occur. The *Times'* publisher accused a Confederate colonel of cowardice in the incident, challenged him in the street, and was fatally shot.[79] An Idaho editor trying to run a Union newspaper in a town with Southern sympathies claimed rebels had fired shots into his office. Other papers insisted that there was no substance to the story, however.[80] Some newspapers closed quietly as publishers realized their communities opposed them, others kept a low profile until the furor quieted. One publisher who had run a Secesh newspaper in a mining camp knew better than to show any Southern sympathies when he moved to the Santa Barbara *Post*.[81]

The chill of libel suits transcended political philosophies, but frontier publishers were rarely cowed by the prospect of being summoned to court, even though libel was commonly treated as a criminal, as well as civil, offense. In Utah in 1880, the owners of the Silver Reef *Miner* were arrested after printing a story that suggested local mines were not all they were purported to be. Noting that the mining company had hired the only lawyers in Silver Reef, the Salt Lake *Herald* commented, "The company's attempt to thus muzzle the press is generally regarded here as a gross outrage," and later, "The Miner, notwithstanding the threats made to demolish it . . . is still firing away briskly."[82] The *Miner* affirmed its original claim about the mine and was eventually acquitted, the Provo *Enquirer* observing approvingly that the jury had not succumbed to intimidation.[83]

The San Francisco *Chronicle* in its heady early days could afford to make light of legal problems. Commenting on a $7,500 award made in a libel case involving the San Francisco *Bulletin*, the youthful *Chronicle* publishers expressed the wish that some "pecunious" person would libel them and give them an easy source of income.[84] After the paper became established and influential, the deYoungs were in and out of the courts with regularity on libel charges. Another San Francisco publisher who was sued for libel planned to make the best of a bad situation by printing 20,000 extra copies of the coverage of his trial so he could expose his opponent's tricks.[85]

Profit and power mixed with a sense of social responsibility in different measures to guide individual publishers facing pressures. After beer sellers pulled their advertising from The Dalles *Times-Mountaineer* for printing a critical communication, the newspaper apologized. This in turn led the Walla Walla *Daily Journal* to chide the *Mountaineer*. The *Journal*, which of course was not threatened with loss of revenue, said the newspaper was not responsible for others' opinions and added that the beer sellers were stupid for taking such criticism seriously.[86] In Utah a story reflecting unfavorably on the management of a mine resulted in a withdrawal of patronage but the publishers refused to retract their statements.[87]

Some of the thinnest-skinned advertisers were the theater people who were, of course, seeking constant praise and approval from the press and were outraged when they did not get it from the publishers to whom they gave so much business. After all, not only did newspapermen expect to attend performances at the theater owner's expense, theatrical events provided a substantial amount of job printing. Usually good reviews were forthcoming, but on one occasion the *Territorial Enterprise* published rave reviews of actress Adah Isaacs Mencken's performance at Tom Maguire's Opera House in Virginia City, ignoring the rest of the play. The angry supporting cast pressured Maguire to ban *Enterprise* journalists from the theater. He complied but the newspaper retaliated by printing only unfavorable reviews which it obtained secondhand. Maguire eventually capitulated and welcomed the writers back to the theater with champagne.[88] The incident failed to convince Maguire of the power of the press, however. In San Francisco he had a similar encounter when the *Chronicle* suggested that a 200-pound actress might not be the best casting for "Camille." The subsequent feud between Maguire and the newspaper helped build circulation, but cost the theater owner audience until he decided again to make his peace with the press.[89]

Mark Twain once told of writing an indignant story for the San Francisco *Morning Call* about ruffians stoning a Chinese man, but the next morning, when he scanned the paper's columns, the story was nowhere to be found. When Twain confronted the newspaper's owner, he learned it had not been printed because, the publisher told him, the *Call* was the newspaper of the poor, and as such could not afford to publish such articles. It had to "respect their prejudices or perish."[90] A Utah publisher courageously attacked local vice lords and was tarred and feathered and soon run out of business for his trouble.[91]

Publishers resented the pressures brought to bear on them. An Idaho man complained, "Some men seem to have a sort of stupid idea that because they pay us the princely sum of $5 a year in support of their local newspaper and get the fullest kind of return on their investment, that it is our bounden duty to puff them 'from July to eternity,' especially if they are before the public in the capacity of office-seekers."[92] A Wyoming man remarked of his first year of publication, "Efforts have not been infrequent, with promises of favor and other reward, to secure the influence of this paper for certain men and measures unacceptable, if not injurious, to the interests of the people of this Territory."[93]

"We are thankful for your patronage and favors, gentlemen," wrote Dryer in the *Oregonian*, "but we deny being your debtor for either, or your right of censorship over our opinions."[94] One of his competitors, the *Oregon Statesman*, carried the slogan, "No favor sways us; no fear shall awe," on its front page, and its publisher's caustic editorials provided evidence of his fearlessness. Newspapermen recognized that, as the San Francisco *Chronicle* put it, "No journal that aspires to wide and permanent influence can afford to yield its independence," and, after profit, influence was, for most of them, what the business was all about.[95]

11

OBLITERATING THE FRONTIER

Frontier publishers scattered to the outermost points of the region; they also concentrated in its developing cities. One historian has suggested that the "primary purpose of the frontier newspaper was to obliterate the frontier," and at least in the major centers, they succeeded.[1] Their triumph was most obvious in San Francisco, but throughout the West towns increasingly supported city-like journalistic conditions. Denver, Portland, Salt Lake City, Los Angeles, and even Walla Walla and Leadville for a time could boast of a newspaper community worthy of their eastern counterparts in terms of diversity and competition.

San Francisco, of course, lead the way and far outdistanced the field. The 1849 gold rush quickly boosted sleepy Yerba Buena into a major seaport and trading center. According to one estimate, California's population grew in 1849 by some 70,000 people, most of whom used San Francisco as their staging center.[2] From two tri-weekly newspapers at the end of 1849, San Francisco journalism went to three dailies by March of 1850, and never looked back. In the next eight years, more than 170 different journals issued forth in the city, exemplifying the great variety of interests characteristic of city journalism. Many lasted only a few issues; some party organs appeared just during campaigns, but names like *California Farmer and Journal of Useful Sciences*, *Satan's Blossom*, and *Pathfinder and Post* testify to the attempts to provide the cosmopolitan community with appealing reading matter.[3]

In 1880, San Francisco, population 233,959, had 21 daily newspapers, placing it third nationally in the ratio of people to newspaper circulation, with 1.63 people for each newspaper copy. The city had more daily newspapers than any other American city except New York (29) and Philadelphia (24). It surpassed Chicago which had twice the population (18 dailies for 503,185 people). A decade later, the number of San Francisco dailies remained at 21, and the city slipped to fourth place nationally but circulation had exceeded the population increase, narrowing the ratio to 1.04 people per copy. New York, with 50 dailies in 1890, issued more newspapers than it had people (.89 people per copy), as Chicago surged into second place with 27, and Philadelphia held onto its 24.

Of San Francisco's 21 dailies, one, the *Alta California*, dated to 1849, four were established in the 1850s, four in the 1860s, and 12 in the 1870s. The latter included a number of daily journals specializing in commercial information and publishing separate morning and evening editions. The city also had 57 weekly newspapers competing for reader attention on topics ranging from religion to sports to literary interests.

A thriving foreign-language press served San Francisco and the West from the gold rush period. Kemble counted 13 newspapers published in French in the mid 1850s, and by 1880 the city had publications in French, Spanish, Chinese, Italian, Danish, German, and Swedish.[4] German-language newspapers were particularly common in major centers around the West; 20 of them were published in 1880.

While San Francisco grew in sophistication, other towns also dealt with the diversity and competitiveness characteristic of city journalism. For some, like Leadville, Colorado, which in 1880 boasted six daily newspapers for a population of 23,563, conditions were temporary, lasting only as long as the mining boom, but for Denver six dailies represented growth that would see the city in 1890 become the West's second city to qualify for listing in the census as a major population center. The same year Sacramento, Portland, and Los Angeles each had four daily newspapers, and Salt Lake City had three. In addition, each city had a number of weeklies—Portland had eleven, Sacramento and Los Angeles seven each, and Denver six, not including the weekly edition the daily newspapers published.

Almost every western daily, regardless of its size, published a weekly that circulated outside the city. The weeklies consisted primarily of material used in the daily editions, with a few up-to-the-minute items from the day of publication. Like the weekly editions of eastern city newspapers that circulated in the West, these weeklies put additional financial pressure on small-town papers who tried to counter their influence by emphasizing local news content.

One kind of weekly seldom produced outside cities was the Sunday paper. A few western papers set Sunday morning for their regular publication time and skipped the Monday edition, but the Sunday paper, as it later developed with special features, belonged to the cities. San Francisco's first Sunday papers started in the 1850s. The *Sunday Dispatch* attempted a few issues in 1851, but the illustrated *Sunday Varieties*, started in 1856, bore a greater resemblance to later papers and had greater success.[5] By 1880, four of the city's major dailies produced Sunday editions. In 1884, the San Francisco *Chronicle*, for example, issued an eight-page Sunday paper with features of the kind common to modern weekend papers.

The 1880 census showed three Sunday papers in Oregon that started in the 1860s and 1870s, but Sunday papers were largely unknown outside San Francisco before the 1880s. The Portland *Oregonian* published a campaign special one Sunday in 1880 and the next year began a regular Sunday edition, an eight-page paper that offered the kind of content that became a staple of the Sunday paper.[6] Seattle readers were greeted with the *Sunday Star* in 1883 which promised to be "light without frivolity, racy without being vulgar," and vowed it would not make the ladies blush.[7] Other larger centers, even Walla Walla, began to experiment with Sunday papers.[8]

Greater competition in the cities also meant more aggressive news gathering. Wealthy city publishers like Frederick MacCrellish of the *Alta California* promoted road, rail, and telegraph routes that would not only bring settlers and business, but also enhance their news acquisition abilities. When steamers arrived at the dock in San Francisco, local papers typically had reporters waiting to collect the news. This was not good enough for the Sacramento *Union* which needed to stay ahead of the San Francisco papers that also circulated in Sacramento, so it sent an agent on a launch to board the steamer as it entered the bay. As soon as the boat docked he rushed to the telegraph office to send whatever news he had been able to gather. The *Union* and the *Alta California* met the overland mail in Placerville where again they used the telegraph to convey the news as quickly as possible.[9] Attempts by the *Alta California* and the *Bulletin* to control San Francisco's news emphasize the value they placed on issuing a timely and exclusive product in competitive conditions.

The scandal-minded reader was more likely to find a publication to his taste in the cities. The *Morning Call* and *Town Talk* in San Francisco printed racy stories to attract a particular clientele, as did another *Town Talk* in Walla Walla, and the *Northwest News* in Portland, which shocked its readers with such headlines as "Mrs. Wiseman Elopes, Goes to Victoria with a Sewing Machine Agent."[10]

Similarly, some city papers accepted advertising other towns might eschew, partly because cities bred more questionable activity interested in purchasing advertising space, partly because the variety of journals allowed a publisher to target his audience. San Francisco's *Town Talk*, for example, looked to the lower classes for its readership and advertised social-disease medicine, cheap auctions, and gold-brick raffles.[11]

Heightened competition in the cities increased publishers' susceptibility to pressure from advertisers and readers. In the 1850s the San Francisco *Herald* completed an agreement for exclusive rights to advertising by city auctioneers. Holding this substantial account, the *Herald* appeared financially secure. However, in 1856 the Vigilance Committee, a group of local businessmen impatient with normal law and order channels, summarily hanged men accused of murdering James King of William, publisher of the *Bulletin*. The *Herald*, perhaps because it had been feuding with the *Bulletin*, condemned the vigilantes' actions, while the *Alta California* and other city papers supported the hanging. Angered by the *Herald*'s effrontery in questioning vigilante authority, 215 merchants signed an advertisement placed in every other San Francisco newspaper warning auctioneers to discontinue their exclusive advertising contract. The *Herald* argued editorially for freedom of speech but opposition was too strong and its financial foundation was destroyed. Meanwhile, the *Alta* came out of the fracas stronger than ever.[12]

Three decades later, the Seattle *Daily Call*, like the *Alta*, found economic benefits in being on the "right" side of a political dispute. After completion of the Northern Pacific Railroad in the 1880s, Pacific Northwest unions perceived a labor threat from the many Chinese who moved into the general job market. The *Call*, started by three young cousins, crusaded to have the Chinese removed from the Seattle area. "The Chinese Must Go!" was repeated in the advertising and news columns of the paper. "The Chinese Must Go. The IXL Store Says So," advertised one merchant. Parades and demonstrations brought a declaration of martial law before some Chinese were evicted and the matter quieted down. Seattle labor supported the *Call* for its efforts on behalf of the white working man, and the newspaper prospered. Its young owners soon sold their publication and went on to other activities.[13]

Bigness also bred strength, and large city papers could tackle problems lesser organs feared to handle. As the San Francisco *Chronicle* grew in power and influence, the deYoung brothers became a major force in San Francisco politics. Their outspoken positions cost Charles deYoung his life in 1880 when one of the *Chronicle*'s editorial foes shot him, but the paper continued to target city graft.[14] While many newspapers accepted bribes from California's railroad barons, publishers of the *Bulletin* and *Examiner* in San Francisco and the Sacramento *Union* challenged their dominance. The papers campaigned, as the *Examiner* said, for railroad safety "at least equal to that of a soldier on the battlefield."[15] The effort eventually cost the *Union* men their newspaper, but the deep pockets of the *Examiner* proved beyond the railroad's control. After young William Randolph Hearst took over the paper, railroad interests found the bribes that had worked so well with other publishers had no effect on the young man with the multimillionaire mother.

The fight for city readers extended to circulation and tended to keep subscription prices somewhat lower than those of the country papers, but papers generally avoided price wars. During heated competition in 1851, the *Alta California* cut its price to a half bit, but one of its competitors, the *Pacific News*, maintained its one-bit price and claimed better circulation growth; the *Pacific News* also published a steamer edition whose 2,000 copies sold like "hotcakes" at two bits.[16] In the 1880s, when eastern newspapers tried to respond to the push by advertisers for higher circulation by reducing subscription rates, Portland was the only western city significantly affected. The *Oregonian* cut its single-copy price to 2 cents, bringing about a brief price war.[17]

San Francisco dominated not only the newspaper business, but the printing industry in general. In 1870 the city had 34 of California's 50 newspapers and 29 of the 32 job shops. The remaining job shops and five of the newspapers were in Sacramento. The high level of competition diluted San Francisco job-printers' income, giving them an average net income of $5,670, well below the state average. Sacramento printers, on the other hand, averaged more than $27,500.

Bigger, wealthier city papers could better take advantage of developing technology. Steam presses and stereotyping arrived first in the cities to meet the demand for printing capacity. By the 1880s, western city papers followed their eastern counterparts in using more illustrations, particularly sketches of famous people to highlight stories. Drawings by editorial cartoonist Thomas Nast—famed as the creator of the Tammany Tiger among other scathing images—appeared in Hearst's *Examiner* in 1889.[18]

City papers also quickly adopted another major development in communication technology, the telephone. The *Deseret News* installed telephones soon after they were introduced in Salt Lake City in 1878; that same year the *Oregonian* was one of the first subscribers in Portland.[19] In 1881 the Los Angeles *Times* made a point of telling readers in its first issue that it was on the local telephone system.[20] An eastern Washington newspaperman was responsible for bringing telephones to his part of the territory. Nevertheless, a fellow publisher was skeptical about the device. "The usefulness of the institution is questionable to us," Spokane publisher Frank M. Dallam wrote, "for it seems rather queer to use a telephone in a place where a small boy can carry a message to any quarter of the business part of the city in two minutes."[21]

The enhanced availability of printing equipment meant that city publishers found it even easier than their country cousins to move from one newspaper venture to another. The concentration of presses in the city allowed a publisher to start a newspaper without having his own equipment; he could rent someone else's facilities or hire the shop to print for him. Or, if he had his own plant, he did not have to move it to find a new, growing market; he had only to think of a new name for his enterprise to get a fresh start.

The Bartlett brothers—Columbus, Julian, and Washington—individually, in concert with one another, or with others, published a series of San Francisco newspapers. Washington transported printing equipment when he moved west from Florida in 1849. His plan to begin the daily *Journal of Commerce* early in 1850 spurred *Alta California* owners to turn their tri-weekly to daily to stay ahead of competition. Bartlett's paper suffered in the May 1850 fire that damaged a number of newspapers; it burned again in June, and finally closed the following February. But the Bartletts' newspaper connections continued. Washington, who edited the *Evening Journal* for a time in 1852, and Julian became editors for the *Daily Evening*

News, started by Columbus with F. W. Pinkham in 1853. Columbus and Washington published the *True Californian* in 1856. Washington later turned to politics and served as mayor of San Francisco and governor of California.[22]

Common Interests

Concentration of newspapermen in cities inevitably led to associations, principally to foster common economic interests. Printers organized in San Francisco in 1850, in Sacramento by 1852, in the Pacific Northwest by 1853, and in Denver by 1860.[23] *Deseret News* printers celebrated their first Typographic Feast in 1852.[24] When the industry was small, distinctions were generally blurred between employee and employer, and most groups initially included printer-publishers; Thornton McElroy attended a printers' convention in Portland while he was publisher of the *Columbian*.[25] As newspapering became more specialized, so, too, their associations: the printers unionized and publishers moved into associations with different kinds of objectives. The journalists were the least organized, sometimes forming social groups, but rarely banding together for economic protection.

Specialization resulted in conflict, each side seeking to protect and strengthen its interests and perceiving the other as a threat. In the early 1850s the *Alta California* accused San Francisco Typographical Society members of failing to acknowledge somewhat depressed economic conditions by accepting a wage cut. When *Alta* owners' efforts to get other publishers to stand behind a cut caught the printers unaware and disorganized, the rate was reduced. The printers in turn developed work rules and reorganized as the San Francisco Typographical Union, so the stubborn *Alta* owners fired all of their union employees and imported eighteen printers from New York City. Local unionists beat up the imported printers who, when they recovered, joined the union. Other publishers failed to give support, so the *Alta* gave in and restored the wage level.[26]

At the same time, printers fought amongst themselves. The SFTU refused to "rat" the *Alta* office—"ratting" was a form of blacklisting used by printers—and the more militant printers formed the Eureka Typographical Union. The Eureka men eventually won out over the first group and gained a national charter in 1854.[27]

Despite occasional successes, early typographical unions found it hard at first to build enough membership to maintain their organizations. San Francisco printers reorganized again in 1859, and Los Angeles Local No. 44 of the National Typographical Union was chartered in 1859 only to succumb in the depression of 1860. As the number of newspapers in the cities increased, however, with accompanying labor needs, the union movement likewise expanded. In the 1860s the San Francisco union grew to 165 members, and chapels organized in Sacramento with about 60 members, in Stockton with about 25.[28]

Unionists became increasingly aggressive and ratted offices that did not meet their demands or tried to use non-union labor. In 1864 printers ratted the offices of the *Argus* and *Daily American Flag* in San Francisco because they were paying printers less than scale.[29] In Denver the typographical union and local publishers compromised on a 10 instead of 20 percent pay cut in 1875, but when the Denver *Tribune* refused to meet the scale, the union ratted the newspaper, pulling a dozen men off the job.[30] It was general union practice to circulate fliers around the country listing ratted offices and blacklisting men who crossed picket lines. In 1873, when the *Territorial Enterprise* fired all ten of its printers and brought in new men from San Francisco, the local union president, referring to one newcomer in particular, said that no local printer would work with "the most notorious 'rat' on the coast."[31] Unionists, concerned about unemployment, also distributed flyers around the country to alert other printers to depressed conditions. An 1878 circular from Denver encouraged the "nomadic manipulator of antimony" to avoid Denver because there were no jobs.[32]

The balance of power between printers and publishers shifted frequently. In Denver where the first typographical union was formed in 1860, publisher John Dailey noted in his diary that the "boys" had "loafed," so he had cut their wages and they had gone out on strike. Three days later, however, he commented that the "boys begin to feel like compromising."[33] California printers called a statewide strike in 1870 when publishers asked them to take a cut in wages, after completion of the transcontinental railroad brought increased competition from the East. The new rates meant about $10 a week less in pay for most printers, but employers' plans to use the railroad to import printers forced the union to give in.[34]

Publishers had their turns capitulating. In 1883 printers struck the morning *Call* and evening *Bulletin* in San Francisco. This time printers wanted a closed shop; when the owners refused, unionists called for a citywide boycott of the newspapers. More than fifty unions supported them, and after a month the owners gave in.[35] In 1885 the Butte *Miner* quickly agreed to a union shop when printers threatened to strike.[36] In 1888 union boycotts hurt the Pasadena *Star* and the San Bernardino *Times*, but labor strife rarely did any permanent damage to either side.[37]

Los Angeles printers, who re-formed into a viable union in the 1870s—the fashionable event of the January 1874 social season was the typographical ball—had similarly checkered success. In 1878, for example, the union protested the failure of the *Daily Star*, a Workingmen's party newspaper, to establish a closed shop. When the *Star* acceded to union demands, the printers ratted the *Daily Commercial* with similar objectives, but lost that effort.[38] In 1884 the union fought successfully to keep boilerplate out of the Los Angeles papers, but the following year had to accept not only boilerplate but also a wage cut.[39]

After Harrison Gray Otis became editor of the Los Angeles *Times* in 1882, the union and the *Times* co-existed uneasily. Otis was unsympathetic toward union printers but the newspaper's economic situation forced him to moderate his animosity until his business was on a surer footing. By 1890 he had sufficient financial security to challenge the union.[40] Although in the meantime the Los Angeles typographical union had become the second largest union in the city with more than 200 members, it was nevertheless weak and susceptible in 1890 to Otis's tactics which included getting the support of a rival union, the Printers' Protective Fraternity. After a two-year strike, during which the PPF sent scabs from Kansas City, Otis agreed to hire union printers, but the union failed to get the closed shop it wanted.[41]

Publishers at small, isolated newspapers had fewer direct union challenges, but the difficulty in attracting labor to some locations had the same effect. The despair some publishers voiced at getting skilled help suggests their willingness to accommodate printers' requests. At the same time, a printer in a remote outpost might well consider his prospects for other employment before walking off the job.

From the earliest days, publishers sought to minimize competition that might impinge on their profits, and they knew that some problems were best solved cooperatively. About sixteen newspapers attended the 1851 California convention at which publishers agreed on wage scales, subscription prices, and rates for job printing.[42] Publishers also attempted to maximize their job-printing profits by cooperative agreements and, when challenged, argued their right to self-protection on the same principle as unionization.

Efforts at rate fixing rarely succeeded, either because not everyone participated at the beginning or because one or more publishers were so hungry for business they could not resist stepping outside the agreement at first opportunity. In the 1870s four Olympia, Washington, publishers agreed to abide by a set of standard prices. They also agreed to take turns bidding on large jobs, a pact with the problem that not all printers were party to the agreement. The publisher of the temperance-oriented *Echo*, Francis Cook, who later started Spokane's first paper, attacked the association as a monopoly and insisted that he would not sacrifice his reputation to join it; there is no indication, however, that he was ever invited.[43]

Employers formed their own associations as early as 1851, although long-lasting, statewide organizations generally waited until the late 1880s. Oregon publishers formed a State Editorial Association in 1878, then regrouped in 1887 to form the Oregon Press Association, the forerunner of the modern Oregon Newspaper Publishers Association.[44] Washington publishers also organized in 1887.[45] Arizona newspapermen tried to form a press club in 1885 and at least thirteen members attended a banquet in Prescott, but it was another five years before a serious association got off the ground.[46] Wyoming organized in 1877, New Mexico in 1880.[47] These were combined social and business groups; publishers and their wives frequently took excursions as guests of the railroad or some other major industry. The third annual meeting of the Washington Press Association in Tacoma included invitations from a land company to visit a lake, railroads for free travel, and a tour company for a harbor ride, as well as free use of the opera house, club rooms, and other amenities.[48] In 1885 an Idaho publisher complained such jaunts were "about what most of them think a press association is organized for, simply to take excursions some where once a year at the expense of some railroad."[49] When the Montana Press Association held its first meeting in Butte in 1885, members received tickets from the Union Pacific and the Northern

Pacific railroads. Copper king William A. Clark, part-owner of the Butte *Miner* and "a sort of one-man host committee," saw to it that the publishers had theater tickets and other hospitality as well.[50]

When not sight-seeing, publishers dealt with matters concerning the operation of their papers, mostly having to do with business, but sometimes with content. Oregonians first met in 1878 to deal with concerns raised by libel and a shooting. Publishers wanted to be able to punish libelers and passed a resolution calling for the press to be held responsible for infringement of private rights.[51] Similarly lofty public objectives accompanied the formation of other state groups. The Montana Press Association, for example, pledged to "elevate its [the press's] tone, purify its expression, enlarge its sphere of usefulness," etc., but the real business of these associations was business. Montana members immediately established committees to keep an eye on the legislature's activities that might affect the press, to watch out for people taking printing business outside the state, and to discourage one printer infringing on the territory of another.[52]

Journalists, the least organized, attempted off and on to form press clubs, and in 1889 the San Francisco Press Club held its first benefit, netting $1,100.[53] In general, writers did not figure prominently in associations except where they served also as editors or publishers.

12

SUCCESS AND FAILURE

Printer Jack Merrick was late with the first issue of his new newspaper, the *Cherry Creek Pioneer*. For a frontier paper, that would normally be par for the course. Getting all the equipment, labor, news, and advertising together for a newspaper often took longer than aspiring publishers anticipated. Weather deluged roads and delayed wagons carrying type and presses. The exchanges failed to arrive. The extra help in the print shop turned out to be no help at all because he drank too much. Anything could hold up a paper, so while frontier residents may have been disappointed, few were surprised when a new paper missed its first deadline. But Merrick wasn't in a typical situation. He was in Cherry Creek—the future Denver—and being late meant he had just lost the race to be the town's pioneer publication.

Merrick reached Denver ahead of the team that planned to publish the *Rocky Mountain News*. He proceeded leisurely to set up his shop, failing to appreciate the urgency of getting his publication under way—until he discovered that bets were being laid among the miners as to whose paper, his or the *News* planned by William Byers, would be first. He hired only two helpers, and although his paper was small format—about 7 by 10 inches—he had to set all of the type before he could concentrate on the printing. Byers and company arrived better equipped and staffed, and they enlisted the aid of a number of townspeople to get the office organized; they also had the foresight to set and print two pages in Omaha.

For all his poor judgment in the first instance, when the great newspaper race concluded, Merrick had the good sense to realize that Denver in 1859 was too small to accommodate two newspapers. He traded his plant to Byers for a $25 grubstake and went prospecting.[1]

Twenty-five dollars, perhaps the best bargain in a printing office on the frontier—but no bargain at all if one couldn't make a living with it. People who wanted to publish newspapers in the West had relatively little difficulty getting started, but survival was another story, one in which failures far outnumbered the successes.

Getting the financing to acquire the necessary equipment was often the easy part of the enterprise. As has been seen, about $1,500 was required to buy a hand press large enough to do a newspaper, perhaps a smaller job-printing press, a few fonts of type, and other necessities. It could be done for less money; some job presses served to print small-format newspapers. But $1,500 allowed a publisher a good start in a small town, even for a modest daily, and this price remained remarkably representative throughout the forty years under review.

From the available figures, we can get an idea of the kinds of calculations a prospective publisher might have made as he contemplated establishing a frontier weekly. Let us assume our publisher, a man in his twenties with some experience with newspapers, has identified a likely town for his enterprise. He wants to be in business for himself and has saved about a thousand dollars toward that end. The chief town booster, delighted at the prospect of a newspaper that will help him sell land, offers assistance, either to provide a lot and help build an office or to find space for the enterprise in an existing building. The booster may also arrange for the additional money needed to purchase equipment and initial stocks of supplies such as ink and paper. Because the publisher knows he will need some funds to pay employees until the money starts rolling in, he borrows a thousand dollars for one year at 1 percent a month.

Labor is the first operating expense he considers. Because he is himself a qualified printer, he is able to manage, at least initially, with the aid of only one other printer. At the going rate of $1 per thousand ems, plus something for the time spent working on the press and some overtime, he will probably have to pay $30 a week. The shop will also need a "devil," an apprentice-level employee, at $12 a week. Labor costs will thus total about $2,700 for a 50-issue year. Given a circulation of 400 to 500, therefore requiring a ream of paper (our printer is expert—he has no waste), plus ink and other materials, he adds another $500 a year. He also has costs related to distribution—postage, express, or carriers—that could add another $1,000. Include a small contingency fund of $300, and expenses total $4,500.[2]

On the revenue side, he can expect $2,000 from 400 subscribers at $5 each a year, assuming he actually collects in advance. In a six-column paper about 15 inches wide by 20 inches long that is 50 percent advertising, he has 240 column inches to sell, and at the flat rate $2 per column inch his advertising income will be $24,960 for the year. The $2 applies only to the first insertion and he will give liberal discounts to long-term advertisers, so let us assume that over the course of the year, allowing for discounts, he averages 75 cents a column inch, or $9,000. Total income from subscriptions and advertising therefore amounts to $11,000. This, less his expenses, leaves him with a net of $6,500.

From this he must pay $1,120 interest and principal on the $1,000 he borrowed to buy his equipment, but his first-year balance sheet still shows more than $5,000 which he can pay himself and call profit, a significant amount considering his initial investment. And this is before he does any job printing.

If, indeed, potential publishers looked at the figures in this way, it is no wonder so many newspapers were started. And sometimes the numbers added up in this promising way. A California publisher wrote his brother that the steamer edition he printed on wrapping paper brought him $650 profit. Four reams of paper cost $32, the press work $16, the composition, $52, and he sold 1,800 copies at 50 cents apiece.[3] Surely the profits were just waiting for an enterprising publisher.

With figures like these one might very well wonder why so many newspapers folded. Certainly, over the years a great deal of money was gambled in unsuccessful newspaper ventures. In Sacramento the *California American* cost its owners about $15,000 in the first six months of its nine-month life.[4] In 1884 George Hearst sought a buyer to take the San Francisco *Examiner* off his hands and stop the $7,000 a month drain.[5] The *Oregonian* estimated that a half million dollars was squandered in Portland in the 1870s and 1880s on unsuccessful newspaper ventures.[6] Typically, as was once said of the Salt Lake City *Tribune*, "there was more exuberance in the editorial office than in the business office."[7] Few publishers made fortunes from their newspapers, although they might make enough to invest profitably in other areas.

Publishers were quick to assure their readers they were not getting rich. The publisher of the *Oregon Statesman*, after calling on his patrons to pay bills that were a year old, said, "These dues are

TABLE 12.1
Net Revenue^a 1890

STATE	TOTAL NET ($)	AVERAGE NET PER NP ($)
Arizona	25,842	1,231
California	1,155,337	3,073
Colorado	449,861	2,829
Idaho	31,508	1,086
Montana	67,800	1,654
Nevada	18,222	1,657
New Mexico	49,866	1,609
Oregon	209,813	1,724
Utah	88,442	4,212
Washington	276,734	2,214
Wyoming	54,922	2,615
WEST	2,409,932	2,547
UNITED STATES	36,575,857	2,958

Source: U.S. Census.
a. Total Product Value less expenses (wages, materials, miscellaneous). Includes all income—newspaper and job printing—reported to the census for all newspapers and periodicals in 1890.

mostly small amounts, and may seem of little importance to individual debtors, but at the aggregate they form a sum which a printing office cannot well do without."[8] An Idaho publisher explained, "The publication of a newspaper is attended with a larger expense than is commonly imagined."[9] Denver readers learned that after seven years of struggle the *Rocky Mountain News* was barely on a paying basis, although in flush times, the paper made a "fair profit."[10] A publisher who said he could not boast of "any favorable pecuniary results," at least could boast that his paper was still alive.[11]

That it lived was the best that could be said for many a newspaper. In 1890, income from advertising, subscriptions, and job printing exceeded basic expenses by only an average of about $2,500 per office (see table 12.1). Given that some newspapers were quite successful, others must have been struggling to account for the modest figure.

We have already noted that the number of failing newspapers more than matched those that succeeded. Newspapers closed for many reasons, some of them purely personal and not directly related to the operation of the newspaper—the need to return to wife and family in the eastern states, health, or other, better business opportunities. In addition, the failure rate is somewhat inflated by inclusion in directories of publications never intended as long-term enterprises. Campaign newspapers, for example, served their political purposes and their publishers moved on to other activities after the election, but the papers sometimes are listed in directories as short-lived newspapers and are considered "failed."

Some newspapers closed prematurely because publishers established them as personal organs and paid little attention to business, concentrating their efforts on quarrels or other objectives. Eldridge Morse in Snohomish, Washington, and Edward Clayson in Seabeck, Washington, cared more about content than monetary remuneration. Morse pursued literary inclinations, Clayson attacked local sawmill owners for restricting his hotel business. Neither succeeded, although both developed a taste for journalism and later enaged in other similarly unsuccessful ventures.[12] In San Francisco, Benjamin R. Buckelew, annoyed when the *Alta California* would not praise him in the manner he thought he deserved, started the *Public Balance*. He subsequently quarreled with an associate who started a second *Public Balance*. Both newspapers sold for 25 cents a week; both died in less than a year. The exercise is said to have cost Buckelew $30,000; the losses of his rivals were not recorded.[13]

Aside from idiosyncratic reasons for ceasing publication, explanations for the demise of most western newspapers fall into three major categories: location, management, and credit. Clearly these factors are not mutually exclusive, but looking at them individually helps define the problems the publisher faced.

Location

Even though the frontier publisher generally took time to examine prospective locations and to make a carefully considered choice of where to establish his newspaper, he frequently erred. Sometimes the population simply moved on when an ore vein, a railroad company, or local politicians failed to live up to expectations. Bellingham Bay, Washington, anticipated becoming a major mining center until the Canadians insisted all prospectors bound for the Fraser River mines get a permit issued only from Vancouver Island; Kalama, Washington, prepared to grow as a railroad hub until the Northern Pacific decided to concentrate its facilities at Tacoma; the Arizona Territory capital shifted between Prescott and Tucson and back, leaving those towns variously in economic quandaries. Such circumstances undercut the best of plans. A newspaperman purchased the Corinne, Utah, *Daily Reporter* at a time when Corinne residents were moving to Salt Lake City. When he committed suicide, other publishers attributed it to financial problems.[14]

Even when the population did not desert towns like Bellingham or Kalama or Prescott, the reduction in business activity often left residents too poor to pay for advertising and subscriptions. More than one publisher reportedly turned in his printer's rule for a saloon keeper's apron: "Of twenty men, nineteen patronize the saloon and one the newspaper, and I am going with the crowd."[15] In small Utah towns, Mormon farmers and businessmen were too busy scraping a subsistence and supporting their church to also support a newspaper, no matter that it had the backing of the church. Even the *Deseret News* in the Utah metropolis, Salt Lake City, struggled because its audience was preoccupied with survival. The newspaper record of New Mexico, too, reflects the territory's relative poverty.

Competition was another consideration in respect of location; one that, curiously enough, publishers often seemed to ignore. We may wonder why a publisher would elect to start a daily newspaper in a relatively small town like Virginia City, Nevada, which already had four dailies, or in Los Angeles which had three when the Los Angeles *Times* began. In some instances, the decision to start the paper had clear political underpinnings. A Democratic campaign daily in Virginia City, Nevada, in 1863, was, for a few months, daily number four, but the only Democratic journal; in contrast, a year later the Republican *Washoe Herald* joined three other Republican-leaning dailies.[16]

The *Montana Post* misjudged the market's capacity when it moved from Virginia City, Montana, to join two other dailies in Helena. When the *Post* closed after about a year, the Helena *Herald* commented, "The truth is . . . two daily newspapers can barely maintain themselves here. The third is the feather that breaks the camel's back."[17] In Salt Lake City, the Salt Lake City *Democrat* tested its mettle against five other dailies in 1885.[18] A writer expressed concern about the "mania of starting new newspapers" and called it "mistaken enterprise."[19]

One explanation for publishers' optimistic market appraisals lies in the technological capacity common to western papers at the time.

Those using a hand press had difficulty producing more than about 500 copies a day, and some towns clearly had greater potential for circulation. A publisher could not simply speed up his press to increase production; he essentially had to double his operation, in terms of both equipment and personnel. He could install a steam press, of course, but in most cases this meant an increase in capacity far beyond his needs and an expenditure well beyond his means. Consequently, most publishers resigned themselves to competition and even welcomed it. When the *Rocky Mountain Star* started in Cheyenne, the *Leader* said of its "twinkle, twinkle" contemporary, "It proposes to 'go for' the interests of Cheyenne. That's all right! Go it!"[20]

Where steam was viable, publishers had a powerful tool against competition. Newspapermen thought Virginia City offered a large enough market in the 1860s that they repeatedly entered into competition with the steam-printed *Territorial Enterprise* but rival papers rarely published more than a few months. When the Provo, Utah, *Enquirer* went to daily publication in 1889, it warned that its steam presses would make competition futile.[21]

Incurable optimism and confidence in his ability to produce a better, more desirable newspaper than the existing contingent also clouded publishers' judgment, leading them into unwise competition. Of course, they were not always wrong. The Los Angeles *Times* has outlived all its competitors and has born out the prediction of a Santa Barbara contemporary that it would become a "fortune to its owner."[22]

Management

Once in business, management policies, or lack thereof, could quickly scuttle a paper. Probably most detrimental was the simple failure to collect what was due from subscribers, advertisers, or job-printing patrons. Publishers too often failed to enforce the "invariably in advance" statements that accompanied the publication of subscription rates. Like modern publishers who offer cheap subscriptions to attract readers, frontier newspapermen knew that they had to maintain a good subscriber count in order to attract advertisers, but in the process of accommodating delinquent readers, some newspapers compiled hefty lists of accounts payable.

The *Deseret News* at one point claimed it was owed some $51,000, while a Walla Walla newspaper told readers it had $2,800 in subscriptions outstanding.[23] The *Idaho Avalanche* reproached its neighbors: "Within a stone's throw, almost, of the spot where this paper is published, we can count up money enough owing us to run this establishment for one year."[24] The *Rio Virgin Times* in southern Utah carried subscribers for six months or so, but when residents experienced a good harvest, the publisher made it clear that he expected them to pay their newspaper bills.[25] Eighty to 90 percent of subscribers in New Mexico were delinquent at any given time.[26]

Some publishers simply took local circumstances, such as the general lack of cash, into account when they failed to insist on payment; others, however, stuck their heads into the financial sand. Dryer at the *Oregonian* took people at their word when they said they had paid their bills; he finally hired a business manager to rescue his accounts. A Washington publisher twice pulled the *Columbia Chronicle* from the "financial morass" into which it had fallen as a result of incompetent management.[27] When E. A. Bentley took over the *Arizona Miner* in 1866, he took immediate measures to tighten fiscal policies, principally by instituting a cash-only system.[28] The Ferndale, California, *Enterprise* was likewise resuscitated when a physician purchased it and reorganized the business, "the most important feature being the collection of bills the first of each month, by a regular collector."[29]

New owners Joseph Goodman and Denis McCarthy put the struggling *Territorial Enterprise* on a cash basis. According to *Enterprise* lore, the proprietors did not keep any books but "conducted their business strictly on a cash basis and carried their dividends home in water buckets at the close of each week."[30] The competent business manager they soon hired to save themselves from their own free-spending ways doubtless took exception to their bucket brand of bookkeeping but not to the cash-only policy.

Poor managers failed to budget adequately and to control expenses. Our overly simple example suggests expenses to operate a weekly would run about $4,500 a year, assuming the publisher actively participated in the operation. Many printer-publishers overestimated their personal capacity for work. If help was unavailable or unaffordable, the publisher's health suffered; if he hired additional labor, his profits disappeared. Not long before he closed his paper, an Idaho publisher complained: "We are a slave to our business and our health has been seriously impaired in a struggle to keep this journal in existence."[31]

Pressures created by competition, or the threat thereof, led publishers into expenses they may not have anticipated when they figured their budgets. Enlargement of the paper, replacement of worn-out type, legal fees in case of libel suits, and payment for telegraph or express news services could cut into otherwise well-laid financial plans. In the 1870s, expenses at the Los Angeles *Express* amounted to as much as $1,600 a month. Despite good circulation, after only six months the publisher was forced to turn the assets over to creditors.[32] A small daily in Olympia recorded expenses four times its revenue.[33]

Credit

Problems of poor location and weak management came to a head when a publisher found himself overextended and deeply in debt. The frontier economy rested on barter and credit, but while barter might ensure that a publisher had food on his table, the day of reckoning always arrived for credit. Creditors demand cash, not pumpkins. Whether a publisher's difficulties originated from circumstances or incompetence, or more likely a combination of the two, his basic problem was commonly one of an inadequate cash flow to service his debt.

Sometimes a publisher could sell the bartered payments to get cash; the *Deseret News* suggested that a bushel of wheat was "very convenient change"[34] that could be sold or converted to cattle which could be driven, rather than hauled, to market. In Oregon for a time, wheat was legal tender for debts, and one paper offered to accept $4 a year in currency or wheat, $3 in coin.[35] But publishers still needed ready cash.

A publisher first incurred debt for the purchase of his plant—press, type, and other materials. As we have seen, boosters or politicians sometimes put up the money, and the publisher then "leased" the materials. These leases often were lease-purchase arrangements; if the paper succeeded, the publisher could buy out his backers. In other cases, the publisher borrowed the money personally. In still others, the publisher bought his equipment on credit, either from a supplier or another publisher, agreeing to a conditional sales contract or chattel mortgage which allowed the seller to retain title until the equipment was paid for. Regardless, the publisher was expected to make payments out of his revenue, and if he could not, he lost his press.

Owners of the *Californian* wanted to sell to Edward Kemble because "their notes were rapidly maturing" on the money they owed. Eventually they simply departed for Hawaii and left Kemble with both the plant and the debts.[36] The Los Angeles *Star* started in 1851, and as of 1858 a correspondent could write that it "asks no favors, and pays expenses easily."[37] Indeed, the *Star* survived longer than many western newspapers, but when it closed in 1873, the publishers said:

> The current depression, the low rates of advertising, together with the accumulation of private debts, have brought about this result. We shall see that the Star property is equally divided among creditors, and expect they will receive at least seventy-five cents on the dollar.
>
> Eighteen months ago, the Star was purchased for $5,000. Three thousand dollars of this amount have been paid by us on account. We abandon the hope of recovery of even part of this sum.[38]

Edward Niles borrowed $2,500 to start the *Carson Daily Times* in Nevada in 1880. During the year in which he operated, he paid $1,200 on material, including freight, and $4,000 for labor. Nervous creditors still closed in, "notwithstanding the fact that they were fully protected and had been paid nearly one-half of the value of the property."[39] In 1856 creditors of the *Southern Californian* foreclosed on an $8,500 mortgage.[40] Credit was such a way of life that San Francisco press and type dealers were surprised when Frank Leach paid $1,400 cash for materials to start the Vallejo *Chronicle*.[41]

The problems of credit are particularly evident in the story of Alf Doten, Comstock journalist and publisher of the Gold Hill *News* for seven years. Doten, who worked for the *Territorial Enterprise* and other local newspapers, joined the *News* in 1867. When its owner died in 1872, Doten scraped together the $10,000 needed to buy the paper, borrowing $7,000 from future senator William Sharon, then manager of the California Bank in Virginia City, and raising the remainder from several lesser sources. On March 9, 1872, he recorded in his diary, "Counted out $10,000 in golden 'twenties'—The proper documents were passed, and I am now editor and proprietor of the Gold Hill News—Rough on me the last day or two, you bet."[42]

Initially prosperous, Doten confided to his diary on January 1, 1875, "Have cleared my property & insured it, have a wife and baby, and am worth $20,000 or more—Am much better fixed than I ever was before in my life."[43] He bought a new press and expanded the paper, but he could not resist speculating on mining stocks and spent much of his time trying to borrow money while watching share prices drop. In 1879, Western Union cut off telegraph service to the *News* for nonpayment of fees, and Doten fell so far behind in wages to his printers that he had to borrow $620 to pay them. Finally, to satisfy his creditors he found a buyer for half interest in the paper, but soon was forced to sell the other half interest as well, and found himself managing editor instead of proprietor.[44]

Before long, he was out of the *News* entirely. He became editor of the *Reese River Reveille* in Austin, but two years later, after ownership changes, he was again unemployed, limited to sending correspondence from Austin to the *Territorial Enterprise*.[45] He turned down one job offer because of inadequate pay; he was holding out for $40 a month.[46] He also rejected an opportunity to become a notary public in Austin. He calculated it would cost him $20 for the seal and commission, and income would be only $2.50 a month, taking him eight months to break even.[47] By 1885 he was back doing locals for the *Territorial Enterprise*, a job he had held twenty years earlier.

Discounting of notes, greenbacks, warrants, and other forms of money aggravated the credit problem and played havoc with a publisher's financial well-being. For every dollar he charged and expected to get, the publisher might find that he actually received much less. The *Owyhee Avalanche* listed its subscription rates in greenbacks at par, but they were trading at only 72 cents on the dollar.[48] When Doten was paid for publishing federal laws in 1874, he received $546 in greenbacks which were accepted by the bank at 89.5 cents on the dollar.[49] But Doten was fortunate in losing only 10 percent on the transaction. California's Jonas Winchester found accepting government payments particularly costly.

In 1850 Winchester brimmed with enthusiasm at prospects for profiting from newspapering and the public printing. His initial calculations had led him to expect even greater gains than those forecast in our modest hypothetical budget. He estimated profits at the *Pacific News*, in which he eventually bought a share, at $10,000 a month; advertising yielded more than $500 a day, and job work paid the office expenses of $1,200 a week.[50] Buying into the business placed him deeply in debt and it was, perhaps, as well that the newspaper

was destroyed by fire in September 1850. Winchester lost his investment but as he was considered bankrupt, he was not liable for
the substantial debt he had accumulated.[51] He revived the *News* and
persisted a few months until he anticipated its imminent collapse.
Winchester then sold the paper and moved to San Jose to publish a
Democratic organ, with the promise of lucrative public-printing contracts that would make his fortune. He received the contracts and
did the printing, but the California government was slow to pay and
issued warrants instead of cash. At one point, Winchester estimated
that he had done $25,000 worth of government printing and had
received nothing.[52] Another time, ruefully acknowledging that the
public printing had not paid expenses, he sold $16,000 worth of state
warrants for 40 cents on the dollar, to meet his own notes. Overall, he
calculated that $125,000 in state printing should have brought him
$60,000 in profit; in the end he failed even to cover costs.[53]

Discounted warrants and currency hurt Winchester, Doten, and
other publishers, but those who had cash available to buy and the
fortitude to speculate could profit. Warrants, notes, and greenbacks
traded like stocks and bonds, and buyers could hold them until—
and if—the price went up. In 1878 Clarence Bagley wrote his father,
"The first spare hour I have to make out my bills I can have [$]1,000
or [$]1,200 currency due me from the Territory and then [you] shall
have all you may want to buy warrants with . . . Get those printing
office warrants as soon as possible."[54]

The Bagleys, frugal frontiersmen, were creditors more often than
debtors. While Clarence was running the *Puget Sound Courier*, he
and his father also held an interest in a Seattle printing office, as
well as in other businesses.[55]

Cutting Costs

These kinds of problems led publishers to look for ways to reduce
operating expenses. Labor being a major cost, they appreciated regular advertisers who took advantage of the substantial discounts
gained by letting their advertisements stand for months. This meant
space that did not need the compositor's attention each issue and
left him or her free to do other things such as job printing. Sometimes other kinds of content ran repeatedly. The *Oregon Statesman*

published the "Law of Newspapers" frequently in the early 1850s, no doubt to fill space as well as to remind subscribers of their obligations, and the Sacramento *Union* repeated a number of stories in its early issues. Surprisingly, these practices did not seem to hurt the newspapers with their subscribers. The *Union*, for example, gathered enough early support to become one of the leading newspapers in California in spite of its repetitive content. Even so, much of the *Union*'s survival stemmed from the fact that its proprietors were all printers and they therefore needed little outside help.

Family involvement improved chances of success as well, because it cut costs, how much so became obvious when a child died. Charles Prosch of the *Puget Sound Herald* lamented the death of his 14-year-old son in the context of the newspaper business: "It is, or should be known to nearly all our readers that the continued publication of the Herald depends upon the costless labor of our children, formerly three in number—now, alas! reduced to two—aged respectively, ten, twelve and fourteen years."[56]

We have also seen how weeklies, in particular, but also some dailies, reduced news-gathering costs by "borrowing" telegraph news from their more affluent cohorts, and how the use of patent 'sides cut labor costs, and excess plant and labor capacity was put to work printing other publications. Collusion and price fixing, for example in San Francisco and Sacramento in 1851 and Olympia in the 1870s, also helped control prices.

In addition, arrangements similar to twentieth-century joint operating agreements helped frontier publishers economize. Two Olympia publishers combined parts of their respective enterprises. "I expect I shall move into [John Miller] Murphy's building," Clarence Bagley wrote his father. "Consolidate our job offices, but keep papers separate. Use all matters possible in common, and see prospects for the future."[57] In central Washington, Legh R. Freeman, of press-on-wheels renown, trying to minimize competition, worked out a co-operative agreement with Charles M. Holton, owner of the *Record*, one of Yakima's two newspapers. The two men pooled their equipment, issued stock in the Capital Publishing Company, and published the *Washington Farmer*. When the agreement collapsed, Holton took back his equipment and resumed publishing his own newspaper.[58]

Local boosters who funded a newspaper sometimes also provided a source of income to fall back on. The booster who lured Charles

Prosch to Steilacoom, Washington, promised the newspaperman would not want for necessities for himself or his family for the first year.[59] Merchants who lent money for the start of the Helena *Herald* also made cash donations to help keep the paper alive for its first six months.[60] When times were difficult for newspapers, however, boosters usually had their own economic problems and maintenance of a newspaper could easily drop on their list of priorities. Dryer was annoyed when Puget Sound merchants failed to support the *Columbian*, a Yakima publisher had difficulty collecting what he said was due him from boosters, and in Idaho, Alonzo Leland suggested promises of support for his Lewiston *Radiator* were not being fulfilled.[61]

Sometimes publishers sought to ensure survival by moving their newspapers to towns with more potential, an action somewhat different from closing the paper and starting somewhere else. When they moved, they generally kept the same name and continued the volume and number of the paper. The *Territorial Enterprise* started in Genoa and moved to Carson City before settling in Virginia City. Threat of competition led publishers of the Como, Nevada, *Sentinel* to discover they had made a mistake in locating in Como; they rectified their error with a quick move to nearby Dayton, the county seat.[62] The *Bellingham Bay Mail* started in Whatcom and moved to LaConner where prospects were better.[63] *Sweetwater Mines* was published at Fort Bridger, South Pass City, Bryan, and again at South Pass City, as its publisher tried to find a niche in its seventeen-month existence.[64]

In 1869 the publisher of the *Kern County Courier*, contemplating a move from Havilah, California, to Bakersfield, told his readers that he wanted to give "the citizens of this place an opportunity to make some arrangements for its [the newspaper's] retention if they so desire; but unless something is done by the citizens here we intend to box it up and remove it. We have given this camp a fair trial, and are satisfied that *we* cannot sustain a paper here with credit to the people or profit to ourself."[65] The citizens did nothing, so the *Courier* moved—without missing an issue.[66]

One publisher moved when his competitor paid him to do so. The Sacramento *Transcript and Times* called Vincent E. Geiger and Benjamin F. Washington "interlopers" when they started the *State Journal* in 1852 and said the town was not big enough for both Democratic newspapers. *Transcript and Times* publisher George Fitch gave the choice of who moved to Geiger and his partner. When they chose to stay in Sacramento, Fitch moved to San Francisco, taking with him a farewell gift of $3,000 from Geiger and Company.[67]

Valuable Properties

The shaky financial underpinnings of most frontier newspapers led a county historian to comment, in 1882, about the La Porte, California, *Mountain Messenger*: "The ground on which the building stands is very rich in gold, which gives the Messenger an advantage not often had by newspapers, of having a solid basis upon which to do business."[68] To be sure, most papers were undercapitalized. The frequent changes of ownership of frontier newspapers sometimes amounted to little more than the publisher turning his plant back to the mortgage holder, or to one of his employees to whom he owed wages. But not all frontier newspapers were bottomless pits into which money was tossed. A few were true survivors, and others were, at least for a time, perceived as valuable properties.

In 1850, the year-old *Alta California* was highly profitable. Receipts were estimated at $15,000 a month, its assistant editor earned $6,000 a year, and its building was valued at $30,000; one partner made enough from the business to buy out another's one-third interest for $25,000. Then fire destroyed the office, and although the *Alta* immediately resumed publishing, it never fully recovered is preeminence in the San Francisco market.[69] In the succeeding decade, the paper changed hands several times, once at auction for $13,500, another time for $8,000, six months later for $10,000.[70] As Winchester reported, the *Pacific News* was another profitable early San Francisco newspaper. Within months of its establishment, one of the partners sold his one-third share for $30,000, but such prosperity was short-lived and the *News* soon closed.[71] When the first daily in Sacramento, the *Placer Times*, changed hands in 1850, it sold for $16,000.[72] The Sacramento *Transcript* started April 1, 1850; that summer several one-fifth interests changed hands for $5,000, one for $10,000.[73] The following year the two papers merged, and in 1852 the combined *Times* and *Transcript* sold for $30,000.[74] In San Francisco, until it got on the wrong side of the Vigilance Committee in the mid-1850s, the *California Chronicle* was said to have been worth $40,000 to $50,000.[75] The *Daily Dramatic Chronicle*'s deYoungs found their small theater giveaway so successful they turned it into a general circulation morning daily without having to borrow.[76]

After four years as publisher of the San Diego *Herald*, John Judson Ames claimed he had been "successful beyond our most ardent hopes."[77] Unfortunately, San Diego's economy declined in the late 1850s, taking the *Herald* with it. Ames moved his press to San Bernardino where he soon turned it over to a creditor in payment of his debts.[78]

When Frank Leach and a partner started the Napa *Daily Reporter* in the 1860s, the venture immediately paid its way, earning the two young men about $30 a week each in profit.[79] Their Vallejo *Chronicle* was similarly successful. After two years, Leach bought out his partner, and his first month as sole owner brought him $300 above expenses. He soon redeemed his note, "with no little feeling of pride and satisfaction."[80] Arizonian John Wasson said he had consistently made a profit and had paid for all improvements without borrowing.[81] The Los Angeles *Times* claimed to have made a profit from its inaugural issue.[82]

The publisher of the Carson City *Daily Appeal* in Nevada in 1865 saluted his readers and said that, because he wanted to avoid the mistakes made by those who had started dailies in the past, he was starting small so he could build.[83] The strategy worked; the *Appeal* still publishes today. Another longtime survivor, the San Francisco *Call*, started in 1856 with expenses estimated at $700 to $800 a month; on its 25th anniversary, its labor bill alone was $23,000 a month.[84] Like the *Appeal*, the Los Angeles *Times*, the Seattle *Post-Intelligencer*, the Salt Lake *Tribune*, and the *Rocky Mountain News*, most western-city newspapers today have endured from the frontier period.

Rocky Mountain News publisher William Byers claimed that a newspaper was difficult to kill, even when it was losing money. "There is a reason for this," said Byers. "The eyes of all the community are upon its proprietor. Should he fail, everybody knows his weakness, and this fact stimulates him to every sacrifice and exertion."[85]

Nevertheless, most frontier publishers lacked Byers' ego and determination. For them, wealth remained a dream, one fringed by the knowledge that all around them, papers were sprouting and, almost as quickly, dying. Aware that theirs might well be next, publishers honored their failing colleagues with sympathetic obituaries and eulogies. The Georgetown, Colorado, *Miner* said good-bye to the *Western Mountaineer* of Golden:

> Mountaineer, farewell! May no hard knocks attend your spirit pilgrimage to the land where the shades of defunct newspapers do congregate, but may the Western glories of the departing sun light you through the dark valley. . . . Alas—that one so gifted should die this early. Was there no balm in Golden City to save thee?[86]

NOTES

Preface

1. William Ames and Dwight Teeter, "Politics, Economics, and the Mass Media" in *Mass Media and the National Experience*, eds. Ronald T. Farrar and John D. Stevens (New York: Harper and Row, 1971), 39.

2. Isaiah Thomas, *The History of Printing in America* (New York: Weathervane Books, 1970; originally published in 1810); Alfred McClung Lee, *The Daily Newspaper in America* (New York: Macmillan Company, 1937).

3. *ANPA Facts About Newspapers '90* (Washington, D.C.: American Newspaper Publishers Association, August 1990).

4. Sidney Warren, *Farthest Frontier: The Pacific Northwest* (Port Washington, New York: Kennikat Press, 1970; originally published in 1949), 329.

5. Lawrence H. Larsen, *The Urban West at the End of the Frontier* (Lawrence, Kansas: The Regents Press of Kansas, 1978), 19.

6. Geoffrey Blainey, *The Tyranny of Distance* (Melbourne, Australia: Sun Books, 1966).

7. Michael P. Malone, "Beyond the Last Frontier: Toward a New Approach to Western History," *Western Historical Quarterly* 20 (November 1989): 417.

8. *Ibid.*

9. William Cronin, "Revisiting the Vanishing Frontier: The Legacy of Frederick Jackson Turner," *Western Historical Quarterly* 18 (April 1987): 173.

10. Arlington Russell Mortensen agrees that the *Deseret News* had "all the appearance and aspirations of a regular newspaper." "The *Deseret News* and Utah, 1850–1867" (Ph.D. dissertation, University of California, Los Angeles, 1949), ii. A considerable amount of useful economic information is available about the *Deseret News*.

11. *El Crepuscula de la Libertad*, the "Dawn of Liberty," was published briefly in Santa Fe in 1834, and there were at least two other attempts at newspapers in New Mexico prior to 1846. See Felix Gutierrez, "Spanish-Language Media in America, Background, Resources, History," *Journalism History* 4 (Summer 1977): 38. Handwritten newspapers also appeared occasionally before 1846. Bernard De Voto, *The Year of Decision, 1846* (Boston: Houghton Mifflin Co., 1942).

12. Frederick Jackson Turner, *The Frontier in American History* (New York: Holt, Rinehart and Winston, 1920).

13. Sherilyn Cox Bennion, *Equal to the Occasion: Women Editors of the Nineteenth-Century West* (Reno: University of Nevada Press, 1990).

14. Ames and Teeter, "Politics, Economics, and the Mass Media," 39.

Chapter 1: The Newspaper Frontier

1. Gold Hill, Nevada, *News*, 13 October 1863.

2. Richard Kielbowicz, *News in the Mail: The Press, Post Office, and Public Information, 1700–1860s* (Westport, Connecticut: Greenwood Press, 1989), 99.

3. Frederic Hudson, *Journalism in the United States From 1690 to 1872* (New York: Harper and Brothers, 1873; Scholarly Press reprint, 1968), 593.

4. Ella Sterling Cummins, *The Story of the Files: A Review of California Writers and Literature* (San Francisco: Co-operative Printing Co., 1893), 79.

5. Quoted in Hudson, 593–594.

6. *Wasatch Wave* (Heber, Utah), 30 March 1889, quoted in J. Cecil Alter, *Early Utah Journalism* (Westport, Connecticut: Greenwood Press, 1970; originally published in 1938), 80–81.

7. *Owyhee Avalanche* (Silver City, Idaho), 4 January 1873.

8. Earl Pomeroy, *The Pacific Slope* (Seattle: University of Washington Press, 1973; originally published in 1965), 40.

9. *Ibid.*

10. Robert L. Perkin, *The First Hundred Years: An Informal History of Denver and the Rocky Mountain News* (Garden City, New York: Doubleday & Company, Inc., 1959), 79.

11. Percival R. Jeffcott, *Nooksack Tales and Trails* (Ferndale, Washington: Sedro-Woolley *Courier-Times*, 1949), 106.

12. Richard C. Wade, *The Urban Frontier: The Rise of Western Cities, 1790–1830* (Cambridge: Harvard University Press, 1959), 130.

13. Louis B. Wright, *Culture on the Moving Frontier* (Bloomington, Indiana: Indiana University Press, 1966), 237. Wright says it was THE most important connection.

14. *Silver Reef Echo* (Utah), 24 February 1877, quoted in Alter, *Early Utah Journalism*, 246.

15. Alter, *Early Utah Journalism*, has re-created a number of newspapers solely on the basis of comments by their contemporaries.

16. Richard E. Lingenfelter and Karen Rix Gash, *The Newspapers of Nevada: A History & Bibliography, 1854–1979* (Reno: University of Nevada Press, 1984), 253–269; I omitted from my count the *Orphans' Appeal*, a paper issued in November each of several years as part of a fund-raiser, but theatrical and foreign language papers are included in the total.

17. Any count of newspapers over time is fraught with difficulty because of name and ownership changes, hence the lack of precision. Washington Territory figures between censuses are from Barbara Cloud, "Start the Presses: The Birth of Journalism in Washington Territory" (Ph.D. dissertation, Uni-

versity of Washington, 1979) and Marlene Mitchell, "Washington Newspapers: Territorial and State, a Bibliography and Checklist" (M.A. thesis, University of Washington, 1964).

18. Lucius Beebe, *Comstock Commotion* (Stanford, California: Stanford University Press, 1954), 3.

19. Unless otherwise cited, statistics used in this study are from the published United States Census. Particular attention is given to the 1880 census, the first to include a special report on the newspaper industry, and to the 1890 census which had similarly extensive coverage of the industry. County rather than city figures are used because that is the unit for which most data are available. However, it should be noted that census data are not infallible. Formation of new counties during this rapidly expanding period creates problems in tracing changes. Information is also dependent on what is reported; not all newspapers provided data.

20. Edward C. Kemble, *A History of California Newspapers, 1846–1858*, ed. Helen Harding Bretnor (Los Gatos, California: The Talisman Press, 1962; reprinted from Sacramento *Union*, 25 December 1858), 13, 64, 81.

21. George S. Turnbull, *History of Oregon Newspapers* (Portland: Binfords & Mort, 1939), 56.

22. Charles Prosch, *Reminiscences of Washington Territory* (Seattle: 1904), 8.

23. Bausman quoted in Lottie Roeder Roth, ed., *History of Whatcom County*, 2 vols. (Chicago: Pioneer Historical Publishing Co., 1926), 1:94.

24. Jeffcott, *Nooksack Tales and Trails*, 121.

25. Portland *Oregonian*, 10 July, 17 July 1852.

26. Perkin, *The First Hundred Years*, 82–83.

27. *Washington Gazette*, 15 August 1863. When Watson went ahead with the paper he called it the *Seattle Gazette*.

28. S. N. D. North, *History and Present Condition of the Periodical Press of the United States*, vol. 8 of Tenth U.S. Census, 1880 (Washington, D.C.: Government Printing Office, 1884), 65.

29. Allan Nevins, *Saturday Review of Literature* 32, 14 May 1949, 52.

30. *Placer Times* (Sacramento), 19 May 1849.

31. Cheyenne *Leader*, 19 September 1867; Reno *Daily Record*, 5 August 1878; Chehalis, Washington, *Bee*, 19 October 1888.

32. Gold Hill *News*, 13 October 1863.

33. Daniel Boorstin, *The Americans: The National Experience* (New York: Vantage Books, 1965), 125.

34. Butte, Montana, *Miner*, 1 June 1876.

35. Frank A. Leach, *Recollections of a Newspaper Man: A Record of Life and Events in California* (San Francisco: Samuel Levinson, 1917), 122.

36. Barbara Cloud, "Establishing the Frontier Newspaper: A Study of Eight Western Territories," *Journalism Quarterly* 61 (Winter 1984): 811. Snohomish County had a modest population (1,500) with a large number of non-whites (26 percent, mostly Indians), few farms, and virtually no active industry because logging was in a slump.

37. Cloud, "Start the Presses," 170; James F. Hamilton, "Economic Growth and Entrepreneurs: The Establishment of the First Daily Newspaper in Seven Washington Territory and State Towns" (Paper presented to West Coast Journalism Historians, San Francisco, February 1986), 17.

38. Myron K. Jordan, "The Golden Age of the Press Revisted," paper presented to West Coast Journalism Historians, San Francisco, February 1987, 4; Mitchell, "Washington Newspapers: Territorial and State," *passim.*

39. Agreement between Thomas Jefferson Dryer and Puget Sound merchants, 8 July 1852, Thornton F. McElroy papers, Manuscript Division, University of Washington Libraries; Martin Hardwick Hall, "The Mesilla *Times*, A Journal of Confederate Arizona," *Arizona and the West* 5 (Winter 1963): 337. Secessionist Mesilla remained in New Mexico, however; Kenneth Leonard Robison, "Idaho Territorial Newspapers" (M.S. thesis, University of Oregon, 1966), 19; Los Angeles *Star*, 16 July 1853; Arthur K. Whyte, "History of the Press in San Diego County," in Carl H. Heilbron, *History of San Diego County* (San Diego: San Diego Press Club, 1936), 164.

40. See Alter, *Early Utah Journalism, passim.*

41. Howard Roberts Lamar, *The Far Southwest: 1846–1912* (New York: W. W. Norton & Co., 1970), 167–168.

42. Barbara Cloud, "A Party Press? Not Just Yet! Political Publishing on the Frontier" *Journalism History* 7 (Summer 1980): 73.

43. Snohomish, Washington, *Northern Star*, 15 January 1876.

44. Seabeck, Washington, *Rebel Battery*, October 1878.

45. Battle Mountain *Central Nevadan*, 3 October 1889.

46. *Idaho Avalanche*, 28 September 1878.

Chapter 2: Ink-Stained Entrepreneurs

1. George Adolf Kubler, *A New History of Stereotyping* (New York: J. J. Little & Ives Company, 1941), 108; Alter, *Early Utah Journalism*, 206.

2. Thornton F. McElroy to his wife, Sally, 4 September 1853, McElroy papers; Cummins, *The Story of the Files*, 413.

3. Alfred Doten, *The Journals of Alfred Doten*, ed. Walter Van Tilburg Clark, 3 vols., 2:1245. Six years later, however, Doten had lost everything.

4. Cloud, "Start the Presses," 61–62, 149.

5. *Ibid.*, 61–62; Lingenfelter and Gash, *The Newspapers of Nevada*, 253; Perkin, *The First Hundred Years*, 32.

6. Kemble, *A History of California Newspapers*, 126, 146–147; John Bruce, *Gaudy Century: The Story of San Francisco's Hundred Years of Robust Journalism* (New York: Random House, 1948), 72–73; Julia Norton McCorkle, "A History of Los Angeles Journalism," *Annual Publication of the Historical Society of Southern California* 10 (1915): 27.

7. Kemble, *A History of California Newspapers*, 88–89.

8. Leach, *Recollections of a Newspaper Man*, 260.

9. James G. McCurdy, *By Juan de Fuca's Strait* (Portland: Metropoli-

tan Press, 1937), 149; Edmond S. Meany, *Newspapers of Washington Territory* (Seattle: University of Washington Press, 1923), 13; *Chronicle Dispatch* (Dayton, Washington), 17 April 1958.

10. Editors sometimes mentioned "subscribers" in their columns in reference to people pledging money toward the paper rather than those ordering copies for personal use.

11. Meany, *Newspapers of Washington Territory*, 81; Frank T. Gilbert, *Historic Sketches of Walla Walla, Whitman, Columbia and Garfield Counties, Washington Territory* (Portland: A. G. Walling, 1882), 360.

12. Myron Angel, ed., *History of Nevada*, (Berkeley: Howell-North Books, 1958; reprint of Thompson & West edition, 1881), 293.

13. *History of Placer County, California* (Oakland: Thompson & West, 1882), 300.

14. Perkin, *The First Hundred Years*, 32, 84.

15. Jonas Winchester to his wife, Susan, 15 April 1850 and 15 March 1851, Jonas Winchester papers, Kemble Collection, California Historical Society Library, San Francisco.

16. Dorothy Gile Firebaugh, "The Sacramento *Union*: Voice of California, 1851–1875," *Journalism Quarterly* 30 (Summer 1953): 322.

17. S. H. Newman III, "The Las Vegas *Weekly Mail*," *New Mexico Historical Review* 44 (April 1969): 156.

18. Kemble, *A History of California Newspapers*, 29; agreement between Dryer and merchants, McElroy papers; Lingenfelter and Gash, *The Newspapers of Nevada*, 20; Robison, "Idaho Territorial Newspapers," 196; Elizabeth Keen, "Wyoming Frontier Newspapers: The Newspapermen," *Annals of Wyoming* 34 (April 1962): 64.

19. Cloud, "Start the Presses," 145–146.

20. Chester Barrett Kennedy, "Newspapers of the California Northern Mines, 1850–1860, A Record of Life, Letters and Culture" (Ph.D. dissertation, Stanford University, 1949), 68–70.

21. No more is heard of him after 1861. Kennedy, "Newspapers of the California Northern Mines," 72–74.

22. Angel, *History of Nevada*, 308. Robison, "Idaho Territorial Newspapers," 20, 24, 110; Alter, *Early Utah Journalism*, 57, 335; Lingenfelter and Gash, *The Newspapers of Nevada*, 6, 66, 164, 165, 228.

23. Turnbull, *History of Oregon Newspapers*, 150, 285, 352.

24. Legh Freeman's odyssey has been ably told by Thomas Heuterman, *Movable Type: Biography of Legh R. Freeman* (Ames, Iowa: Iowa State University Press, 1979). See also John A. Lent, "The Press on Wheels: A History of the Frontier Index," *Journal of the West* 10 (October 1971): 662–699.

25. *Rocky Mountain News* (Denver), 17 May 1878; Kennedy, "Newspapers of the California Northern Mines," 79; Rex C. Myers, ed., *Lizzie: The Letters of Elizabeth Chester Fisk, 1864–1893* (Missoula, Montana: Mountain Press Publishing Co., 1989), 156; Murphy's obituary, *Post-Intelligencer*, Seattle, 21 December 1916.

26. William B. Rice, *The Los Angeles Star, 1851–1864: The Beginnings*

of Journalism in Southern California (Berkeley: University of California Press, 1947), 13–14.

27. Kemble, *A History of California Newspapers*, 324; Roth, *History of Whatcom County*, 1:573.

28. McElroy to his mother, May 1850, McElroy papers.

29. Kemble, *A History of California Newspapers*, 68–70.

30. Murphy's obituary, Seattle *Post-Intelligencer*, 21 December 1916.

31. Wilbur Fisk Stone, ed., *History of Colorado*, 4 vols. (Chicago: S. J. Clarke Publishing Co., 1918): 1:810.

32. Pat M. Ryan, "Trail-Blazer of Civilization: John P. Clum's Tucson and Tombstone Years," *Journal of Arizona History* 6 (Summer 1965): 53; Don Schellie, *The Tucson Citizen: A Century of Arizona Journalism* (Tucson, Arizona: Tucson Daily Citizen, 1970), 25.

33. Cloud, "Start the Presses," 148.

34. Barron Beshoar, "The Strife and Struggle of a Newspaper in the Old West," *American West* 10 (September 1973): 46.

35. Alter, *Early Utah Journalism*, 164.

36. James Bryce, *Reflections on American Institutions* (Greenwich, Connecticut: Fawcett Publications, 1961, from *The American Commonwealth*, 1893): 228.

37. Clarence B. Bagley, *History of Seattle*, 3 vols. (Chicago, 1916), II, 665; I, 293–294; Orange Jacobs, *Memoirs of Orange Jacobs* (Seattle, 1908), 225–227; *Puget Sound Semi-Weekly*, Seattle, 5 April 1866; *Puget Sound Daily*, 23 April 1866; *Puget Sound Weekly*, 30 April, 21 May 1866.

38. *Puget Sound Weekly Gazette*, 25 March, 10 June 1867; *Weekly Intelligencer* (Seattle), 5 August 1867.

39. *Territorial Dispatch and Alaska Times*, 22 May, 14 August 1871.

40. See Barbara Cloud, "Laura Hall Peters, Pursuing the Myth of Equality," *Pacific Northwest Quarterly* 74 (January 1983): 28–36.

41. William Farrand Prosser, *A History of the Puget Sound Country*, 2 vols. (New York: The Lewis Publishing Co., 1903), 1:419–420; Gilbert, *Historic Sketches*, 365; Porter A. Stratton, *The Territorial Press of New Mexico, 1834–1912* (Albuquerque: University of New Mexico Press, 1969), 11.

42. Thomas Donaldson, *Idaho of Yesterday* (Westport, Connecticut: Greenwood Press, 1970, reprint of Caxton Press edition, 1941), 125; Warren J. Brier, "A History of Newspapers in the Pacific Northwest, 1846–1896" (Ph.D. dissertation, State University of Iowa, 1957), 51, lists law, education, and the ministry as the most likely alternative careers for newspapermen.

43. Lamar, *The Far Southwest*, 39; Gilbert, *Historic Sketches*, 422–423.

44. Keen, "Wyoming Frontier Newspapers: The Newspapermen," 77–79; William T. Ellis, *Memories: My Seventy-Two Years in the Romantic County of Yuba, California* (Eugene: University of Oregon, 1939), 43; Anthony Jennings Bledsoe, *History of Del Norte County* (Eureka, California: Wymer & Co., 1881), no page, but actually 177.

45. Stratton, *The Territorial Press of New Mexico*, 11.

46. Keen, "Wyoming Frontier Newspapers," 61–62.

47. Cloud, "Start the Presses," 156. Seven of the 31 publishers studied served in the legislature.

48. *Ibid.*, 151.

49. Robert L. Houseman, "Boy Editors of Frontier Montana," *Pacific Northwest Quarterly* 27 (July 1936): 219.

50. Cloud, "Start the Presses," 151.

51. *Oregon Statesman* (Salem), 4 April 1851; Keen, "Wyoming Frontier Newspapers: The Newspapermen," 77. Asa Shinn Mercer had a bachelor's degree from Franklin College in Ohio when he became the first president and only teacher at the new University of Washington. It should be noted that during this period college degrees were not necessary for either teaching or the practice of law, both of which publishers frequently did.

52. Cloud, "Start the Presses," 155.

53. Daughters of the American Revolution, "Family Records and Reminiscences of Washington Pioneers," vol. 2 (1929–1930): 288–289.

54. *Territorial Republican* (Olympia), 12 July 1869.

55. Francis H. Cook, *The Territory of Washington, 1879*, ed. with an introduction by J. Orin Oliphant (Fairfield, Washington: Ye Galleon Press, 1972; originally published 1925), 109.

56. Keen, "Wyoming Frontier Newspapers: The Newspapermen," 61–84.

57. Kalama, Washington, *Beacon*, 19 May 1871.

58. Robert E. Lance, "First Lady of Arizona Journalism" (unpublished paper, 1979), 2.

59. Arthur K. Whyte, "History of the Press in San Diego County" in *History of San Diego County* by Carl H. Heilbron (San Diego: San Diego Press Club, 1936), 165.

60. Bennion, *Equal to the Occasion*, 14–15.

61. *Ibid.*, 4, 29.

62. Cloud, "Start the Presses," 156.

63. Jeffery B. Rutenbeck, "The Rise of Independent Newspapers in the 1870s: A Transformation in American Journalism" (Ph.D. dissertation, University of Washington, 1990), 199.

64. *Ibid.*, 79.

65. Gerald J. Baldasty, "The Press and Politics in the Gilded Age," (paper presented to the West Coast Journalism Historians Conference, 1987), 7.

66. Grass Valley *Tidings*, 10 January 1874, quoted in Rutenbeck, "The Rise of Independent Newspapers," 299.

67. Alexis de Tocqueville, *Democracy in America*, 2 vols. (New York: Alfred A. Knopf, 1953; first published in 1835), I:187–188.

68. Baldasty, "The Press and Politics in the Gilded Age," 12.

69. Legal Documents, 13 December 1869, Clarence Bagley papers, Manuscript Division, University of Washington Libraries.

70. Clarence Bagley to Daniel Bagley, 7 April 1869, Bagley papers.

71. Selucius Garfielde to Clarence Bagley, 28 March 1873, Bagley papers.

72. Doten, *Journals*, 2:1329. Republican Doten also helped a Democrat write a political letter to a newspaper; 2:1238–1239.

73. *Puget Sound Semi-Weekly Gazette*, 3 March 1866, 6 May–3 June 1867. Even with party backing, Hall's election was not guaranteed. He tied with his opponent and had to draw straws for the position.

74. *Illustrated History of Plumas, Lassen and Sierra Counties* (San Francisco: Fariss & Smith, 1882), 390; William H. Lyon, "Louis C. Hughes, Arizona's Editorial Gadfly," *Journal of Arizona History* 24 (Summer 1983): 172; Lance, "First Lady of Arizona Journalism," 2.

75. *History of Contra Costa County, California* (San Francisco: W. A. Slocum & Co., 1882), 403.

76. Kemble, *A History of California Newspapers*, 227.

77. Oscar Lewis, ed., *The Life and Times of the Virginia City Territorial Enterprise: Being the Reminiscences of Five Distinguished Comstock Journalists* (Ashland, Oregon: Lewis Osborne, 1971), 27.

78. *Esmeralda Star* (Aurora, Nevada), 17 May 1862.

79. *Daily Index* (Carson City, Nevada), 26 December 1880.

80. *Independent* (Vancouver, Washington), 9 April 1875.

81. Seattle *Post-Intelligencer* quoted in *An Illustrated History of Southeastern Washington* (Spokane: Western Historical Publishing Co., 1906), 807.

82. San Diego *Herald*, 21 April 1855, quoted in Millard F. Hudson, "A Pioneer Southwestern Newspaper and Its Editor," *Historical Society of Southern California* 8 (1911): 18.

83. Doten, *Journals*, 2:1498.

Chapter 3: Building Circulation

1. Nevada City, California, *Daily Transcript*, 22 January 1867, quoted in Rutenbeck, "The Rise of Independent Newspapers in the 1870s," 233.

2. Belmont, Nevada, *Courier*, 28 February 1874.

3. *Lewis County Nugget* (Chehalis, Washington), 4 August 1883.

4. *North Idaho Radiator* (Lewiston) 18 February 1865, quoted in Robison, "Idaho Territorial Newspapers," 28.

5. *Weekly Rocky Mountain Herald* (Denver) 1 February 1868, quoted in David Fridtjof Halaas, *Boom Town Newspapers: Journalism on the Rocky Mountain Mining Frontier, 1859–1881* (Albuquerque: University of New Mexico Press, 1981), 32. Halaas notes an almost identical statement in the *Weekly Helena Herald* a month earlier, 9 January 1868.

6. Cheyenne, Wyoming, *Leader*, 19 September 1867.

7. Douglas W. Staples, "The Calico *Print*, Pioneer Newspaper of the Mojave Desert," *Historical Society of Southern California Quarterly* 42 (September 1960): 229.

8. Belmont *Courier*, 21 February 1874.

9. Prosch, *Reminiscences*, 11.

10. *Deseret News* (Salt Lake City), 15 June 1850.

11. *Oregon Statesman*, 22 June 1852.

12. *Ibid.*, 6 November 1852.

13. Belmont *Courier*, 7 March 1874.

14. Sacramento *Daily Union*, 19 March 1851.

15. *Deseret News*, 15 June 1850.

16. Leach, *Recollections of a Newspaper Man*, 180–181.

17. Butte, Montana, *Miner*, 5 June 1877.

18. *Mountain Echo* (Downieville, California), quoted in Kennedy, "Newspapers of the California Northern Mines," 141.

19. Ralph E. Dyar, *News for an Empire* (Caldwell, Idaho: Caxton Printers Inc., 1952), xlix.

20. Gilbert, *Historic Sketches*, 352.

21. Leach, *Recollections of a Newspaper Man*, 91.

22. Robison, "Idaho Territorial Newspapers," 134.

23. Doten, *Journals*, 1:730–731; 2:945.

24. B. R. Stone to Bion Kendall, 22 October 1862, Kendall papers, Manuscript Division, University of Washington Libraries.

25. Newspapers commonly listed their agents in the paper. For the *Deseret News* see also Wendell J. Ashton, *Voice in the West: Biography of a Pioneer Newspaper* (New York: Duell, Sloan & Pearce, 1950), 83.

26. In their study of newspaper circulation practices, William J. Thorn and Mary Pat Pfeil, *Newspaper Circulation: Marketing the News* (New York: Longman, 1987), 147, link the start of subscription premiums to the Pulitzer era in New York (after 1883), but Frank Presbey, *The History and Development of Advertising* (New York: Doubleday & Co., 1929; reprint, Westport, Connecticut: Greenwood Press, 1968), 260, says the weekly New York *Tribune* used them in the late 1860s. In any case, western newspapers adopted the practice in the 1860s.

27. Olympia, Washington, *Echo*, 24 September 1868.

28. San Francisco *Chronicle* miniature, 31 August 1885, San Francisco *Chronicle* collection, California Historical Society Library, San Francisco.

29. Port Townsend, Washington, *Argus*, 29 December 1870.

30. San Francisco *Chronicle*, 2 September 1878.

31. Seattle *Fin-Back*, 15 December 1879.

32. Kalama *Semi-Weekly Beacon*, 23 May 1871.

33. *Puget Sound Courier* (Olympia, Washington), 2 January 1875.

34. *Lewis County Nugget*, 21 July, 11 August 1883.

35. Perkin, *The First Hundred Years*, 34.

36. Copies of miniatures are in the San Francisco *Chronicle* Collection, California Historical Society Library.

37. *Deseret News*, 30 November 1850.

38. *The Journalist*, 4 February 1888, 5.

39. *Ibid.*, 22 June, 2, and 2 March 1889, 5.

40. *Deseret News*, 12 July 1851.

41. Doten, *Journals*, 2:889.

42. *Ibid.*, 3:1620.

43. Mesilla, New Mexico, *Times*, 2 March 1866, quoted in Hall, "The Mesilla *Times*," 341.

44. *Reese River Reveille* (Austin, Nevada) 31 December 1877, quoted in Robert D. Armstrong, *Nevada Printing History* (Reno: University of Nevada Press, 1981), 310.

45. Turnbull, *History of Oregon Newspapers*, 60.

46. Thorn and Pfeil, *Newspaper Circulation*, 45, describes different circulation plans.

47. Bruce, *Gaudy Century*, 148–149.

48. Alice Starbuck Spencer, "Newspapers in Gunnison County, 1879–1900" (Master of Arts thesis, Western State College of Colorado, 1932), 24.

49. "Frontier Journalism in San Francisco," Works Projects Administration "History of Journalism in San Francisco" Project (San Francisco, 1940), 2:51, California Historical Society Library, San Francisco.

50. Los Angeles *Times*, 4 December 1881.

51. Firebaugh, "The Sacramento *Union*," 328.

52. Robison, "Idaho Territorial Newspapers," 132.

53. Sacramento *Daily Union*, 19 March, 22 July, 1851.

54. Early figures are based on rates given in the newspapers or collected by other historians; the 1880 figures are from the census.

55. *Daily Inland Empire* (Hamilton, Nevada), 27 March 1869.

56. *Republican* (Pomeroy, Washington), 8 May 1882.

57. *Carson Valley News* (Genoa, Nevada), 20 February 1875; 18 February 1876.

58. *Placer Times*, 24 November 1849.

59. *Spirit of the West* (Walla Walla, Washington), 25 December 1874.

60. *Carson Valley News*, 18 February 1876.

61. *Weekly Rocky Mountain News*, 27 October 1859, quoted in Halaas, *Boom Town Newspapers*, 32.

62. Port Townsend, Washington, *Register*, 18 January 1860.

63. *Oregon Statesman*, 22 June 1852.

64. *Puget Sound Weekly Gazette*, 25 March 1867.

65. *Rio Virgin Times* (St. George, Utah), 2 September 1868, quoted in Alter, *Early Utah Journalism*, 226.

66. *The Advertiser* (Ione, Nevada), 1 October 1864.

67. *Idaho Avalanche*, 28 December 1878.

68. *Rocky Mountain News*, 1 March 1873.

69. *Ibid.*, 1 January 1874.

70. Alter, *Early Utah Journalism*, 308, suggests this was a "quaint" practice.

71. Chehalis, Washington, *Bee*, 16 October 1888.

72. *Idaho Avalanche*, 28 September 1878.

73. *Deseret News*, 8 February 1851.

74. *Washington Statesman* (Walla Walla), 10 May 1862.

75. Perkin, *The First Hundred Years*, 40.

76. *Deseret News*, 8 February 1851.

77. *Ibid.*, 3 May 1851.

78. *The Southern Utonian*, n.d., quoted by the Salt Lake *Democrat*, 14 December 1886, then in Alter, *Early Utah Journalism*, 33.

79. Wilbur, Washington, *Register*, 22 June 1939.

80. *Deseret News*, 12 July 1851.

81. *Columbian* (Olympia, Washington), 11 September 1852.

82. Alter, *Early Utah Journalism*, 282.

83. *Territorial Enterprise* (Genoa, Nevada), 1 January 1859; a similar statement appeared in the *Oregon Statesman* several times in 1853; I also saw versions in the *Puget Sound Weekly*, 30 April 1866, and *Idaho Avalanche*, 14 December 1878.

84. Kennedy, "Newspapers of the California Northern Mines," 160.

85. *Churchill News* (White Plains, Nevada), 31 March 1888; the *News* was the only newspaper in the county.

86. A century later, average daily and weekly circulation totaled 115,569,064, according to American Newspaper Publishers Association, *Facts About Newspapers* (August 1990). Based on an estimated U.S. population of 250 million, daily circulation (62,649,218) equaled about 25 percent of the population in 1989. This is not readership; ANPA estimates that 64 percent of adults read a daily newspaper.

87. Perkin, *The First Hundred Years*, 40.

88. Rice, *The Los Angeles Star*, 66.

89. Wells Drury, *An Editor on the Comstock Lode* (New York: Farrar & Rinehart, Inc., 1936), 182; Lucius Beebe, *Comstock Commotion: The Story of the Territorial Enterprise* (Stanford: Stanford University Press, 1954), 35.

90. Robert J. Chandler, "The California News-Telegraph Monopoly, 1860–1870," *Southern California Quarterly* 58 (Winter 1976): 469; Bruce, *Gaudy Century*, 141.

91. Ashton, *Voice in the West*, 399.

92. Chandler, "The California News-Telegraph Monopoly," 469.

Chapter 4: Advertising

1. Alex Ayres, *The Wit and Wisdom of Mark Twain* (New York: Harper & Row, 1987), 4–5.

2. Gold Hill *Daily News*, 12 October 1863.

3. Seattle *Gazette*, 29 March 1864.

4. Boorstin, *The National Experience*, 126.

5. *The Weekly Commonwealth* (Denver), 6 August 1863, quoted in Halaas, *Boom Town Newspapers*, 35.

6. Laramie *Daily Sentinel*, 22 June 1870, quoted in Halaas, *Boom Town Newspapers*, 35.

7. *Boulder County News* (Colorado), 2 February 1872, quoted in Halaas, *Boom Town Newspapers*, 35.

8. San Francisco *Daily Dramatic Chronicle*, 16 January 1865.

9. *Ibid.*, 21 January 1865.

10. Oakland *Daily Tribune*, 21 February 1874.

11. *Daily Dramatic Chronicle*, 15 February 1865.

12. Butte *Miner*, 1 June 1876.

13. *Carson Free Lance* (Nevada), 2 March 1885.

14. Doten, *Journals*, 2:1259.

15. *Territorial Enterprise*, 26 March 1859.

16. Leach, *Recollections of a Newspaper Man*, 124.

17. Millard F. Hudson, "A Pioneer Southwestern Newspaper and its Editor," *Historical Society of Southern California* 8 (1911): 16.

18. Hudson & Monet to Frederick J. Stanton, 7 September 1868, Frederick J. Stanton papers, Western History Department, Denver Public Library.

19. Ralph M. Hower, *The History of an Advertising Agency* (Cambridge: Harvard University Press, 1949), 13–16, describes four relationships: the newspaper agency, space jobbing, the space wholesaler, and the advertising concession agency that bought the entire space of a publication and resold it. The latter system was rarely used by the general press.

20. S. M. Pettengill & Co.'s Newspaper Advertising Agency, printed form letter to Antioch, California *Ledger*, 1874. Antioch *Ledger* records, Kemble Collection.

21. Ashton, *Voice in the West*, 157.

22. Doten, *Journals*, 2:1236.

23. Samuel Hill, San Francisco, to Antioch *Ledger*, 20 February 1871, Antioch *Ledger* records, Kemble Collection.

24. Eureka, Nevada, *Daily Leader*, 24 April 1879.

25. Reno, Nevada, *Daily Record*, 5 August 1878.

26. Mark Twain, *Mark Twain's West: The Author's Memoirs About His Boyhood, Riverboats and Western Adventures*, ed. Walter Blair (Chicago: Lakeside Press, 1983), 290.

27. *Deseret News*, 14 March 1855.

28. Ashton, *Voice in the West*, 141.

29. *Carson Daily Index*, 25 December 1880.

30. Ashton, *Voice in the West*, 73.

31. *Idaho Register* (Eagle Rock, now Idaho Falls), 4 April 1885.

32. Mark Twain, *Roughing It* (New York: Holt, Rinehart and Winston, Inc., 1953), 228; Henry Winfred Splitter, "Newspapers of Los Angeles: The First Fifty Years, 1851–1900," *Journal of the West* 2 (October 1963): 436.

33. Sherman & Hyden to Antioch *Ledger*, n.d., Antioch *Ledger* records, Kemble Collection.

34. Samuel Hill, San Francisco, to Antioch *Ledger*, 20 February 1871, Antioch *Ledger* records, Kemble Collection.

35. S. M. Pettengill & Co.'s Newspaper Advertising Agency to Antioch *Ledger*, 8 June 1874, Antioch *Ledger* records, Kemble Collection.

36. Jonas Winchester to his wife Susan Winchester, 15 October 1850, Jonas Winchester papers, Kemble Collection.

37. *Ibid.*, 15 November 1850.

38. Victor J. Farrar, "Barter: Mainstay of the First State Newspapers," *Washington Historian* 3 (April 1918): 193.

39. Grant C. Angle, "Rambling Reminiscences of Fifty Years of Newspapering," *Washington Newspaper* 21 (August 1936): 2.

40. Doten, *Journals*, 2:1193.

41. *Rocky Mountain News*, 1 March 1873.

42. *Oregon Statesman*, 4 April 1851.

43. Kemble, *A History of California Newspapers*, 60, 63.

44. *Columbian*, 11 September 1852.

45. Robert D. Armstrong, "Newspapering in Nineteenth Century Nevada," *Proceedings of the Nevada Newspaper Conference*, ed. Karen Rix Gash (Reno: Oral History Program, University of Nevada, Reno, 1990), 14.

46. Ashton, *Voice in the West*, 83.

47. Robert E. Huffman, "Newspaper Art in Stockton, 1850–1892," *California Historical Society Quarterly* 34 (December 1955): 349.

48. Turnbull, *History of Oregon Newspapers*, 36.

49. Marysville, California, *Appeal*, 29 September 1860.

50. *Placer Times*, 22 September 1849.

51. *Oregon Statesman*, 7 February 1854.

52. *Nevada National* (Grass Valley, California), 7 May 1859, quoted in Kennedy, "Newspapers of the California Northern Mines," 156.

53. *Territorial Enterprise*, 26 March 1859.

54. Albuquerque, New Mexico, *Daily Journal*, 31 January 1882; Los Angeles *Times*, 8 December 1881.

55. Butte *Miner*, 11 December 1877.

56. *Borax Miner* (Columbus, Nevada), 27 February 1875.

57. Oakland *Tribune*, 21 February 1874.

58. *Borax Miner* (Columbus, Nevada), 27 February 1875.

59. Sacramento *Union*, 1 March 1860.

60. *Territorial Enterprise*, 16 July 1859.

61. *Measure for Measure* (Battle Mountain, Nevada), 26 June 1875.

62. *Daily Dramatic Chronicle*, 15 February 1865.

63. *Arizona Miner* (Prescott), 9 March 1867.

64. *Boulder County Pioneer* (Colorado), quoted in Halaas, *Boom Town Newspapers*, 37.

65. *Ibid.*, 37.

66. *Owyhee Avalanche*, 7 January 1871.

67. Albuquerque *Daily Journal*, 20 September 1882.

68. Bruce, *Gaudy Century*, 73, 101.

69. Doten, *Journals*, 2:1164.

70. *Annual Proceedings of the Washington Press Association* 1889, 1890 (Hoquiam, Washington: Washington Steam Book, News and Job Printing, 1891), 91.

71. William Whitfield, ed. *History of Snohomish County, Washington*, 2 vols. (Chicago: Pioneer Historical Publishing Co., 1926), 1:785.

72. Ione *Advertiser*, 17 September 1864.

73. *The Journalist*, 21 January 1888, 6.

74. Stratton, *The Territorial Press of New Mexico*, 45; *Idaho Register* printed the brands on drawings of cattle, 1885–1886.

75. For example, *Borax Miner*, 15 September 1877.

76. *History of Santa Barbara County, California* (Oakland: Thompson & West, 1883), 112.

77. Sam Gilluly, *The Press Gang: A Century of Montana Newspapers, 1885–1985* (Helena: Montana Press Association, 1985), 30.

78. Lee, *The Daily Newspaper in America*, 321; Linda Lawson, "Advertisements Masquerading as News in Turn-of-the-Century American Periodicals," *American Journalism* 5 (2:1988): 82.

79. Cheyenne *Leader*, 28 September 1867.

80. *Central Nevadan*, 23 January 1885.

81. *Carson Valley News*, 20 March 1875.

82. *Reese River Reveille*, 13 January 1882.

83. *Arizona Miner*, 28 February 1866.

84. *Carson Daily Appeal*, 24 December 1876.

85. Virginia City, Nevada, *Daily Independent*, 5 January 1875.

86. Geo. P. Rowell & Co. to publisher of the Denver Gazette [Frederick J. Stanton], 19 September 1868. Stanton papers.

87. E. A. Wilson to Frederick J. Stanton, 13 March 1867. Stanton papers.

88. Turnbull, *History of Oregon Newspapers*, 74; see also Lawson, "Advertisements Masquerading as News," 90.

89. Cheyenne *Leader*, 19 September 1867.

90. Mitchell Stephens, *A History of News: From the Drum to the Satellite* (New York: Viking Penguin Inc., 1988), 202.

91. *Daily Dramatic Chronicle*, 17 April 1865.

92. *History of San Bernardino County* (San Francisco: Wallace W. Elliott & Co., 1883), 120.

93. Oakland *Tribune*, 21 February, 21 August 1874.

94. Julia Norton McCorkle, "A History of Los Angeles Journalism," *Annual Proceedings of the Historical Society of Southern California* 10 (1915): 27–28.

95. Richard Kielbowicz, "The Growing Interaction of the Federal Bureaucracy and the Press: The Case of a Postal Rule, 1879–1917," *American Journalism* 4 (1987): 6.

Chapter 5: Job Printing

1. Gutierrez, "Spanish Language Media in America," 38.

2. Perkin, *The First Hundred Years*, 40.

3. Beshoar, "The Strife and Struggle of a Newspaper in the Old West," 46.

4. Perkin, *The First Hundred Years*, 35.

5. Leach, *Recollections of a Newspaper Man*, 114, 136.

6. Jonas Winchester to Heman Winchester, 22 August 1849, Jonas Winchester papers.

7. Ashton, *Voice in the West*, 75–76.

8. Thornton F. McElroy to his mother, 24 July 1864. McElroy papers.

9. Doten, *Journals*, 2:1296.

10. Myers, *Lizzie: The Letters of Elizabeth Chester Fisk*, 46.

11. L. B. Andrews to Clarence Bagley, 12 January 1875, Clarence Bagley papers, Manuscript Division, University of Washington Libraries.

12. Sacramento *Union*, 19 March 1851.

13. *Daily Inland Empire*, 27 March 1869.

14. Aurora *Daily Times*, 12 December 1863.

15. Cheyenne *Leader* Job Book, 1868–1869. Wyoming State Archives, Museum and Historical Department.

16. Ashton, *Voice in the West*, 177.

17. Splitter, "Newspapers of Los Angeles," 439.

18. Dyar, *News for an Empire*, 10; Kemble, *A History of California Newspapers*, 180; Splitter, "Newspapers of Los Angeles," 441.

19. Seattle *Leader*, 5 September 1889.

20. Splitter, "Newspapers of Los Angeles," 438–439.

21. Edgar Eugene Eaton, "A History of Olympia Newspapers from 1852–1885" (Master of Arts thesis, University of Washington, 1964), 135.

22. Ashton, *Voice in the West*, 177.

23. Virginia City *Daily Independent*, 5 January 1875.

24. Doten, *Journals*, 2:1332–1333.

25. *Ibid.*, 2:1285.

26. *Illustrated History of Plumas, Lassen and Sierra Counties*, 390.

27. Prosch, *Reminiscences*, 7; *Puget Sound Herald* (Steilacoom, Washington), 12 March 1858; *Puget Sound Courier*, 19 May 1855. The Indian Wars also contributed to the *Courier*'s failure.

28. Charles Prosch, "The Press of Washington Territory," *Annual Proceedings of the Washington Press Association, 1889* (Hoquiam, Washington: Washington Steam Book, News and Job Printing, 1891), 36.

29. Dorothy Gile Firebaugh, "The Sacramento *Union*: Voice of California, 1851–1875," *Journalism Quarterly* 30 (Summer 1953): 325.

30. *Oregon Statesman*, 10 July 1852.

31. Angel, *History of Nevada*, 323, 325; Doten, *Journals*, 2:867; Lingenfelter and Gash, *Newspapers of Nevada*, 255–256.

32. *Washington Democrat* (Olympia), 15 July 1865.

33. Gilbert, *Historic Sketches*, 352–353, 356; Walla Walla *Union*, 22 May 1869.

34. Angel, *History of Nevada*, 310; Lingenfelter and Gash, *Newspapers of Nevada*, 19.

35. Robert C. Notson, *Making the Day Begin: A Story of the Oregonian* (Portland: Oregonian Publishing Co., 1976), 8.

36. *An Illustrated History of Plumas, Lassen and Sierra Counties*, 312; Gilbert, *Historic Sketches*, 364.

37. *History of Idaho Territory* (San Francisco: Wallace W. Elliott & Co., 1884), 204; Robison, "Idaho Territorial Newspapers," 36.

38. Lamar, *The Far Southwest*, 105, 125, 443.

39. *Oregon Statesman*, 28 May 1851.

40. *History of Clarke County* (Portland: A. G. Walling, 1885), 276.

41. *Washington Standard* (Olympia), 17 November 1860.

42. William Armstrong Katz, "Public Printers of Washington Territory, 1853–1863," *Pacific Northwest Quarterly* 51 (July 1960): 104, 113. After 1873 the amount decreased to about $4,000 per biennium, and interest among printers declined accordingly.

43. Jonas Winchester to Susan Winchester, 13 May 1850. Jonas Winchester papers, Kemble Collection.

44. *Ibid.*, 14 August 1850.

45. Jonas Winchester to Ebenezer Winchester, 13 January 1851. Jonas Winchester papers, Kemble Collection.

46. *Ibid.*, 1 February, 28 February, 1 May 1851.

47. Thornton F. McElroy to his mother, 24 July 1864. McElroy papers.

48. Rice, *The Los Angeles Star*, 137.

49. Doten, *Journals*, 2:1189.

50. Personal notes, 1908, Clarence Bagley papers.

51. *Oregon Statesman*, 28 May 1851.

52. Armstrong, *Nevada Printing History*, 228.

53. *Ibid.*, 3.

54. John G. Nicolay to Thornton McElroy, 3 June 1861, McElroy papers.

55. Robert D. Armstrong, "Nevada's Public Printing, Chiefly in 1869: Additional Notes to Armstrong, *Nevada Printing History*," *The Papers of the Bibliographic Society of America*, 81 (1987): 471.

56. Quoted in Armstrong, "Nevada's Public Printing," 466.

57. William Armstrong Katz, "Public Printers of Washington Territory, 1863–1889," *Pacific Northwest Quarterly* 51 (October 1960): 175.

58. Armstrong, "Nevada's Public Printing," 469.

59. Turnbull, *History of Oregon Newspapers*, 161–162.

60. Leach, *Recollections of a Newspaper Man*, 176.

61. *Columbia Chronicle* (Dayton, Washington), 18 May 1878.

Chapter 6: Setting Up Shop

1. Keith Wheeler, *The Chroniclers* (New York: Time-Life Books, 1976), 61.

2. *History of Placer County, California*, 298.

3. Kenneth Hufford, "The Arizona Gazette: A Forgotten Voice in Arizona Journalism," *Journal of Arizona History* 7 (Winter 1966), *passim*.

4. Quoted in Bruce, *Gaudy Century*, 5.

5. Ashton, *Voice in the West*, 370–371; Roby Wentz, *Western Printing: A Selective and Descriptive Bibliography of Books and Other Materials on the*

History of Printing in the Western States, 1822–1975, (Los Angeles: Dawson's Book Shop, 1975), 16. Ashton cites sources that say the original Monterey press was sold by the *Alta* to the founders of the Portland *Oregonian,* but Wentz's sources are more recent.

6. Perkin, *The First Hundred Years,* 32.

7. Millard Hudson, "A Pioneer Southwestern Newspaper and Its Editor," *Historical Society of Southern California* 8 (1911): 13. The 1860 census listed fourteen printing press manufacturers in five states: Massachusetts, Rhode Island, New York, Pennsylvania, and Ohio.

8. Ashton, *Voice in the West,* 17; Myers, *Lizzie: The Letters of Elizabeth Chester Fisk,* 10.

9. *History of Idaho Territory,* 204.

10. Turnbull, *History of Oregon Newspapers,* 50.

11. Alter, *Early Utah Journalism,* 233.

12. Quoted in Kemble, *A History of California Newspapers,* 57.

13. *Ibid.,* 60.

14. Turnbull, *History of Oregon Newspapers,* 48.

15. Kemble, *A History of California Newspapers,* 137; Perkin, *The First Hundred Years,* 49.

16. Twain, *Mark Twain's West,* 289. These were the days when type was set one letter at a time; the stories were assembled in a frame called a chase on the imposing stone. It was important for the imposing stone to be smooth and even because the type had to be fitted into the chase securely enough that the chase could be lifted and carried to the press without the pieces falling out; the type also had to be free from any wobble if the final impression was to be clean.

17. Robison, "Idaho Territorial Newspapers," 34.

18. Beebe, *Comstock Commotion,* 4.

19. W. D. Lyman, *History of the Yakima Valley* (Chicago: S. J. Clarke Publishing Co., 1919), 497.

20. Quoted in Kemble, *A History of California Newspapers,* 59.

21. *Ibid.,* 93.

22. Rice, *The Los Angeles Star,* 129–130.

23. *Overland Press* (Olympia), 23 March 1863.

24. Pioneer Washington publisher Thomas Prosch says two men could do 1,000 single pages in ten hours; "The Pioneer Press and Publishers of Seattle," Typescript #15 (c. 1900), Northwest Collection, University of Washington Libraries. George H. Himes, in a speech, "Some Historical Events," reported in the *Olympian* (Olympia, Washington), 20 November 1910, said 50 to 60 complete papers an hour. Wentz, *Western Printing,* 38, says 60 to 70 an hour, and Ashton, *Voice in the West,* 41, estimates about two sheets a minute.

25. Santa Barbara *Post,* 24 March 1869, quoted in Havilah *Weekly Courier,* 27 April 1869, and then by Ralph S. Kuykendall, "History of Early California Journalism" (Master of Arts thesis, University of California, 1918), 9.

26. Wentz, *Western Printing*, 38.

27. Notson, *Making the Day Begin*, 7; Splitter, "Newspapers of Los Angeles," 436.

28. Turnbull, *History of Oregon Newspapers*, 107; Twain, *Roughing It*, 228.

29. Splitter, "Newspapers of Los Angeles," 438–439. W. D. Lyman, *An Illustrated History of Walla Walla County* (W. H. Lever, 1901), 229.

30. Leach, *Recollections of a Newspaper Man*, 273.

31. Notson, *Making the Day Begin*, 8. Presses could print as many as 20,000 copies an hour by 1860.

32. Thorn and Pfeil, *Newspaper Circulation*, 50.

33. Leach, *Recollections of a Newspaper Man*, 135.

34. Dyar, *News for an Empire*, 14; Robison, "Idaho Territorial Newspapers," 114; Stratton, *The Territorial Press of New Mexico*, 44.

35. Robison, "Idaho Territorial Newspapers," 129.

36. Doten, *Journals*, 2:1291.

37. Splitter, "Newspapers of Los Angeles," 442; see also Stratton, *The Territorial Press of New Mexico*, 44.

38. Armstrong, "Newspapering in Nineteenth-Century Nevada," 18.

39. Beebe, *Comstock Commotion*, 10.

40. Gold Hill, Nevada, *News*, 23 October 1873.

41. Doten, *Journals*, 3:2252.

42. Staples, "The Calico *Print*," 230.

43. Robert F. Karolevitz, *Newspapering in the Old West* (New York: Bonanza Books, 1965), 23. In the next five years the Linotype was introduced into every western state except Idaho, which installed its first machine in 1898, and Nevada, which mechanized in 1901.

44. Kubler, *A New History of Stereotyping*, 174.

45. Ashton, *Voice in the West*, 176; *History of San Bernardino County*, 120; *Rocky Mountain News*, 22 April 1934.

46. On at least one occasion, the *Deseret News* asked subscribers to bring in molasses so more rollers could be made. Ashton, *Voice in the West*, 63.

47. WPA Writers Program, "History of the Colorado Press Association and Early Newspapers in Colorado," *Colorado Editor* 17 (June 1942): 11.

48. *Arizona Miner*, 10 January 1866; Kemble, *A History of California Newspapers*, 138.

49. Lyman, *History of the Yakima Valley*, 497.

50. Clarence B. Bagley, *History of King County, Washington*, 3 vols. (Seattle: S. J. Clarke Publishing Co., 1929), 1:467.

51. *Lewis County Nugget*, 4 August 1883.

52. *Arizona Miner*, 10 January 1866.

53. Perkin, *The First Hundred Years*, 33.

54. Effie Mack, *Mark Twain in Nevada* (New York: Scribner's, 1947), 208–209.

55. Ryan, "Trail-Blazer of Civilization," 58.

56. Kemble, *A History of California Newspapers*, 15, 137.

57. *Ibid.*, 80.

58. *Ibid.*, 87.

59. Splitter, "Newspapers of Los Angeles," 435.

60. Twain, *Roughing It*, 228.

61. Kemble, *A History of California Newspapers*, 93.

62. Oakland *Tribune*, 18 May 1874.

63. Perkin, *The First Hundred Years*, 32.

64. Leach, *Recollections of a Newspaper Man*, 142–143.

65. Spokane *Daily Chronicle*, 8 August 1933.

66. *Deseret News*, 22 February 1851.

67. *Empire County Argus* (Coloma, California), 21 June 1856, quoted in Kennedy, "Newspapers of the California Northern Mines," 141.

68. St. George, Utah, *Enterprise*, May 1873, quoted in Alter, *Early Utah Journalism*, 233.

69. Splitter, "Newspapers of Los Angeles," 437–438.

70. Kemble, *A History of California Newspapers*, 94, 100.

71. Seattle *Morning Journal*, 7 June 1889.

72. Angel, *History of Nevada*, 299.

73. Perkin, *The First Hundred Years*, 39.

74. William A. Katz, "The *Columbian*, Washington Territory's First Newspaper," *Oregon Historical Quarterly* 64 (March 1963): 37; *History of Stanislaus County, California* (San Francisco: Elliott & Moore Publishers, 1881), 131.

75. This account of the flood is from the *Reese River Reveille*, 13 August– 9 September 1878.

76. *History of Contra Costa County*, 402.

77. Bruce, *Gaudy Century*, 75.

78. Drury, *An Editor on the Comstock Lode*, 203; Doten, *Journals*, 3:2232.

79. Warren J. Brier, "A History of Newspapers in the Pacific Northwest," 94.

80. Kubler, *A New History of Stereotyping*, 119.

81. *Arizona Miner*, 26 October 1867.

82. Kemble, *A History of California Newspapers*, 93.

83. Wheeler, *The Chroniclers*, 61.

84. Ione *Advertiser*, 17 September 1864.

85. Belmont *Courier*, 28 February 1874.

86. Angel, *History of Nevada*, 304. The *Reese River Reveille* at one point had nine columns, the size of the Sacramento *Union*, but it reduced to five columns in an economic downturn.

87. Doten, *Journals*, 2:1231; *Daily Inland Empire* (Hamilton, Nevada), 13 April 1869.

88. Angel, *History of Nevada*, 317.

89. Because of the idiosyncratic way publishers treated names, I have adhered to the practice of not including the city in the name. Thus the "Los Angeles Times" is the Los Angeles *Times*. I have also emphasized the better-known usage, such as Sacramento *Union*, rather than *Daily Union*.

90. *Deseret News*, 14 March 1855.

91. *Arizona Miner*, 13 January 1867.

92. Huffman, "Newspaper Art in Stockton," 345.

93. Kennedy, "Newspapers of the California Northern Mines," 156.

94. *Idaho Weekly Avalanche*, 1 January 1876.

95. *History of Idaho Territory*, 218.

96. *Central Nevadan*, 23 January 1885.

97. For example, *Daily Inland Empire*, 1869; Kalama *Beacon*, 1871; Yakima *Signal*, 1883.

Chapter 7: Staffing the Newspaper

1. Kuykendall, "History of Early California Journalism," quoting the *California Star*, 20 May 1848.

2. Turnbull, *History of Oregon Newspapers*, 45.

3. Spencer, "Newspapers in Gunnison County, Colorado," 33.

4. Kuykendall, "History of Early California Journalism," 30.

5. Ira B. Cross, *A History of the Labor Movement in California* (Berkeley: University of California Press, 1935), 26.

6. *Northern Star*, 22 January 1876.

7. Salt Lake City *Tribune*, 29 December 1874, quoted in Alter, *Early Utah Journalism*, 23.

8. Alter, *Early Utah Journalism*, 226.

9. "A History of the Colorado Press Association," *Colorado Editor* 17 (December 1942): 13.

10. Boise *News*, 29 September 1863, quoted in Robison, "Idaho Territorial Newspapers," 34.

11. Doten, *Journals*, 3:2253.

12. Roth, *History of Whatcom County*, 1:577.

13. U.S. Census returns for California were incomplete in 1850, hence the estimate.

14. Angel, *History of Nevada*, 309; *History of Fresno County, California* (San Francisco: Wallace W. Elliott & Co., 1882), 202.

15. *Directory of the City of Placerville* (Placerville, California: Placerville Republican Printing Office, 1862).

16. "Historical Sketch and essay on the resources of Montana: including a business directory of the metropolis [Helena]" (Helena, Montana: Herald Book and Job Printing Office, 1868).

17. Sidney Kobre, *Development of American Journalism* (Dubuque, Iowa: Wm. C. Brown Company Publishers, 1969), 314; Lewis, *Life and Times*, 14. Twain, *Roughing It*, 228, says 23.

18. Staples, "The Calico *Print*," 230.

19. Bagley, *King County*, 1:467.

20. Leach, *Recollections of a Newspaper Man*, 90.

21. Lee, *Daily Newspaper in America*, 137.

22. Clarence Bagley to Daniel Bagley, 8 December 1873, Clarence Bagley papers.

23. Doten, *Journals*, 2:1165.

24. Ashton, *Voice in the West*, 205.

25. *History of Contra Costa County*, 404.

26. Belmont *Courier*, 28 February 1874.

27. Doten, *Journals*, 2:1369.

28. Jonas Winchester to Ebenezer Winchester, 11 July 1851, Jonas Winchester papers, Kemble Collection, says $2 a thousand; Cross, *A History of the Labor Movement in California*, 299, quoting the *Alta California* in 1853, says $1.50; Lee, *Daily Newspaper in America*, 151, says New York pay was $3 for 10-hour day in 1865–1871, which works out to 30 to 40 cents a thousand.

29. John Damon, one of the fastest compositors in the Pacific Northwest, could keep up a pace of 1,800 ems an hour. Turnbull, *History of Oregon Newspapers*, 116.

30. Jonas Winchester to Ebenezer Winchester, 11 July 1851, Jonas Winchester papers, Kemble Collection; also Cross, *A History of the Labor Movement in California*, 229 and 297.

31. Sacramento *Union*, 19 March 1851.

32. Cross, *A History of the Labor Movement in California*, 12, 299.

33. William A. Katz, "The Western Printer and His Publications, 1850–1890," *Journalism Quarterly* 44 (Winter 1967): 513.

34. Carolyn Stewart Dyer, "Economic Dependence and Concentration of Ownership Among Antebellum Wisconsin Newspapers," *Journalism History* 7 (Summer 1980): 42, says Wisconsin shops averaged $25 per employee per month.

35. Clarence Bagley to Daniel Bagley, 22 November 1868, Clarence Bagley papers. In Hamilton, Nevada, in 1869, $50 a month put the printer on a par with a city assessor, but at about half the wages of the city treasurer or street commissioner. *Daily Inland Empire*, 14 April 1869.

36. Leach, *Recollections of a Newspaper Man*, 111.

37. Doten, *Journals*, 2:1165, 1225.

38. Schellie, *The Tucson Citizen*, 40.

39. Bruce, *Gaudy Century*, 255; Evelyn Wells, *Fremont Older* (New York: D. Appleton-Century Company, 1936), 52, 55, 65, 68. Older had difficulty keeping a job because of his "impetuous" nature.

40. Grace Heilman Stimson, *Rise of the Labor Movement in Los Angeles* (Berkeley: University of California Press, 1955), 48.

41. Cross, *A History of the Labor Movement in California*, 297; Twain, *Roughing It*, 228.

42. Clarence Bagley, personal notes, Clarence Bagley papers; see also Cross, *A History of the Labor Movement in California*, 207.

43. *Ibid.*, 37, 148.

44. Robison, "Idaho Territorial Newspapers," 49.

45. Jonas Winchester to Heman Winchester, 26 February 1850; to Susan Winchester, 28 February 1850. Jonas Winchester papers, Kemble Collection.

46. Gold Hill *News*, 13 October 1863.

47. Leach, *Recollections of a Newspaper Man*, 116, 134.

48. Clarence Bagley to Daniel Bagley, 29 [no month] 1870. Clarence Bagley papers.

49. Doten, *Journals*, 3:2253.

50. Butte *Miner*, 25 December 1877.

51. Angle, "Rambling Reminiscences," 1; Caroline Gale Budlong, *Memories of Pioneer Days* (Eugene, Oregon: The Picture Press Printers, 1949), 15, 40.

52. Turnbull, *History of Oregon Newspapers*, 51; Robison, "Idaho Territorial Newspapers," 129.

53. Alter, *Early Utah Journalism*, 225.

54. Ashton, *Voice in the West*, 41.

55. *Ibid.*, 179.

56. Alter, *Early Utah Journalism*, 24.

57. Doten, *Journals*, 2:1419, 1422; *The History of Wallowa County, Oregon* (Wallowa County, Oregon: Wallowa County Museum Board, 1983), 80.

58. Quoted in Bruce, *Gaudy Century*, 76–77.

59. Levette Jay Davidson, "O. J. Goldrick, Pioneer Journalist," *Colorado Magazine* 18 (January 1936): 27.

60. Leach, *Recollections of a Newspaper Man*, 260.

61. Twain, *Roughing It*, 213.

62. Ashton, *Voice in the West*, 64.

63. John Denton Carter, "Before the Telegraph: The News Service of the San Francisco *Bulletin*, 1855–1861," *Pacific Historical Review* 11 (September 1942): 304–306. Hudson lists several western representatives in Washington, 701–702.

64. Pataha, Washington, *Spirit*, 25 January 1881.

65. John P. Young, *Journalism in California* (San Francisco: Chronicle Publishing Company, 1915), 40.

66. Turnbull, *History of Oregon Newspapers*, 117.

67. Twain, *Mark Twain's West*, 293–294.

68. *Wallowa Chieftain* (Enterprise, Oregon), 15 May 1884, quoted in *History of Wallowa County*, 80.

69. Beshoar, "The Strife and Struggle of a Newspaper in the Old West," 46.

70. Doten, *Journals*, 3:1649.

71. Leach, *Recollections of a Newspaper Man*, 134.

72. Twain, *Mark Twain's West*, 296.

73. Jonas Winchester to Susan Winchester, 29 October 1850. Jonas Winchester papers, Kemble Collection.

74. Doten, *Journals*, 2:1209.

75. *Ibid.*, 2:1272, 1279, 1293.

76. Cummins, *The Story of the Files*, 420.

77. Edward N. Fuller, "Washington Press History," *Annual Proceedings of the Washington Press Association*, 1892, 13.

78. Cummins, *The Story of the Files*, 378–379.

79. Twain, *Mark Twain's West*, 421.

80. Clifford Weigle, "San Francisco Journalism, 1847–1851," *Journalism Quarterly* 14 (June 1937): 156; Splitter, "Newspapers of Los Angeles," 436; Splitter also notes that the editor received $20 a week more than a compositor even though the latter worked twice as long.

81. Lewis, *Life and Times*, 25.

82. Doten, *Journals*, 2:1487. His wife was offered $65 a month to teach school.

83. Ashton, *Voice in the West*, 180; Keen, "Wyoming Frontier Newspapers," 34:74.

84. *The Journalist*, 19 April 1884.

85. Doten, *Journals*, 2:1014, 1044, 1094, 1228.

86. Twain, *Roughing It*, 222.

87. *Ibid.*, 223.

88. Doten, *Journals*, 2:1066.

89. *Ibid.*, 3:1582.

90. Leach, *Recollections of a Newspaper Man*, 139.

91. Doten, *Journals*, 2:1129.

92. Henry Nash Smith, *Mark Twain of the Enterprise* (Berkeley: University of California Press, 1957), 211–212; Sacramento *Union*, 21 April–1 May 1860.

93. Quoted in Beebe, *Comstock Commotion*, 85.

94. Lewis, *Life and Times*, 12, says the business manager of the *Territorial Enterprise* built an estate worth $600,000.

95. Turnbull, *History of Oregon Newspapers*, 110. When Dryer received a government appointment in Hawaii, he gave Pittock the paper as payment for his work.

96. *Ibid.*, 169.

97. Doten, *Journals*, 2:1341.

98. Ashton, *Voice in the West*, 68, 180.

99. *Ibid.*

100. *Territorial Enterprise*, 1 January 1859.

101. Leach, *Recollections of a Newspaper Man*, 123.

102. *Daily Inland Empire*, 27 March 1869.

103. Aurora, Nevada, *Daily Times*, 30 November 1863.

104. Doten, *Journals*, 3:1588, 1601.

Chapter 8: News Across the Miles

1. Ashton, *Voice in the West*, 59.

2. Thornton McElroy to Sally McElroy, 11 January 1853. McElroy family papers.

3. *Arizona Miner*, 16 January 1867; *Daily Inland Empire*, 27 March 1869; Butte *Miner*, 1 June 1876.

4. Perkin, *The First Hundred Years*, 86–88.

5. Douglas C. McMurtrie, "The Pioneer Press in Montana," *Journalism Quarterly* 9 (1932): 172.

6. N. W. Durham, *History of the City of Spokane and Spokane County, Washington*, 3 vols. (Spokane: S. J. Clarke Publishing Co., 1912), 358; Dyar, *News for an Empire*, xlix.

7. Robison, "Idaho Territorial Newspapers," 167.

8. Laura Homsher, "Guide to Wyoming Newspapers, 1867–1967," typescript, n.d., v. Joseph Jacobucci Collection, University of Wyoming Western History Research Center, University of Wyoming Library.

9. Thornton McElroy to Sally McElroy, 10 August 1852. McElroy family papers.

10. Oscar Lewis, *The Town that Died Laughing: The Story of Austin, Nevada, Rambunctious Early Day Mining Camp, and of Its Renowned Newspaper, 'The Reese River Reveille'* (Reno: University of Nevada Press, 1986, reprint of 1955 edition), 16.

11. Walla Walla *Watchman*, quoted in the *Spokan Times*, 28 August 1880, and quoted again in Francis H. Cook, *The Territory of Washington, 1879*, J. Orin Oliphant, ed. (Fairfield, Washington: Ye Galleon Press, 1972, reprint of 1925 edition), 7.

12. *Territorial Enterprise*, 19 and 26 March 1859.

13. Wesley Norton, "'Like a Thousand Preachers Flying,' Religious Newspapers on the Pacific Coast to 1865," *California Historical Quarterly* 56 (Fall 1977): 197; Arthur C. Carey, "Effects of the Pony Express and the Transcontinental Telegraph Upon Selected California Newspapers," *Journalism Quarterly* 51 (Summer 1974): 320.

14. Rice, *The Los Angeles Star*, 26; San Francisco *Evening News*, 5 November 1853.

15. Cloud, "Start the Presses," 168.

16. Ashton, *Voice in the West*, 60.

17. Angel, *History of Nevada*, 104, 106.

18. Donaldson, *Idaho of Yesterday*, 93, 131–132.

19. Bruce, *Gaudy Century*, 141.

20. Robison, "Idaho Territorial Newspapers," 46.

21. Ashton, *Voice in the West*, 140–141.

22. John L. Dailey, Diary, September 1859. Western History Department, Denver Public Library.

23. Butte *Miner*, 12 September 1876.

24. *Oregon Statesman*, 30 October 1852.

25. See Kielbowicz, *News in the Mail*.

26. Walter Colton, *Three Years in California* (New York: A. S. Barnes & Co., 1854), 53.

27. *Reese River Reveille*, 20 August 1878.

28. *Ibid.*, 23 August 1878.

29. Phillip I. Earl, "Story on glowing tree made saps of readers," *Nevadan* magazine, 6T, *Las Vegas Review-Journal*, 1 April 1990.

30. *Reese River Reveille*, 19 August 1878.

31. *Placer Times*, 26 January 1850.

32. *Daily Inland Empire*, 27 March 1869.

33. Belmont *Courier*, 28 February 1874.

34. *Deseret News*, 19 October 1850.

35. Robison, "Idaho Territorial Newspapers," 35.

36. Sacramento *Union*, 19 March 1851.

37. Carson *Daily Independent*, 1 September 1863.

38. Kennedy, "Newspapers of the California Northern Mines," 171.

39. *Deseret News*, 31 May 1851.

40. William Lightfoot Visscher, *A Thrilling and Truthful History of the Pony Express* (Chicago: Charles T. Pownes, Co., 1946, originally published 1908), 28.

41. The story of the news consortium formed by the Sacramento *Union*, the San Francisco *Bulletin*, and the *Alta California* is told by Robert J. Chandler, "The California News-Telegraph Monopoly, 1860–1870," *Southern California Quarterly* 58 (Winter 1976): 459–484.

42. Meany, *Newspapers of Washington Territory*, 27.

43. Ashton, *Voice in the West*, 112, 115.

44. Visscher, 26, 29. Even so, the Pony Express lost an estimated $200,000 during its short life.

45. Ashton, *Voice in the West*, 118–119.

46. Kennedy, "Newspapers of the California Northern Mines," 142.

47. Angel, *History of Nevada*, 105.

48. Rice, *The Los Angeles Star*, 141.

49. Ashton, *Voice in the West*, 120.

50. Perkin, *The First Hundred Years*, 206; Notson, *Making the Day Begin*, 8; Seattle *People's Telegram*, 3 November 1864.

51. Ashton, *Voice in the West*, 142–143.

52. *History of Humboldt County, California* (San Francisco: Wallace W. Elliott & Co., 1881), 215; Robison, "Idaho Territorial Newspapers," 128.

53. *Rocky Mountain News*, 7 May 1859, quoted in LeRoy Reuben Hafen, *The Overland Mail, 1849–1869: Promoter of Settlement, Precursor of Railroads* (Cleveland: Arthur C. Clark Company, 1926), 145–146, 148.

54. Joseph Umans, "The Territorial Press of Northern and Central Colorado" (Master of Arts thesis, University of Colorado, 1928), 45.

55. Carson *Daily Independent*, 1 September 1863.

56. Ione *Advertiser*, 17 September 1864.

57. Notson, *Making the Day Begin*, 8.

58. *Daily Inland Empire*, 27 March 1869.

59. Doten, *Journals*, 2:1027–1028, 1331.

60. Robison, "Idaho Territorial Newspapers," 146.

61. Keen, "Wyoming Frontier Newspapers," 33:136–137.

62. *The Footlight* (Virginia City, Nevada), 9 November 1875. *The Footlight* frequently took jabs at the Virginia City *Chronicle*.

63. *Daily Rocky Mountain News*, 10 December 1860, quoted in Halaas, *Boom Town Newspapers*, 66.

64. *Weekly Montana Post* (Virginia City, Montana), 8 December 1866, quoted in Halaas, *Boom Town Newspapers*, 66.

65. Chandler, "The California News-Telegraph Monopoly," 462.

66. *Ibid.*

67. *Ibid.*, 464–468.

68. *Ibid.*, 468.

69. *Ibid.*, 469.

70. *Ibid.*, 471.

71. Richard Schwarzlose, *The Nation's Newsbrokers*, 2 vols. (Evanston, Ill.: Northwestern University Press, 1989–1990), 2:75.

72. Chandler, "The California News-Telegraph Monopoly," 477.

73. Schwarzlose, *The Nation's Newsbrokers*, 2:76; he also discusses the politics of the fighting between the news services, 2:63.

74. Hubert Howe Bancroft, *History of Utah* (San Francisco: The History Company, 1890), 770–771.

75. Rice, *The Los Angeles Star*, 141; Ashton, *Voice in the West*, 118–119.

76. Robison, "Idaho Territorial Newspapers," 38.

77. *Central Nevadan*, 18 July 1885.

78. Spokane Falls *Evening Review*, 10 June 1884.

79. Dyar, *News for an Empire*, 18, 22.

80. *The Journalist*, 23 March 1889, 12.

81. Stratton, *The Territorial Press of New Mexico*, 41.

82. *People's Telegram*, 3 November 1864; Meany, *Newspapers of Washington Territory*, 45, 51. The *People's Telegram* and *Citizen's Dispatch* are listed as separate papers although Meany also calls them "extras."

83. Angel, *History of Nevada*, 105.

84. Ashton, *Voice in the West*, 121.

85. Doten, *Journals*, 2:1286, 1289.

86. Seattle *Morning Dispatch*, 11 July 1871.

87. St. George, Utah, *Evening Telegram*, 12 April 1879, quoted in Alter, *Early Utah Journalism*, 240.

88. Spokane *Times*, 29 April 1882.

89. Spencer, "Newspapers in Gunnison County, Colorado," 24, 26.

90. *Daily Inland Empire*, 30 March 1869; Oakland *Evening Tribune*, 19 May 1874.

91. Quoted in Turnbull, *History of Oregon Newspapers*, 150.

92. *Owyhee Avalanche*, 30 October 1874; *History of Humboldt County*, 215.

93. Spokane *Daily Review*, 10 June 1884. Bradford W. Scharlott, "Influence of Telegraph on Wisconsin Newspaper Growth," *Journalism Quarterly* 66 (Autumn 1989): 710–715, found that the telegraph contributed to the start of weekly papers as well.

94. Butte *Miner*, 1 June 1876.

95. *Ibid.*, 12 September 1876. A weekly edition of a daily paper might carry more reading matter than other editions because it sometimes had less advertising. For example, the *Owyhee Weekly Avalanche* carried little advertising. A tri-weekly might actually have more reading matter if its ad-

vertising had to be spread over the week instead of concentrated in one issue. Obviously, it depended on the overall level of advertising.

96. Ashton, *Voice in the West*, 204.

97. Doten, *Journals*, 2:1321.

98. Rice, *The Los Angeles Star*, 15.

99. Ashton, *Voice in the West*, 74.

100. Doten, *Journals*, 2:1066.

101. Hubert Howe Bancroft, *History of Nevada, Colorado, and Wyoming 1540–1888*, vol. 25, *Works of Hubert Howe Bancroft* (San Francisco: The History Company, Publishers, 1890), 528.

102. Doten, *Journals*, 2:831.

103. Robison, "Idaho Territorial Newspapers," 5.

104. George N. Belknap, "Oregon Sentinel Extras—1858–1864," *Pacific Northwest Quarterly* 70 (October 1979): 178–180.

105. *Ibid.* As noted elsewhere, the enterprising *Statesman* publisher also sold printed supplements of the federal statutes.

106. Bruce, *Gaudy Century*, 11.

107. Rice, *The Los Angeles Star*, 134–135.

108. Leach, *Recollections of a Newspaper Man*, 117.

Chapter 9: Supplies and Services

1. Huffman, "Newspaper Art in Stockton," 342.

2. Rice, *The Los Angeles Star*, 16; Los Angeles *Star*, 16 October 1852.

3. *Oregon Statesman*, 25 September 1852.

4. *Deseret News*, 19 October 1850; Ashton, *Voice in the West*, 55.

5. *Daily Inland Empire*, 13 April 1869.

6. Hall, "The Mesilla *Times*," 345.

7. *The Journalist*, 4 and 25 February 1888.

8. Los Angeles *Star*, 16 October 1852; Ashton, *Voice in the West*, 99.

9. Alfred Lawrence Lorenz, "'Out of Sorts and Out of Cash': Problems of Publishing in Wisconsin Territory, 1833–1848," *Journalism History* 3 (Summer 1976): 37.

10. *Arizona Miner*, 13 January 1867.

11. *Deseret News*, 30 November 1850.

12. Ashton, *Voice in the West*, 53–58.

13. *Ibid.*, 122–123.

14. *Ibid.*, 124–125.

15. *Deseret News*, 28 April 1876, quoted in Ashton, *Voice in the West*, 387.

16. Ashton, *Voice in the West*, 201–202.

17. Alter, *Early Utah Journalism*, 111, 224, 236.

18. W. Claude Adams, "History of Papermaking in the Pacific Northwest: I," *Oregon Historical Quarterly* 52 (March 1951): 27; David C. Smith, "The Paper Industry in California to 1900," *Southern California Quarterly* 57 (Summer 1975): 129.

19. Adams, "History of Papermaking in the Pacific Northwest," 22; Arthur L. Throckmorton, *Oregon Argonauts: Merchant Adventurers on the Western Frontier* (Portland: Oregon Historical Society, 1961), 311; Smith, "The Paper Industry in California to 1900," 129.

20. *Deseret News*, 6 March 1880, quoted in Alter, *Early Utah Journalism*, 248.

21. Firebaugh, "The Sacramento *Union*," 322; Ashton, *Voice in the West*, 55. New York *Tribune* figures are from Lee, *Daily Newspaper in America*, 743.

22. Bonnell to Thornton McElroy, 25 January 1867. McElroy family papers.

23. Smith, "The Paper Industry in California to 1900," 132, 140. Fourdrinier was a brand of papermaking machine.

24. *Ibid.*, 136, 138.

25. *Ibid.*, 140.

26. *Ibid.*, 141–142.

27. Adams, "History of Papermaking in the Pacific Northwest," 24–29; Throckmorton, *Oregon Argonauts*, 311.

28. Elmo Scott Watson, *History of Auxiliary Newspaper Service in the United States* (Champaign, Illinois: Illini Publishing Co., 1923), 5–9. See also Eugene C. Harter, *Boilerplating America: The Hidden Newspaper*, ed. Dorothy Harter (Lanham, Maryland: University Press of America, 1991).

29. *American Newspaper Reporter*, 1 January 1872.

30. S. N. D. North, *History and Present Condition of the Newspaper and Periodical Press of the United States*, vol. 8, *Tenth Census of the United States, 1880* (Washington: Government Printing Office, 1884), 94. When Kellogg died in 1886, his company's customers were estimated at 1,600, according to *The Journalist*, 3 April 1886.

31. Robison, "Idaho Territorial Newspapers," 196.

32. *History of San Bernardino County*, 121; Spencer, "Newspapers in Gunnison County," 13–14; Alter, *Early Utah Journalism*, 32. Where not otherwise indicated, identification of patent 'sides is by author's observation and determination or statement by the newspaper itself.

33. Turnbull, *History of Oregon Newspapers*, 165.

34. J. F. Atkinson to Clarence Bagley, 12 January 1875. Bagley papers.

35. *Skagit News* (Mt. Vernon, Washington), quoted in Brier, "A History of Newspapers in the Pacific Northwest," 28.

36. A. N. Kellogg to Frederick J. Stanton, July 22, 1868. Stanton papers.

37. Kubler, *A New History of Stereotyping*, 340.

38. Albuquerque *Review*, 8 July 1876, about the *New Mexico Co-operator*, quoted in Stratton, *The Territorial Press of New Mexico*, 42.

39. *Reese River Reveille*, 1 July 1878, about the *Carson Valley News*.

40. Yakima *Record*, 10 February 1883, quoted in Thomas H. Heuterman, "A History of Newspapering in Yakima, Washington" (Master of Arts thesis, University of Washington, 1961), 14–15.

41. Clip in Morse Scrapbook 5, n.d. but probably 8 June 1876. Northwest Collection, University of Washington Libraries.

42. Eaton, "A History of Olympia Newspapers," 128.

43. *The Journalist*, 5 April 1884.

44. North, *History and Present Condition of the Newspaper and Periodical Press*, 95–96.

45. *Palouse Gazette* (Colfax, Washington), 6 June 1879; *Columbia Chronicle*, 7 February 1880.

46. Eaton, "A History of Olympia Newspapers," 128.

47. A. N. Kellogg obituary, *The Journalist*, 3 April 1886.

48. Brier, "A History of Newspapers in the Pacific Northwest," 28.

49. Jonathan Edwards, *An Illustrated History of Spokane County* (W. H. Lever, 1900), 208.

50. Alter, *Early Utah Journalism*, 111.

51. Kubler, *A New History of Stereotyping*, 339.

52. *Ibid.*, 320.

53. Jonas Winchester to Heman Winchester, 22 August 1849. Jonas Winchester papers, Kemble Collection. Jonas said he would have some furniture made but complained that it would be expensive because most San Francisco craftsmen were panning for gold in the Sierra.

54. Bonnell to Thornton F. McElroy, 16 April 1864, McElroy family papers; *Arizona Miner*, 29 February 1866.

55. *Daily Dramatic Chronicle*, 16 January 1865.

56. Beshoar, "The Strife and Struggle of a Newspaper in the Old West," 45.

57. *History of Contra Costa County*, 403.

58. Reno *Evening Gazette*, 8 March 1876.

59. Ashton, *Voice in the West*, 58.

Chapter 10: Pressures on the Press

1. David J. Russo, "The Origins of Local News in the U.S. Country Press, 1840s–1870s," *Journalism Monographs* 65 (February 1980): 2; Thomas H. Heuterman, "Assessing the 'Press on Wheels': Individualism in Frontier Journalism," *Journalism Quarterly* 53 (Autumn 1976): 426; John Cameron Sim, *The Grass Roots Press: America's Country Newspapers* (Ames, Iowa: Iowa State University Press, 1969), 33. Sim says local news was not regularly printed in country papers until around 1890 and that readers didn't expect to find local news. Similarly, William H. Lyon, *The Pioneer Editor in Missouri, 1808–1860* (Columbia, Missouri: University of Missouri Press, 1965), 47, says the pioneer editor was not a chronicler of his local community. However, Henry King, *American Journalism* (address to Kansas Editors and Publishers Assn., 1871, Arno Press Inc. reprint, 1970), 13, said that "home news should be first and most sedulously sought."

2. *Owyhee Avalanche*, 4 January 1873.

3. Ione *Advertiser*, 17 September 1864; Carson *Daily Independent*, 1 September 1863.

4. *Daily Inland Empire*, 30 March 1869.

5. *Deseret News*, 14 March 1855; Alter, *Early Utah Journalism*, 236.

6. Vivian Paladin, "Henry N. Blake: Proper Bostonian, Purposeful Pioneer," *Montana: The Magazine of Western History* 14 (August 1974): 41. Interestingly, the speaker delivered his annotated speech to the newspaper before he delivered it to the audience.

7. *Oregonian*, 12 July 1856, quoted in Turnbull, *History of Oregon Newspapers*, 69.

8. Butte *Miner*, 11 December 1877.

9. Virgil Delbert Reed, "A Last Hurrah for the Frontier Press," *American Journalism* 6 (1989): 69.

10. Kennedy, "Newspapers of the California Northern Mines," 465.

11. Quoted in Paladin, "Henry N. Blake: Proper Bostonian, Purposeful Pioneer," 38.

12. *Reese River Reveille*, 21 January 1882.

13. *Daily Dramatic Chronicle*, 18 March 1865.

14. *Idaho Weekly Avalanche*, 5 September 1878.

15. *Oregon Statesman*, 28 May 1851.

16. Drury, *An Editor on the Comstock Lode*, 185.

17. Heuterman, "A History of Newspapering in Yakima, Washington," 19.

18. *Daily Bee* (Carson City, Nevada), 18 November 1882.

19. *Owyhee Avalanche*, 23 November 1867.

20. Roger W. Lotchin, *San Francisco, 1846–1856: From Hamlet to City* (New York: Oxford University Press, 1974), 339.

21. Doten, *Journals*, 3:1623; the story was printed in the 15 April 1886 issue of the *Territorial Enterprise*.

22. *The Journalist*, 20 September 1884. On 5 September 1884, the San Francisco *Chronicle* ran more than six columns of Barnes's testimony.

23. Beebe, *Comstock Commotion*, 33.

24. Douglas D. Martin, *Tombstone's Epitaph* (Albuquerque: University of New Mexico Press, 1951), 101–103.

25. Jordan, "The Golden Age of the Press Revisited," Table I.

26. *Palouse Gazette*, 29 September, 6 October 1877.

27. Gold Hill *News*, 13 October 1863.

28. *Reese River Reveille*, 3 January 1882.

29. Splitter, "Newspapers of Los Angeles," 439.

30. Glenn Chesney Quiett, *They Built the West* (New York: D. Appleton-Century Co., 1934), 505; Spokane *Chronicle*, 29 June 1881; Edwards, *An Illustrated History of Spokane County*, 203.

31. Reed, "A Last Hurrah for the Frontier Press," 67, 74.

32. Lamar, *The Far Southwest*, 168.

33. Stratton, *The Territorial Press of New Mexico*, 19, 47.

34. *History of Santa Barbara County*, 112.

35. Alter, *Early Utah Journalism*, 297.

36. Mortensen, "The *Deseret News* and Utah," 49, 51.

37. Quoted in Lamar, *The Far Southwest*, 375.

38. Alter, *Early Utah Journalism*, 201.

39. Thomas G. Alexander and James B. Allen, *Mormons & Gentiles: A History of Salt Lake City* (Boulder, Colorado: Pruett Publishing Co., 1984), 114–115.

40. Alter, *Early Utah Journalism*, 209.

41. *Ibid.*, 275; Ashton, *Voice in the West*, 99.

42. Notson, *Making the Day Begin*, 8.

43. Kalama *Beacon*, 19 May 1871.

44. Tacoma, Washington, *Herald*, 21 January 1879.

45. Oscar Lewis, *The Big Four* (New York: Alfred A. Knopf, 1966), 316.

46. Firebaugh, "The Sacramento *Union*," 329.

47. Lewis, *The Big Four*, 316.

48. *Ibid.*, 252; Lewis does not detail the "railroad-controlled" press.

49. Lamar, *The Far Southwest*, 175.

50. Lingenfelter and Gash, *The Newspapers of Nevada*, 237.

51. Gilluly, *The Press Gang*, 28; Lamar, *The Far Southwest*, 452.

52. Paul Harvey, *Tacoma Headlines* (Tacoma, Washington: Tribune Publishing Co., 1962), 25; W. P. Bonney, *History of Pierce County, Washington*, 3 vols. (Chicago: Pioneer Historical Publishing Co., 1927), 2:1042.

53. Barbara Boyd Voltmer, *Kern County's Courier, 1866–1887: A Newspaper in a Period of Economic and Political Transition* (Bakersfield, California: Kern County Historical Society, 1968), 25, 28.

54. Cloud, "A Party Press," 54.

55. *Illustrated History of Plumas County*, 390.

56. *Washington Pioneer* (Olympia), 3 December 1853.

57. *Placer Times*, 22 December 1849.

58. *Puget Sound Courier*, 19 May 1855.

59. Boise *News*, 22 October 1863, quoted in Robison, "Idaho Territorial Newspapers," 42.

60. Notson, *Making the Day Begin*, 8.

61. Stratton, *The Territorial Press of New Mexico*, 199.

62. Robison, "Idaho Territorial Newspapers," 22.

63. Newman, "The Las Vegas *Weekly Mail*," 162.

64. Hudson, *Journalism in the United States*, 699; Hufford, "The Arizona Gazette," 25.

65. Turnbull, *History of Oregon Newspapers*, 44–45.

66. Angel, *History of Nevada*, 317.

67. Kemble, *A History of California Newspapers*, 155–156.

68. Leach, *Recollections of a Newspaper Man*, 261–262.

69. Allen Weir to Clarence Bagley, 4 August 1880. Bagley papers. Weir became Washington State's first secretary of state.

70. Bancroft, *History of Nevada, Colorado and Wyoming*, 527.

71. Myers, *Lizzie: The Letters of Elizabeth Chester Fisk*, 30, 54.

72. Lingenfelter and Gash, *The Newspapers of Nevada*, 121–122.

73. Myers, *Lizzie: The Letters of Elizabeth Chester Fisk*, 54.

74. *History of Humboldt County, California*, 217.

75. Aurora *Daily Times*, 27 November 1863.

76. Bruce, *Gaudy Century*, 136, 138.

77. *Daily Dramatic Chronicle*, 22 April 1865.

78. *History of Amador County, California* (Oakland: Thompson & West, 1881), 274.

79. Hall, "The Mesilla *Times*," 349–350.

80. Robison, "Idaho Territorial Newspapers," 17.

81. *History of Santa Barbara County*, 328.

82. Salt Lake City *Herald*, 8 April and 21 April 1880, quoted in Alter, *Early Utah Journalism*, 249.

83. Provo *Enquirer*, 21 July 1880, quoted in Alter, *Early Utah Journalism*, 250.

84. *Daily Dramatic Chronicle*, 28 February 1865.

85. *Owyhee Avalanche*, 5 March 1870, about the San Francisco *Evening Tribune*.

86. Walla Walla *Daily Journal*, 6 August 1883.

87. Alter, *Early Utah Journalism*, 248.

88. Beebe, *Comstock Commotion*, 45–46.

89. Young, *Journalism in California*, 68; Bruce, *Gaudy Century*, 28–31.

90. Twain, *Mark Twain's West*, 346–347.

91. Alter, *Early Utah Journalism*, 170.

92. *Owyhee Avalanche*, 28 September 1878.

93. Cheyenne *Leader*, 19 September 1868.

94. *Oregonian*, 12 April 1851, quoted in Turnbull, *History of Oregon Newspapers*, 73–74.

95. Olympia *Transcript*, 30 November 1867, quoting the *Daily Dramatic Chronicle*.

Chapter 11: Obliterating the Frontier

1. Lyon, "The Significance of Newspapers on the American Frontier," *Journal of the West* (1980): 9.

2. *Placer Times*, 8 December 1849.

3. Kemble, *A History of California Newspapers*, 272–296.

4. *Ibid.*, 119.

5. *Ibid.*, 124. Kemble calls it "disreputable."

6. Turnbull, 477, 481.

7. Seattle *Sunday Star*, 11 Nov. 1883.

8. Gilbert, 359; *Sunday Epigram*, 10 June, 30 Sept. 1883.

9. Chandler, 461.

10. Bruce, *Gaudy Century*, 72–73; Meany, *Newspapers of Washington Territory*, 84; Turnbull, *History of Oregon Newspapers*, 171.

11. Bruce, *Gaudy Century*, 72–73.

12. *Ibid.*, 58–60; Young, *Journalism in California*, 24–32.

13. Seattle *Daily Call*, 27 June 1885–10 February 1886; see also the *Post-Intelligencer* for the same period.

14. Young, *Journalism in California*, 214.

15. Lewis, *The Big Four*, 349.

16. Jonas Winchester to Ebenezer Winchester, 1 January 1851, Jonas Winchester papers, Kemble Collection.

17. Ted Curtis Smythe, "The Advertisers' War to Verify Newspaper Circulation, 1870–1914," *American Journalism* 3 (1986): 176. Robert L. Bishop, Katherine Sharma, and Richard J. Brazee, "Determinants of Newspaper Circulation: A Pooled Cross-Section Time-Series Study in the United States, 1850–1970," *Communication Research* 7 (January 1980): 7, concluded that price may have been the most important factor in determining circulation over a 120-year period in the United States. However, as the authors acknowledge, the conclusion is simplistic and largely reflects the limitations of the data.

18. *The Journalist*, 30 March 1889, 4.

19. Ashton, *Voice in the West*, 203; E. D. Smith Jr., "Communication Pioneering in Oregon," *Oregon Historical Quarterly* 39 (December 1938): 360.

20. Los Angeles *Times*, 4 December 1881.

21. Quoted in Dyar, *News for an Empire*, 14.

22. Kemble, *A History of California Newspapers* 100–101; 110–111; 114; 124; 323.

23. Cross, *A History of the Labor Movement in California*, 15, 21; Katz, *The Columbian*, 38; Perkin, *The First Hundred Years* 33.

24. *Deseret News*, 6 March 1852.

25. Katz, "The Columbian," 38.

26. Bruce, *Gaudy Century*, 56–57.

27. Cross, *A History of the Labor Movement in California*, 24. Unions circulated lists of non-union employers and anyone who worked for them to dissuade union shops from hiring "rats" or "scabs," to ostracize them from fellow printers, and to keep union members from getting involved with either non-union shops or scabs. See for example, the Denver Typographical Union "Rat Circular" in the Denver Typographical Union papers in the Western History Department of the Denver Public Library.

28. Cross, *A History of the Labor Movement in California*, 28, 303.

29. *Ibid.*, 304.

30. Denver Typographical Union circular, 5 November 1875. Denver Typographical Union papers.

31. Quoted by Doten, *Journals*, 2:1212.

32. Denver Typographical Union, semi-annual circular, January 1878. Denver Typographical Union papers.

33. Dailey, Diary, April 1860, 2, Denver Public Library.

34. Cross, *A History of the Labor Movement in California*, 67.

35. *Ibid.*, 179.

36. Gilluly, *The Press Gang*, 28.

37. *The Journalist*, 4 August 1888.

38. Stimson, *Rise of the Labor Movement in Los Angeles*, 33–34.

39. *Ibid.*, 40–41.

40. *Ibid.*, 104.

41. *Ibid.*, 109–115.

42. WPA Writers Program, "History of San Francisco Journalism," 2:51.

43. Eaton, "A History of Olympia Newspapers," 130.

44. Turnbull, *History of Oregon Newspapers*, 159, 387.

45. *Annual Proceedings of the Washington Press Association*, 1889, 3.

46. Lyon, "Louis C. Hughes, Arizona's Editorial Gadfly," 188–190.

47. Hubert Howe Bancroft, *The History of Arizona and New Mexico* (Albuquerque: Horn and Wallach, 1962, reprint of 1889 edition), 777; Keen, "The Newspaper Men," 66.

48. *Annual Proceedings of the Washington Press Association, 1889*, 21.

49. *Idaho Register*, 4 April 1885; see also Doten, *Journals*, 3:1634.

50. Gilluly, 28.

51. Turnbull, *History of Oregon Newspapers*, 159.

52. Gilluly, 26. In organizing, western publishers shared the objectives with the American Newspaper Publishers' Association formed in 1887 to protect members from fraud as well as to share information and assistance. *The Journalist*, 26 March 1887.

53. *The Journalist*, 16 March 1889.

Chapter 12: Success and Failure

1. Perkin, *The First Hundred Years*, 31–35.

2. Budget figures have been rounded for convenience.

3. Jonas Winchester to Ebenezer Winchester, 28 February 1850. Jonas Winchester papers, Kemble Collection.

4. Kemble, *A History of California Newspapers*, 160.

5. *The Journalist*, 16 August 1884.

6. *Ibid.*, 15 January 1887.

7. Orvin Nebecker Malmquist, *The First 100 Years: A History of the Salt Lake Tribune, 1871–1971* (Salt Lake City: Utah State Historical Society, 1971), 54.

8. *Oregon Statesman*, 22 June 1852.

9. *Owyhee Avalanche*, 16 July 1870.

10. *Rocky Mountain News*, 25 October 1866.

11. *Idaho Avalanche*, 24 August 1878.

12. *An Illustrated History of Skagit and Snohomish Counties* (Interstate Publishing Co., 1906), 434; Seabeck, Washington, *Rebel Battery*, October 1878.

13. Kemble, *A History of California Newspapers*, 108.

14. Alter, *Early Utah Journalism*, 57.

15. Angel, *History of Nevada*, 302. Variations of this story were common around the West. For example, the Cheyenne *Leader*, 28 September 1867, put it this way: "The question why printers do not succeed as well as brewers, was answered thus: 'Because printers work for the head and brewers for the stomach, and where twenty men have stomachs but one has brains.'"

16. Lingenfelter and Gash, *The Newspapers of Nevada*, 256.

17. Helena *Herald*, 17 June 1869, quoted in Halaas, *Boom Town Newspapers*, 65.

18. Alter, *Early Utah Journalism*, 278.

19. *Owyhee Avalanche*, 28 December 1878.

20. Cheyenne *Leader*, 10 December 1867.

21. Alter, *Early Utah Journalism*, 206; some semi- and tri-weeklies challenged that notion, but dailies stayed away.

22. Los Angeles *Times*, 9 December 1881.

23. Alter, *Early Utah Journalism*, 298; *Spirit of the West* (Walla Walla), 25 December 1874.

24. *Idaho Avalanche*, 24 August 1878.

25. Alter, *Early Utah Journalism*, 226.

26. Stratton, *The Territorial Press of New Mexico*, 19.

27. *An Illustrated History of Southeastern Washington*, 810.

28. *Arizona Miner*, 10 January 1866.

29. *History of Humboldt County*, 217.

30. Drury, *An Editor on the Comstock Lode*, 182.

31. *Idaho Avalanche*, 24 August 1878.

32. Splitter, "Newspapers of Los Angeles," 439.

33. Eaton, "A History of Olympia Newspapers," 123.

34. *Deseret News*, 8 February 1851.

35. Turnbull, *History of Oregon Newspapers*, 51.

36. Kemble, *A History of California Newspapers*, 85–86.

37. Quoted in *ibid.*, 234.

38. Splitter, "Newspapers of Los Angeles," 454.

39. Angel, *History of Nevada*, 316.

40. Rice, *The Los Angeles Star*, 68.

41. Leach, *Recollections of a Newspaper Man*, 121.

42. Doten, *Journals*, 2:1157.

43. *Ibid.*, 2:1245.

44. *Ibid.*, 2:1231–1342.

45. *Ibid.*, 2:1396.

46. *Ibid.*, 2:1487.

47. *Ibid.*, 2:1510.

48. *Owyhee Avalanche*, 16 November 1867.

49. Armstrong, *Nevada Printing History*, 228.

50. Jonas Winchester to Ebenezer Winchester, 27 March 1850. Jonas Winchester papers, Kemble Collection.

51. Jonas Winchester to Susan Winchester, 1 October 1850. Jonas Winchester papers, Kemble Collection.

52. *Ibid.*, 16 July 1850.

53. *Ibid.*, 30 March 1851.

54. Clarence Bagley to Daniel Bagley, 5 May 1878. Clarence Bagley papers.

55. See, for example, Daniel Bagley to Clarence Bagley, 13 February 1874; 3 March 1874, 17 May 1877; Clarence Bagley to Daniel Bagley, 28 October 1877. Clarence Bagley papers.

56. Quoted in Marysville *Appeal*, 29 September 1860.

57. Clarence Bagley to Daniel Bagley, no date. Clarence Bagley papers.

58. Heuterman, *Movable Type*, 100–104.

59. Charles Prosch, *Reminiscences*, 8.

60. Halaas, *Boom Town Newspapers*, 36.

61. Thomas Jefferson Dryer to Thornton McElroy, 26 September 1853. McElroy papers; Yakima *Record*, 6 September 1879; Robison, "Idaho Territorial Newspapers," 28.

62. Doten, *Journals*, 1:795.

63. Meany, *Newspapers of Washington Territory*, 18.

64. Keen, "Wyoming Frontier Newspapers," 33:150–151.

65. Barbara Boyd Voltmer, *Kern County's Courier, 1866–1876*, 18.

66. *Ibid.*, 20.

67. Bruce, *Gaudy Century*, 70–71. Kemble, *A History of California Newspapers*, 152, says the amount was $6,000.

68. *History of Plumas County*, 483.

69. Kemble, *A History of California Newspapers*, 92–94.

70. Bruce, *Gaudy Century*, 58.

71. Kemble, *A History of California Newspapers*, 99.

72. *Ibid.*, 142.

73. *Ibid.*, 143.

74. Bruce, *Gaudy Century*, 71.

75. Kemble, *A History of California Newspapers*, 116. Not as aggressive as the *Herald*, the *California Chronicle* refused to support the vigilantes, thus earning their wrath.

76. Bruce, *Gaudy Century*, 141.

77. Hudson, "A Pioneer Southwestern Newspaper and Its Editor," 18.

78. *Ibid.*, 19–20.

79. Leach, *Recollections of a Newspaper Man*, 118.

80. *Ibid.*, 134.

81. Schellie, *The Tucson Citizen*, 40.

82. Los Angeles *Times*, 1 January 1882.

83. *Carson Daily Appeal*, 16 May 1865.

84. Los Angeles *Times*, 8 December 1881.

85. *Rocky Mountain News*, 25 October 1866.

86. Quoted in "History of the Colorado Press Association," 17:12–13.

SELECTED BIBLIOGRAPHY

Manuscript Sources

California Historical Society Library

Kemble Collection
Jonas Winchester papers
Antioch *Ledger* collection
San Francisco *Chronicle* collection

Denver Public Library

Western History Department
William N. Byers papers
John L. Dailey diary
Frederick I. Stanton papers
Denver Typographical Union scrapbook
Owen J. Goldrick papers

University of Washington Libraries

Manuscript Division
Clarence Bagley papers
Thornton F. McElroy family papers
Bion Kendall papers

Northwest Collection
Eldridge Morse Scrapbooks

Wyoming State Archives, Museum and Historical Department
Cheyenne *Leader* Job Book, 1868–1869

Books and Articles

Adams, W. Claude. "History of Papermaking in the Pacific Northwest: I," *Oregon Historical Quarterly* 52 (March 1951): 21–37.

Alexander, Thomas G., and James B. Allen. *Mormons & Gentiles: A History of Salt Lake City*. Boulder, Colorado: Pruett Publishing Co., 1984.

Allen, Eric W. "Oregon Journalism in 1887," *Oregon Historical Quarterly* 38 (September 1937): 251–264.

Alter, J. Cecil. *Early Utah Journalism*. Westport, Connecticut: Greenwood Press, 1970; reprint of 1938 edition published by Utah State Historical Society.

American Newspaper Publishers Association. *Facts About Newspapers '90*. Washington, D.C.: ANPA, August 1990.

Ames, William, and Dwight Teeter. "Politics, Economics and the Mass Media." In *Mass Media and the National Experience: Essays in Communications History*, Ron T. Farrar and John D. Stevens, eds. New York: Harper & Row, 1971.

Angel, Myron, ed. *History of Nevada, 1881*. Berkeley: Howell-North Books, 1958; originally published by Thompson & West, 1881.

Angle, Grant C. "Rambling Reminiscences of Fifty Years of Newspapering," *The Washington Newspaper* 21 (August 1936): 1–3.

Annual Proceedings of the Washington Press Association, 1889, 1890, 1892. Hoquiam, Washington: Washington Steam Book, News and Job Printing, 1891.

Armstrong, Robert D. *Nevada Printing History*. Reno: University of Nevada Press, 1981.

———. "Nevada's Public Printing, Chiefly in 1869: Additional Notes to Armstrong, *Nevada Printing History*," *The Papers of the Bibliographic Society of America*, 81 (1987): 465–478.

———. "Newspapering in Nineteenth Century Nevada," in *Proceedings of the Nevada Newspaper Conference*, 1–24, ed. Karen Rix Gash. Reno: Oral History Program, University of Nevada, Reno, 1990.

Ashton, Wendell J. *Voice in the West: Biography of a Pioneer Newspaper*. New York: Duell, Sloan & Pearce, 1950.

Atherton, Lewis E. *The Frontier Merchant in Mid-America*. Columbia: University of Missouri Press, 1971.

Ayres, Alex. *The Wit and Wisdom of Mark Twain*. New York: Harper & Row, 1987.

Bagley, Clarence. *History of King County Washington*, 3 vols. Seattle: S. J. Clarke Publishing Co., 1929.

———. *History of Seattle*. 3 vols. Chicago: 1916.

Bancroft, Hubert Howe, and Frances Fuller Victor. *History of Nevada, 1540–1888*. Reno: University of Nevada Press, 1981; reprint of 1890 edition.

———. *History of Arizona and New Mexico*. Albuquerque: Horn and Wallach, 1962; reprint of 1889 edition.

———. *History of Nevada, Colorado, and Wyoming, 1540–1880*. San Francisco: The History Company, 1890.

———. *History of Utah*. San Francisco: The History Co., 1890.

Beales, Benjamin Bronston. "San Jose Mercury and the Civil War," *California Historical Society Quarterly* 22 (September 1943): 223–234.

Beebe, Lucius. *Comstock Commotion: The Story of the Territorial Enterprise.* Stanford: Stanford University Press, 1954.

Belknap, George N. "Oregon Sentinel Extras—1858–1864," *Pacific Northwest Quarterly* 70 (October 1979): 178–180.

Bennion, Sherilyn Cox. *Equal to the Occasion: Women Editors of the Nineteenth-Century West.* Reno: University of Nevada Press, 1990.

———. "The Woman's Exponent: Forty-two Years of Speaking for Women," *Utah Historical Quarterly* 44 (Summer 1976): 222–239.

Beshoar, Barron. "The Strife and Struggle of a Newspaper in the Old West," *American West* 10 (September 1973): 45–47, 62–63.

Bingham, Edwin R. "American West Through Autobiography and Memoir," *Pacific Historical Review* 56 (February 1987): 1–24.

Bishop, Robert L.; Sharma, Katherine; and Brazee, Richard J. "Time-Series Study in the United States, 1850–1970," *Communication Research* 7 (January 1980): 3–22.

Blackmon, Robert E. "Noah Brooks: Reporter in the White House," *Journalism Quarterly* 32 (Summer 1955): 301–310, 374.

Blainey, Geoffrey. *The Tyranny of Distance.* Melbourne, Australia: Sun Books, 1966.

Blair, Walter, ed. *Mark Twain's West.* Chicago: R. R. Donnelley & Sons Co., 1983.

Bledsoe, Anthony Jennings. *History of Del Norte County, California.* Eureka: Wymer & Co., 1881.

Bonney, W. P. *History of Pierce County, Washington.* 3 vols. Chicago: Pioneer Historical Publishing Co., 1927.

Boorstin, Daniel J. *The Americans: The National Experience.* New York: Vantage Books, 1965.

Boyd, David. *A History: Greeley and the Union Colony of Colorado.* Greeley, Colorado: The Greeley Tribune Press, 1890.

Brier, Warren J., and Blumberg, Nathan B., eds. *A Century of Montana Journalism.* Missoula, Montana: Mountain Press Publishing Co., 1971.

Brinegar, David F. "Arizona's First Chain Journalists," *Journal of Arizona History* 24 (Spring 1983): 73–88.

Broadbent, T. L. "The German-Language Press in California: Record of a German Immigration," *Journal of the West* 10 (October 1971): 637–661.

Bruce, John. *Gaudy Century: The Story of San Francisco's Hundred Years of Robust Journalism.* New York: Random House, 1948.

Bryce, James. *Reflections on American Institutions.* Greenwich, Connecticut: Fawcett Publications, 1961. (From *The American Commonwealth*, published 1893.)

Budlong, Caroline Gale. *Memories of Pioneer Days.* Eugene, Oregon: The Picture Press Printers, 1949.

Carey, Arthur C. "Effects of the Pony Express and the Transcontinental Telegraph Upon Selected California Newspapers," *Journalism Quarterly* 51 (Summer 1974): 320–323.

Carter, John Denton. "Before the Telegraph: The News Service of the San

Francisco Bulletin, 1855–1861," *Pacific Historical Review* 11 (September 1942): 301–317.

Chandler, Robert J. "The California News-Telegraph Monopoly 1860–1870," *Southern California Quarterly* 58 (Winter 1976): 459–484.

Chapman, Arthur. *The Pony Express: The Record of a Romantic Adventure in Business*. New York: A. L. Burt Company, 1932.

Clark, Thomas D. *The Southern Country Editor*. New York: The Bobbs-Merrill Company, 1948.

Cloud, Barbara. "Establishing the Frontier Newspaper: A Study of Eight Western Territories," *Journalism Quarterly* 61 (Winter 1984): 805–811.

————. "A Party Press? Not Just Yet! Political Publishing on the Frontier," *Journalism History* 7 (Summer 1980): 54–55, 72–73.

————. "Laura Hall Peters: Pursuing the Myth of Equality," *Pacific Northwest Quarterly* 74 (January 1983): 28–36.

Colton, Walter. *Three Years in California*. New York: A. S. Barnes & Co., 1854.

Cook, Francis. *The Territory of Washington, 1879*. Edited with an introduction by J. Orin Oliphant. Fairfield, Washington: Ye Galleon Press, 1972; first published 1925.

Cronin, William. "Revisiting the Vanishing Frontier: The Legacy of Frederick Jackson Turner," *Western Historical Quarterly* 18 (April 1987): 157–176.

Cross, Ira B. *A History of the Labor Movement in California*. Berkeley: University of California Press, 1935.

Cummins, Ella Sterling. *The Story of the Files: A Review of California Writers and Literature*. San Francisco: Co-operative Printing Co., 1893.

Dary, David. *Entrepreneurs of the Old West*. New York: Alfred A. Knopf, 1986.

Davidson, Levette Jay. "O. J. Goldrick, Pioneer Journalist," *Colorado Magazine* 18 (January 1936): 26–37.

DeVoto, Bernard. *The Year of Decision, 1846*. Boston: Houghton Mifflin Co., 1942.

Directory of the City of Placerville. Placerville: Placerville Republican Printing Office, 1862.

Donaldson, Thomas. *Idaho of Yesterday*. Westport, Connecticut: Greenwood Press, 1970; reprint of 1941 edition, Caxton Press.

Doten, Alfred. *The Journals of Alfred Doten, 1849–1903*, edited by Walter Van Tilburg Clark. Reno: University of Nevada Press, 1973.

Drury, Wells. *An Editor on the Comstock Lode*. New York: Farrar & Rinehart, Inc., 1936.

Durham, N. W. *History of the City of Spokane and Spokane County, Washington*. 3 vols. Spokane: S. J. Clarke Publishing Co., 1912.

Dyar, Ralph E. *News for an Empire*. Caldwell, Idaho: Caxton Publishers Inc., 1952.

Dyer, Carolyn Stewart. "Economic Dependence and Concentration of Ownership Among Antebellum Wisconsin Newspapers," *Journalism History* 7 (Summer 1980): 42–46.

———. "Political Patronage of the Wisconsin Press, 1849–1860: New Perspectives on the Economics of Patronage," *Journalism Monographs* 109 (February 1989).

———. "Quantitative Analysis in Journalism History: Some Examples and Advice." *Clio*, 1980.

Earl, Phillip I. "Story on glowing tree made saps of readers." *Nevadan* magazine, *Las Vegas Review-Journal*, 1 April 1990, 6T.

Edwards, Jonathan. *An Illustrated History of Spokane County*. W. H. Lever, 1900.

Ellis, L. Ethan. *Print Paper Pendulum: Group Pressures and the Price of Newsprint*. New Brunswick: Rutgers University Press, 1948.

Ellis, William T. *Memories: My Seventy-Two Years in the Romantic County of Yuba, California*. Eugene: University of Oregon, 1939.

Ellison, Rhoda Coleman. "Newspaper Publishing in Frontier Alabama," *Journalism Quarterly* 23 (September 1946): 269–301.

Farrar, Victor J. "Barter: Mainstay for the First State Newspapers," *Washington Historian* 3 (April 1918): 193–195.

Firebaugh, Dorothy Gile. "The Sacramento *Union*: Voice of California, 1851–1875," *Journalism Quarterly* 30 (Summer 1953): 321–330.

Gilbert, Frank T. *Historic Sketches of Walla Walla, Whitman, Columbia and Garfield Counties, Washington Territory*. Portland: A. G. Walling, 1882.

Gilluly, Sam. *The Press Gang: A Century of Montana Newspapers, 1885–1985*. Helena: Montana Press Association, 1985.

Goldrick, Owen J. "The First School in Denver," *Colorado Magazine* 6 (March 1929): 72–76.

Goodwin, Charles C. *As I Remember Them*. Salt Lake City: Salt Lake Commercial Club, 1913.

Goss, Helen Rocca. "The Fourth Estate in Old Tuolumne," *Historical Society of Southern California Quarterly* 40 (June 1958): 120–137.

Gower, Calvin W. "Kansas 'Border Town' Newspapers and the Pike's Peak Gold Rush," *Journalism Quarterly* 44 (Summer 1967): 281–288.

Gurian, Jay. "Sweetwater Journalism and Western Myth," *Annals of Wyoming* 36 (April 1964): 79–88.

Gutierrez, Felix. "Spanish-Language Media in America, Background, Resources, History," *Journalism History* 4 (Summer 1977): 34–41, 65–67.

Hafen, LeRoy Reuben. *The Overland Mail, 1849–1869: Promoter of Settlement, Precursor of Railroads*. Cleveland: Arthur H. Clark Company, 1926.

Hage, George S. *Newspapers on the Minnesota Frontier*. St. Paul: Minnesota Historical Society, 1967.

Halaas, David Fridtjof. *Boom Town Newspapers: Journalism on the Rocky Mountain Mining Frontier, 1859–1881*. Albuquerque: University of New Mexico Press, 1981.

Hall, Mark W. "Journalism in California: the Pioneer Period, 1831–1849," *Journal of the West* 10 (October 1971): 624–636.

Hall, Mark W. "1831–49: The Pioneer Period for Newspapers in California,"

Journalism Quarterly 49 (Winter 1972): 648–655.

Hall, Martin Hardwick. "The Mesilla *Times,* A Journal of Confederate Arizona," *Arizona and the West* 5 (Winter 1963): 337–351.

Harvey, Paul. *Tacoma Headlines.* Tacoma, Washington: Tribune Publishing Co., 1962.

Heuterman, Thomas H. "Assessing the 'Press on Wheels': Individualism in Frontier Journalism," *Journalism Quarterly* 53 (Autumn 1976): 423–428.

———. *Movable Type: Biography of Legh R. Freeman.* Ames, Iowa: Iowa State University Press, 1979.

Himes, George H. "History of the Press of Oregon, 1839–1850," *Oregon Historical Quarterly* 3 (December 1902): 327–370.

History of Amador County, California. Oakland: Thompson & West, 1881.

History of the City of Denver, Arapahoe County, and Colorado. Chicago: O. L. Baskin and Co., 1880.

History of Clarke County (Washington). Portland: A. G. Walling, 1885.

"History of the Colorado Press Association and Early Newspapers in Colorado," WPA Writers Program, *Colorado Editor* 17 (June 1942): 11–15; (July 1942): 13–15; (August 1942): 12–15; (September 1942): 14–15; (October 1942): 16–19; (November 1942): (11–15); (December 1942): 13–15.

History of Contra Costa County, California. San Francisco: W. A. Slocum & Co., 1882.

History of Fresno County, California. San Francisco: Wallace W. Elliott & Co., 1882.

History of Humboldt County, California. San Francisco: Wallace W. Elliott & Co., 1881.

History of Idaho Territory. San Francisco: Wallace W. Elliott & Co., 1884.

History of Napa and Lake Counties, California. San Francisco: Slocum, Bowen & Co., 1881.

History of Placer County, California. Oakland: Thompson & West, 1882.

History of San Bernardino County (California). San Francisco: Wallace W. Elliott & Co., 1883.

History of Santa Barbara County, California. Oakland: Thompson & West, 1883.

History of Stanislaus County, California. San Francisco: Elliott & Moore Publishers, 1881.

The History of Wallowa County, Oregon. Wallowa County, Oregon: Wallowa County Museum Board, 1983.

Houseman, Robert L. "Frontier Journals of Western Montana," *Pacific Northwest Quarterly* 29 (July 1938): 269–276.

———. "Pioneer Montana's Journalistic Ghost Camp—Virginia City," *Pacific Northwest Quarterly* 29 (January 1938): 53–59.

———. "Boy Editors of Frontier Montana," *Pacific Northwest Quarterly* 27 (July 1936): 219–226.

———. "The End of Frontier Journalism in Montana," *Journalism Quarterly* 12 (1935): 133–145.

Hower, Ralph M. *The History of an Advertising Agency*. Cambridge: Harvard University Press, 1949.

Hudson, Frederic. *Journalism in the United States*. New York: Harper & Brothers, 1873; Scholarly Press reprint, 1968.

Hudson, Millard. "A Pioneer Southwestern Newspaper and Its Editor," *Historical Society of Southern California* 8 (1911): 9–23.

Huffman, Robert E. "Newspaper Art in Stockton, 1850–1892," *California Historical Society Quarterly* 34 (December 1955): 341–356.

Hufford, Kenneth. "The Arizona Gazette: A Forgotten Voice in Arizona Journalism," *Journal of Arizona History* 7 (Winter 1966): 182–187.

———. "P. W. Dooner, Pioneer Editor of Tucson," *Arizona and the West* 10 (Spring 1968): 25–42.

Huntzicker, William E. "Historians and the American Frontier," *American Journalism* 5 (1988): 28–45.

Illustrated History of Plumas, Lassen and Sierra Counties. San Francisco: Fariss & Smith, 1882.

Illustrated History of Southeastern Washington, An. Spokane: Western Historical Publishing Co., 1906.

Illustrated History of Southern California, An. Chicago: The Lewis Publishing Co., 1890.

Innis, Harold A. "The Newspaper in Economic Development," *Journal of Economic History* 2 Supplement (December 1942): 1–33.

Jacobs, Orange. *Memoirs of Orange Jacobs*. Seattle, 1908.

Jeffcott, Percival R. *Nooksack Tales and Trails*. Ferndale, Washington: Sedro-Woolley *Courier-Times*, 1949.

Karolevitz, Robert F. *From Quill to Computer: The Story of America's Community Newspapers*. National Newspaper Foundation, 1985.

———. *Newspapering in the Old West*. New York: Bonanza Books, 1965.

Katz, William A. "The Western Printer and His Publications, 1850–1890," *Journalism Quarterly* 44 (Winter 1967): 708–714.

———. "Benjamin F. Kendall, Territorial Politician," *Pacific Northwest Quarterly* 49 (January 1958): 29–39.

———. "The Columbian: Washington Territory's First Newspaper," *Oregon Historical Quarterly* 64 (March 1964): 33–40.

———. "Public Printers of Washington Territory, 1853–1863," *Pacific Northwest Quarterly* 51 (July 1960): 103–114.

———. "Public Printers of Washington Territory, 1863–1889," *Pacific Northwest Quarterly* 51 (October 1960): 171–181.

Keen, Elizabeth. "Wyoming Frontier Newspapers," *Annals of Wyoming* 33 (October 1961): 133–158.

———. "Wyoming Frontier Newspapers: The Newspaper as Historical Record," *Annals of Wyoming* 34 (October 1962): 218–233.

———. "Wyoming Frontier Newspapers: The Newspapermen," *Annals of Wyoming* 34 (April 1962): 61–84.

———. "Wyoming Frontier Newspapers: The Newspaper as Historical Record," *Annals of Wyoming* 35 (April 1963): 88–101.

Kemble, Edward C. *A History of California Newspapers, 1846–1858*, Helen Harding Bretnor, ed. Los Gatos, California: The Talisman Press, 1962; reprinted from the Sacramento *Union*, 25 December 1858.

Kemble, John Haskell. "Pacific Mail Service between Panama and San Francisco, 1849–1851," *Pacific Historical Review* 2 (1933): 404–417.

Kielbowicz, Richard Burket. "Speeding the News by Postal Express, 1825–1861: The Public Policy of Privileges for the Press," *Social Science Journal* 22 (January 1985): 49–63.

—————. "The Growing Interaction of the Federal Bureaucracy and the Press: The Case of a Postal Rule, 1879–1917," *American Journalism* 4 (1987): 5–18.

—————. *News in the Mail: The Press, Post Office, and Public Information, 1700–1860s*. Westport, Connecticut: Greenwood Press Inc., 1989.

King, Henry. *American Journalism*. New York: Arno Press, 1970; reprint of address to Kansas Editors and Publishers Association, 1871.

Knight, Oliver. "The Owyhee Avalanche: The Frontier Newspaper as a Catalyst in Social Change," *Pacific Northwest Quarterly* 58 (April 1967): 74–81.

Knights, Peter R. "Competition in the U.S. Daily Newspaper Industry, 1865–68," *Journalism Quarterly* 45 (Autumn 1968): 473–480.

Kobre, Sidney. *Development of American Journalism*. Dubuque, Iowa: Wm. C. Brown Company Publishers, 1969.

Kubler, George Adolf. *A New History of Stereotyping*. New York: J. J. Little & Ives Company, 1941.

Lamar, Howard Roberts. *The Far Southwest: 1846–1912*. New York: W. W. Norton & Co., Inc., 1970.

Larsen, Lawrence H. *The Urban West at the End of the Frontier*. Lawrence, Kansas: The Regents Press of Kansas, 1978.

Lawson, Linda. "Advertisements Masquerading as News in Turn-of-the-Century American Periodicals," *American Journalism* 5 (1988): 81–96.

Leach, Frank A. *Recollections of a Newspaper Man: A Record of Life and Events in California*. San Francisco: Samuel Levinson, 1917.

Lee, Alfred McClung. *The Daily Newspaper in America*. New York: The Macmillan Company, 1937.

Lent, John A. "The Press on Wheels: A History of The Frontier Index," *Journal of the West* 10 (October 1971): 662–699.

Letter, Otho Clarke. "Scott and the Oregonian," *Journalism Quarterly* 5 (January 1929): 1–10.

Lewis, Oscar, ed. *The Big Four*. New York: Alfred A. Knopf, 1966.

—————. *The Life and Times of the Virginia City Territorial Enterprise: Being Reminiscences of Five Distinguished Comstock Journalists*. Ashland, Oregon: Lewis Osborne, 1971.

—————. *The Town that Died Laughing: The Story of Austin, Nevada, Rambunctious Early-Day Mining Camp, and of Its Renowned Newspaper, 'The*

Reese River Reveille'. Reno: University of Nevada Press, 1986; originally published 1955.

Lingenfelter, Richard E., and Karen Rix Gash. *The Newspapers of Nevada: A History and Bibliography, 1854–1979*. Reno: University of Nevada Press, 1984.

Lorenz, Alfred Lawrence. "Harrison Reed: An Editor's Trials on the Wisconsin Frontier," *Journalism Quarterly* 53 (Autumn 1976): 417–422, 462.

———. "'Out of Sorts and Out of Cash': Problems of Publishing in Wisconsin Territory, 1833–1848," *Journalism History* 3 (Summer 1976): 34–39, 63.

Lotchin, Roger W. *San Francisco, 1846–1856: From Hamlet to City*. New York: Oxford University Press, 1974.

Lyman, W. D. *History of the Yakima Valley*. Chicago: S. J. Clarke Publishing Co., 1919.

———. *An Illustrated History of Walla Walla County*. W. H. Lever, 1901.

Lyon, William H. "Louis C. Hughes, Arizona's Editorial Gadfly," *Journal of Arizona History* 24 (Summer 1983): 171–200.

———. *The Pioneer Editor in Missouri, 1808–1860*. Columbia, Missouri: University of Missouri Press, 1965.

———. "The Significance of Newspapers on the American Frontier," *Journal of the West* (1980): 3–13.

Mack, Effie. *Mark Twain in Nevada*. New York: Scribner's, 1947.

Malmquist, Orvin Nebecker. *The First 100 Years: A History of the Salt Lake Tribune 1871–1971*. Salt Lake City: Utah State Historical Society, 1971.

Malone, Michael P. "Beyond the Last Frontier: Toward a New Approach to Western American History," *Western Historical Quarterly* 20 (November 1989): 409–427.

Martin, Douglas D. *Tombstone's Epitaph*. Albuquerque: University of New Mexico Press, 1951.

McCorkle, Julia Norton. "A History of Los Angeles Journalism," *Annual Publication of the Historical Society of Southern California* 10 (1915): 24–43.

McCurdy, James G. *By Juan de Fuca's Strait*. Portland: Metropolitan Press, 1937.

McIntyre, Jerilyn. "Communication on a Western Frontier—Some Questions About Context," *Journalism History* 3 (Summer 1976): 53–55, 63.

McMurtrie, Douglas C. "The Pioneer Press in Montana," *Journalism Quarterly* 9 (1932): 170–181.

———. "The Sweetwater Mines: A Pioneer Wyoming Newspaper," *Journalism Quarterly* 12 (1935): 164–165.

Meany, Edmond S. *Newspapers of Washington Territory*. Seattle: University of Washington Press, 1923.

Myers, Rex C., ed. *Lizzie: The Letters of Elizabeth Chester Fisk, 1864–1893*. Missoula, Montana: Mountain Press Publishing Co., 1989.

Nevada, A Guide to the Silver State. Writers' Program of the Works Projects Administration. Portland, Oregon: Binfords & Mort, 1940.

Newman, S. H. III. "The Las Vegas Weekly Mail," *New Mexico Historical Review* 44 (April 1969): 155–166.

North, S. N. D. *History and Present Condition of the Newspaper and Periodical Press of the United States*, vol. 8 of Tenth Census, 1880: Washington: Government Printing Office, 1884.

Norton, Wesley. " 'Like a Thousand Preachers Flying,' Religious Newspapers on the Pacific Coast to 1865," *California Historical Quarterly* 56 (Fall 1977): 194–209.

Notson, Robert C. *Making the Day Begin: A Story of the Oregonian*. Portland: Oregonian Publishing Co., 1976.

Paladin, Vivian. "Henry N. Blake: Proper Bostonian, Purposeful Pioneer," *Montana: The Magazine of Western History* 14 (August 1974): 31–56.

Perkin, Robert L. *The First Hundred Years: An Informal History of Denver and the Rocky Mountain News*. Garden City, New York: Doubleday & Company, Inc., 1959.

Pioneer Directory of the Metropolis of Montana. Helena: Herald Book & Job Printing Office, 1868.

Pomeroy, Earl. *The Pacific Slope*. Seattle: University of Washington Press, 1973; originally published in 1965.

Presbey, Frank. *The History and Development of Advertising*. New York: Doubleday & Co., 1929; Greenwood Press reprint, 1968.

Printers' Rollers, A Better Understanding of the Composition Roller. New York: The National Association of Printers' Roller Manufacturers, 1932.

Prosch, Charles. *Reminiscences of Washington Territory*. Seattle: 1904.

Prosser, William Farrand. *A History of the Puget Sound Country*. 2 vols. New York: The Lewis Publishing Co., 1903.

Purcell, Mae Fisher. *History of Contra Costa County*. Berkeley: The Gillick Press, 1940.

Quiett, Glenn Chesney. *They Built the West*. New York: D. Appleton-Century Co., 1934.

Reed, Virgil Delbert. "A Last Hurrah for the Frontier Press," *American Journalism* 6 (1989): 65–84.

Rice, William B. *The Los Angeles Star, 1851–1864: The Beginnings of Journalism in Southern California*. Berkeley: University of California Press, 1947.

Roth, Lottie Roeder, ed. *History of Whatcom County*. 2 vols. Chicago: Pioneer Historical Publishing Co., 1926.

Russo, David J. "The Origins of Local News in the U.S. Country Press, 1840s–1870s," *Journalism Monographs* 65 (February 1980).

Ryan, Pat M. "Trail-Blazer of Civilization: John P. Clum's Tucson and Tombstone Years," *Journal of Arizona History* 6 (Summer 1965): 53–70.

Scharlott, Bradford W. "Influence of Telegraph on Wisconsin Newspaper Growth," *Journalism Quarterly* 66 (Autumn 1989): 710–715.

Schellie, Don. *The Tucson Citizen: A Century of Arizona Journalism*. Tucson, Arizona: Tucson Daily Citizen, 1970.

Schwarzlose, Richard A. *The Nation's Newsbrokers*. 2 vols. Evanston, Illinois: Northwestern University Press, 1989–1990.

Silver, Rollo G. *The American Printer 1787–1825*. Charlottesville, Virginia: University Press of Virginia, 1967.

Sim, John Cameron. *The Grass Roots Press: America's Country Newspapers*. Ames, Iowa: Iowa State University Press, 1969.

Smith, David C. "The Paper Industry in California to 1900," *Southern California Quarterly* 57 (Summer 1975): 129–146.

Smith, E. D. Jr. "Communication Pioneering in Oregon," *Oregon Historical Quarterly* 39 (December 1938): 352–371.

Smith, Henry Nash, ed. *Mark Twain of the Enterprise*. Berkeley: University of California Press, 1957.

Smythe, Ted Curtis. "The Advertisers' War to Verify Newspaper Circulation, 1870–1914," *American Journalism* 3 (1986): 163–180.

Snell, Ralph M., and McBain, B. T. "Early Pulp and Paper Mills of the Pacific Coast," *Paper Trade Journal* 99 (October 11, 1934): 42–50.

Splitter, Henry Winfred. "Newspapers of Los Angeles: The First Fifty Years, 1851–1900," *Journal of the West* 2 (October 1963): 435–458.

Staples, Douglas W. "The Calico *Print*, Pioneer Newspaper of the Mojave Desert," *Historical Society of Southern California Quarterly* 42 (September 1960): 227–238.

Stephens, Mitchell. *A History of News: From the Drum to the Satellite*. New York: Viking Penguin Inc., 1988.

Stimson, Grace Heilman. *Rise of the Labor Movement in Los Angeles*. Berkeley: University of California Press, 1955.

Stone, Wilbur Fisk, ed. *History of Colorado*. 4 vols. Chicago: S. J. Clarke Publishing Co., 1918–1919.

Stratton, Porter A. *The Territorial Press of New Mexico, 1834–1912*. Albuquerque: University of New Mexico Press, 1969.

Thomas, Isaiah. *The History of Printing in America*. New York: Weathervane Books, 1970; originally published 1810.

Thorn, William J., with Mary Pat Pfeil. *Newspaper Circulation: Marketing the News*. New York: Longman, 1987.

Throckmorton, Arthur L. *Oregon Argonauts: Merchant Adventurers on the Western Frontier*. Portland: Oregon Historical Society, 1961.

Tocqueville, Alexis de. *Democracy in America*. 2 vols. New York: Alfred A. Knopf, 1953; first published in 1835.

Turnbull, George S. *History of Oregon Newspapers*. Portland, Oregon: Binfords & Mort, 1939.

Turner, Frederick Jackson. *The Frontier in American History*. New York: Holt, Rinehart and Winston, 1920.

Twain, Mark. *Roughing It*. New York: Holt, Rinehart and Winston, Inc., 1953; originally published 1872.

————. *Mark Twain's West: the author's memoirs about his boyhood, riverboats and western adventures*. Walter Blair, ed. Chicago: Lakeside Press, 1983.

————. *The Man That Corrupted Hadleyburg and Other Essays and Stories*. New York: Harper and Brothers, 1900.

Visscher, William Lightfoot. *A Thrilling and Truthful History of the PONY*

EXPRESS. Chicago: Charles T. Pownes Co., 1946; originally published in 1908.

Voltmer, Barbara Boyd. *Kern County's Courier, 1866–1876: A Newspaper in a Period of Economic and Political Transition.* Bakersfield, California: Kern County Historical Society, 1968.

Wade, Richard C. *The Urban Frontier: The Rise of Western Cities, 1790–1830.* Cambridge: Harvard University Press, 1959.

Warren, Sidney. *Farthest Frontier: The Pacific Northwest.* Port Washington, New York: Kennikat Press, 1970; originally published in 1949.

Watson, Elmo Scott. *History of Auxiliary Newspaper Service in the United States.* Champaign, Illinois: Illini Publishing Co., 1923.

Weigle, Clifford F. "San Francisco Journalism, 1847–1851," *Journalism Quarterly* 14 (June 1937): 151–157.

Wells, Evelyn. *Fremont Older.* New York: D. Appleton-Century Company, 1936.

Wentz, Roby. *Western Printing: A Selective and Descriptive Bibliography of Books and Other Materials on the History of Printing in the Western States, 1822–1975.* Los Angeles: Dawson's Book Shop, 1975.

Wheeler, Keith. *The Chroniclers.* New York: Time-Life Books, 1976.

Whitfield, William, ed. *History of Snohomish County, Washington.* 2 vols. Chicago: Pioneer Historical Publishing Co., 1926.

Whyte, Arthur K. "History of the Press in San Diego County," in *History of San Diego County*, pp. 164–168. Ed. by Carl H. Heilbron. San Diego: San Diego Press Club, 1936.

Works Projects Administration, Nevada. *A Guide to the Silver State.* Portland: Binfords & Mort, 1940.

Wright, Donald K. "Hiram Brundage and Wyoming's First Newspaper," *Journalism History* 2 (Spring 1975): 15, 32.

Wright, Louis B. *Culture on the Moving Frontier.* Bloomington, Indiana: Indiana University Press, 1966.

Young, John P. *Journalism in California.* San Francisco: Chronicle Publishing Company, 1915.

Theses and Dissertations

Brier, Warren J. "A History of Newspapers in the Pacific Northwest, 1846–1896." Ph.D. dissertation, State University of Iowa, 1957.

Cloud, Barbara. "Start the Presses: The Birth of Journalism in Washington Territory," Ph.D. dissertation, University of Washington, 1979.

Eaton, Edgar Eugene. "A History of Olympia Newspapers from 1852–1885." M.A. thesis, University of Washington, 1964.

Heuterman, Thomas H. "A History of Newspapering in Yakima, Washington." M.A. thesis, University of Washington, 1961.

Kennedy, Chester Barrett. "Newspapers of the California Northern Mines, 1850–1860, A Record of Life, Letters and Culture," Ph.D. dissertation, Stanford University, 1949.

Kuykendall, Ralph S. "History of Early California Journalism." M.A. thesis, University of California, Berkeley, 1918.

Mitchell, Marlene. "Washington Newspapers: Territorial and State, a Bibliography and Checklist." M.A. thesis, University of Washington, 1964.

Mortensen, Arlington Russell. "The Deseret News and Utah, 1850–1867." Ph.D. dissertation, University of California at Los Angeles, 1949.

Robison, Kenneth Leonard. "Idaho Territorial Newspapers." M.S. thesis, University of Oregon, 1966.

Rutenbeck, Jeffery B. "The Rise of Independent Newspapers in the 1870s: A Transformation in American Journalism." Ph.D. dissertation, University of Washington, 1990.

Spencer, Alice Starbuck. "Newspapers in Gunnison County, 1879–1900." M.A. thesis, Western State College of Colorado, 1932.

Umans, Joseph. "The Territorial Press of Northern and Central Colorado." M.A. thesis, University of Colorado, 1928.

Other Unpublished Sources

Atwood, Roy Alden. "The 'Critical Mass' for the Frontier Press: Demographics, Economics and Newspapers During Idaho's Territorial Period." Paper presented to American Journalism Historians Association convention, Atlanta, Georgia, October 1989.

Baldasty, Gerald J. "Modern Industrialism, the Press and News in Late 19th Century America." Paper presented to West Coast Journalism Historians, San Francisco, 1985.

———. "The Press and Politics in the Gilded Age." Paper presented to West Coast Journalism Historians, San Francisco, 1987.

Daughters of the American Revolution. "Family Records and Reminiscences of Washington Pioneers." Seattle, 1929–1930. Northwest Collection, University of Washington Libraries.

Hamilton, James F. "Economic Growth and Entrepreneurs: The Establishment of the First Daily Newspaper in Seven Washington Territory and State Towns." Paper presented to West Coast Journalism Historians, San Francisco, February 1986.

Homsher, Laura. "Guide to Wyoming Newspapers, 1867–1967," n.d., Joseph Jacobucci Collection, University of Wyoming Western History Research Center, University of Wyoming Library.

Jordan, Myron K. "The Golden Age of the Press Revisited," Paper presented to West Coast Journalism Historians, San Francisco, 1987.

Lance, Robert. "First Lady of Arizona Journalism." Unpublished paper, 1979.

Prosch, Thomas. "The Early History of Tacoma." Address to the Association of Pierce County Pioneers, Tacoma, Washington, 12 April 1905. Typescript #11, Northwest Collection, University of Washington Libraries.

Works Projects Administration. *History of San Francisco Journalism*. San Francisco, 1940. Project 10008. California Historical Society Library.

Newspapers

The following newspapers were consulted and cited by the author; for specific dates see the endnotes. The endnotes also include a number of newspaper citations gleaned from others' works.

Albuquerque *Daily Journal*
Aurora, Nevada, *Daily Times*
Aurora *Esmeralda Star*
Austin, Nevada, *Reese River Reveille*
Battle Mountain *Central Nevadan*
Battle Mountain *Measure for Measure*
Belmont, Nevada, *Courier*
Butte, Montana, *Miner*
Carson City, Nevada, *Daily Bee*
Carson City *Daily Appeal*
Carson City *Daily Index*
Carson City *Free Lance*
Chehalis, Washington, *Bee*
Chehalis, Washington, *Lewis County Nugget*
Cheyenne, Wyoming, *Daily Leader*
Colfax, Washington, *Palouse Gazette*
Columbus, Nevada, *Borax Miner*
Dayton, Washington, *Columbia Chronicle*
Denver *Rocky Mountain News*
Eagle Rock (Idaho Falls) *Idaho Register*
Eureka, Nevada, *Daily Leader*
Genoa, Nevada, *Carson Valley News*
Gold Hill, Nevada, *News*
Hamilton, Nevada, *Daily Inland Empire*
Ione, Nevada, *Advertiser*
Kalama, Washington, *Beacon*
Los Angeles *Star*
Los Angeles *Times*
Marysville, California, *Appeal*
Oakland *Tribune*
Olympia, Washington, *Overland Press*
Olympia *Columbian*
Olympia *Echo*
Olympia *Transcript*
Olympia *Washington Democrat*
Olympia *Washington Pioneer*
Olympia *Washington Standard*
Pataha, Washington, *Spirit*
Pomeroy, Washington, *Republican*
Portland *Oregonian*

Port Townsend, Washington, *Argus*
Port Townsend *Register*
Prescott *Arizona Miner*
Reno *Daily Record*
Reno *Evening Gazette*
Sacramento *Placer Times*
Sacramento *Union*
Salem *Oregon Statesman*
Salt Lake City *Deseret News*
San Francisco *Chronicle*. Also the *Daily Dramatic Chronicle*
San Francisco *Evening News*
Seabeck, Washington, *Rebel Battery*
Seattle *Daily Call*
Seattle *Fin-Back*
Seattle *Gazette*. Also the *Washington Gazette*
Seattle *Morning Dispatch*
Seattle *Morning Journal*
Seattle *People's Telegram*
Seattle *Post-Intelligencer*
Seattle *Puget Sound Weekly Gazette*; also the daily and semi-weekly editions
Seattle *Sunday Star*
Silver City, Idaho, *Owyhee Avalanche*. Also the *Idaho Avalanche*
Snohomish, Washington, *Northern Star*
Spokane Falls *Evening Review*
Spokane *Times*
Steilacoom, Washington, *Puget Sound Courier*
Tacoma *Herald*
Unionville, Nevada, *Silver State*
Vancouver, Washington, *Independent*
Virginia City, Nevada, *The Footlight*
Virginia City *Daily Independent*
Virginia City *Territorial Enterprise*; also published in Genoa and Carson City, Nevada.
Walla Walla, Washington, *Spirit of the West*
Walla Walla *Daily Journal*
Walla Walla *Sunday Epigram*
Walla Walla *Washington Statesman*
White Plains, Nevada, *Churchill News*
Wilbur, Washington, *Register*
Yakima *Signal*

INDEX